THE
NAKED
NUDE

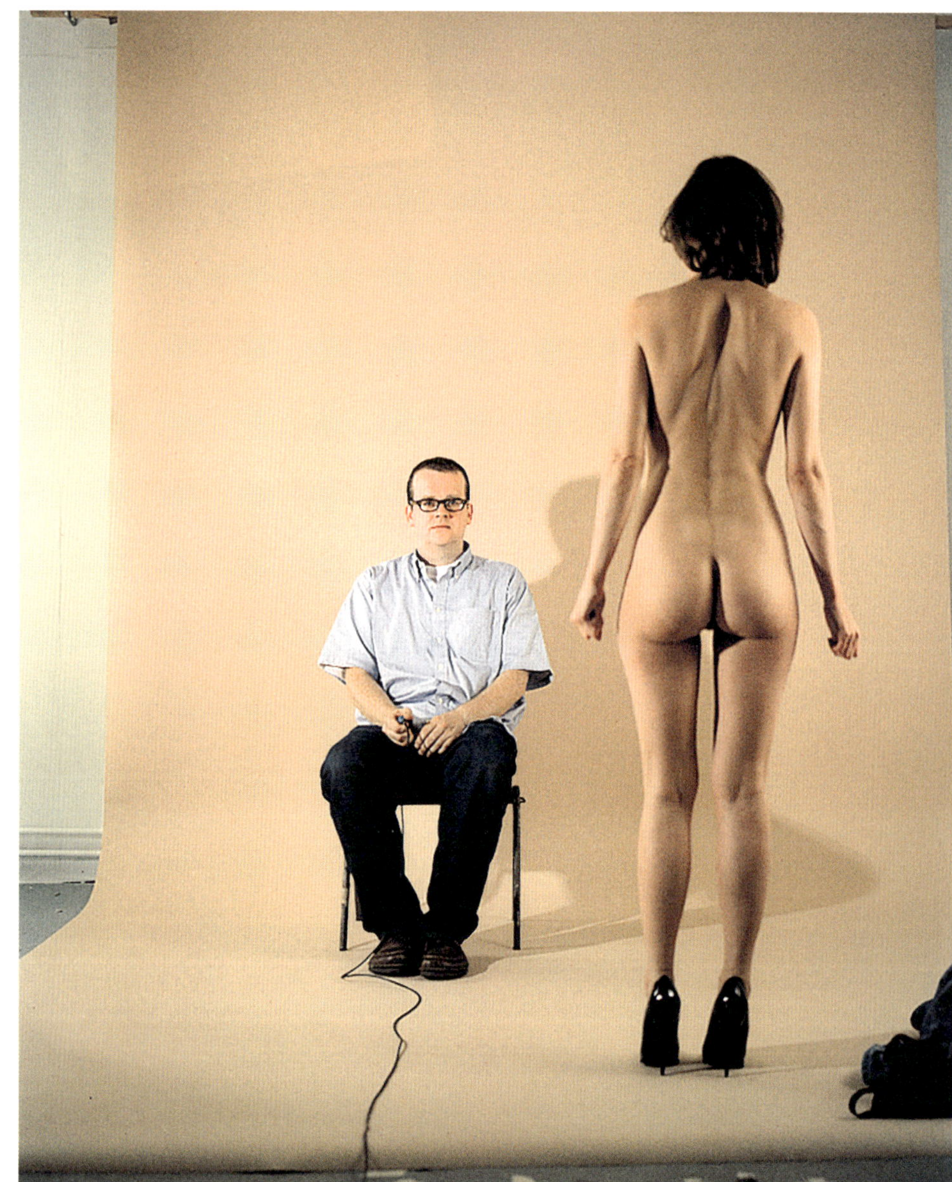

Frances Borzello

THE NAKED NUDE

With 126 illustrations

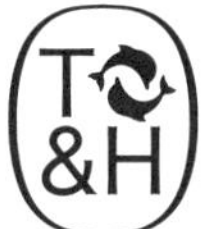

FRONTISPIECE: Jemima Stehli, *Strip No. 7*, 1999 (see pages 52–3)

First published in the United Kingdom in 2012 by
Thames & Hudson Ltd, 181A High Holborn, London WC1V 7QX

This revised and expanded edition 2022

The Naked Nude © 2012 and 2022 Thames & Hudson Ltd

Text © 2012 and 2022 Frances Borzello

Designed by Anna Perotti, www.bytheskydesign.com

British Library Cataloguing-in-Publication Data
A catalogue record for this book is available from the British Library

ISBN 978-0-500-29667-7

Printed and bound in China by C&C Offset Printing Co., Ltd.

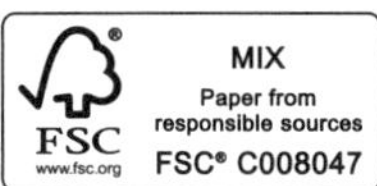

Be the first to know about our new releases,
exclusive content and author events by visiting
thamesandhudson.com
thamesandhudsonusa.com
thamesandhudson.com.au

CONTENTS

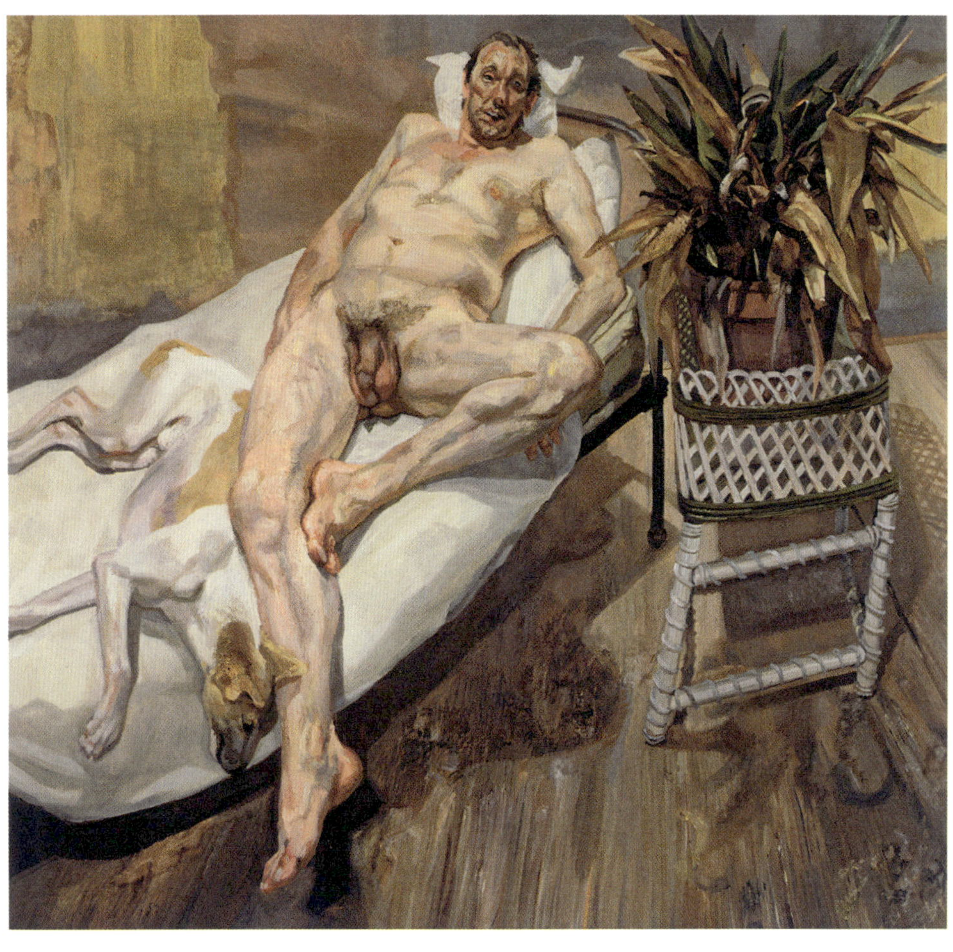

Lucian Freud, *David and Eli*, 2003–4, oil on canvas. With the sitter's inelegant, though believable, sprawl and his sunburn, veins and lumps and bumps, Freud presents us with a thoroughly contemporary nude who bears no relationship to the heroically posed ideal male nudes of the past.

THE RECYCLED NUDE

THE REPRESENTATION OF THE NUDE in art is a victory of fiction over fact. Its great success has been to distance the unclothed body from any uncomfortably explicit taint of sexuality, eroticism or imperfection. There are visual areas where these particular aspects of the body are dealt with. Sexuality is the subject of pornography; its images show the secret, excessive and occasionally illegal sides of human desires. Eroticism sees itself as a cut above, a kind of sex-lite dressed in a hat and black lace that can be discussed in public and ventures into bookshops, art galleries and even, when the work is made by famous artists like Egon Schiele or Gustav Klimt, into galleries and the catalogues of reputable publishers. Imperfection finds a home in medical illustration, with its case histories of the obese and underweight and its diagnostic images of disease, malfunction and diversion from the norm. But fine art is the place to view the ideal body, the perfect body, the young body, the body that has been cleansed of its everyday reality.

When art historian Kenneth Clark, a former director of the National Gallery in London, wrote *The Nude* in 1956, he suggested a rationale that has since taken on the status of one of the 'great statements' of art history: 'To be naked is to be deprived of our clothes … The word nude, on the other hand, carries, in educated usage, no uncomfortable overtone.'[1] No one who considers nudity, the nude, nakedness or the body in art has been able to ignore Clark's definition. What they understand is that the nude is art with a capital 'A', the culturally acceptable face of the human figure with no clothes on. Or, as Clark put it: 'The vague image it projects into the mind is not of a huddled and defenceless body, but of a balanced, prosperous and confident body: the body re-formed.'[2] With great elegance and brilliant simplicity, Clark cleverly subtracted the embarrassment factor from the nude.

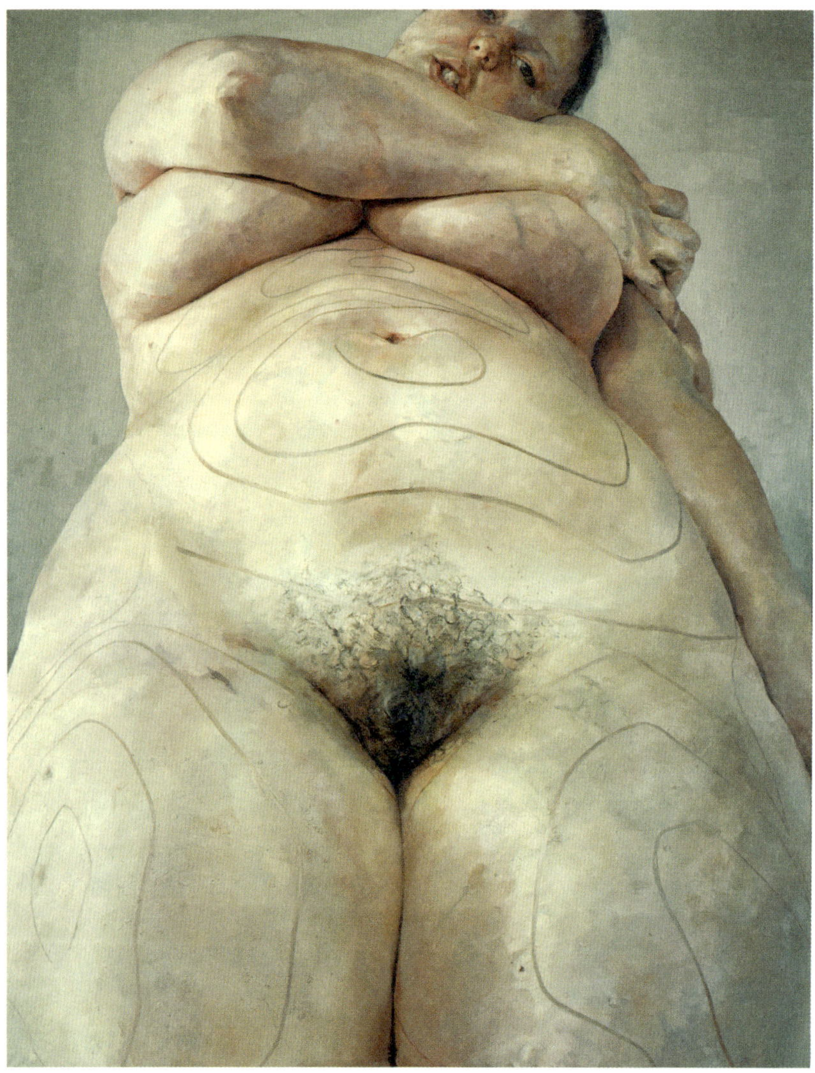

ABOVE **Jenny Saville**, *Plan*, 1993, oil on canvas. Saville's nude, based on her own self-portrait, replaces the smooth perfection of the old masters with a confrontational lived-in body. The contour lines covering her body are suggestive of both those used in cartography and the guides drawn out by a doctor before surgery.

OPPOSITE **Philip Pearlstein**, *Female Nude on a Platform Rocker*, 1977–8, oil on canvas. From the start of the 1960s, Pearlstein devoted five decades to painting men and women without clothes. But the harsh light, everyday poses, and ruthlessly detailed bony knees and working hands take them far from the traditional nude of fine art.

Why is it, then, that viewing the nudes on display in galleries of contemporary art can be anything but comfortable? Lucian Freud's realistic male and female bodies, with their excess flesh and patchy colour, have been disturbing viewers for decades. Jenny Saville's oversized paintings of naked women were recognized as the expression of a new and defiantly female talent from their first exhibition in 1994. Louise Bourgeois's suggestive sexual shapes connect uneasily in our subconscious. John Currin's female grotesques are painted with breasts so large they threaten to bring their owners to the floor. Philip Pearlstein has made everyday nudity the subject of his art, while Marc Quinn explores bodily differences.

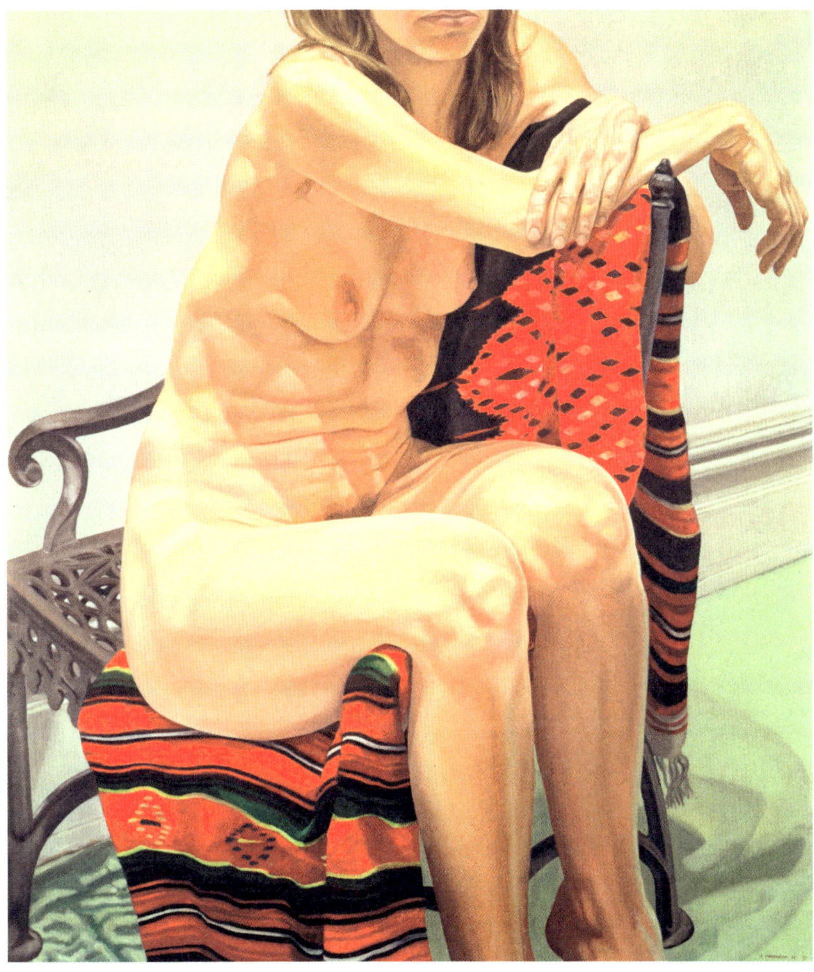

All these artists have turned their backs on the conventional presentation of the ideal nude in favour of something grittier imbued with contemporary concerns.

The ideal body for our times, the perfect body, give or take a national quirk or two, is a slim body. But this contemporary ideal nude is not to be seen in the art that finds its home on serious collectors' walls, in the media that take art seriously or in museums and art galleries. Artists today do not produce up-to-date versions of the reclining nude or of the strong, upright hero, the Venuses and Hercules of past centuries. There are luscious bodies aplenty, of course, but they tend to be the work of artists who cater to fringe desires and the rarefied world of fine art refuses to pay them serious attention. The male nudes of Tom of Finland aimed at gay men, the female nudes of Robert Lenkiewicz, which sell for thousands of pounds, have a sizeable specialist audience but are viewed with glazed eyes by taste-makers.

These days, the representation of the slim and perfect nude is the property of photographers. The young men who model for underwear advertisements are the ideal male bodies for our time; the young stars of film and TV, snapped on the beach in their bikinis, their female equivalent. These pin-ups display the bodies most lusted after in our day, more perfect than real life, their veins and blotches non-existent, their breasts and bottoms as pneumatic as the bodies of the painted nudes of the past. Alongside commercial and fashion photography, a category called the 'artistic' nude has been a staple of photography books aimed at the amateur practitioner from the start of the 20th century. Here we find images of flatteringly lit, voluptuous young women, coyly hiding their sexuality as the reclining nudes of fine art fame have done for centuries.

While the nude in commercial photographs is beautiful, handsome, sexy, perfect, the nude that interests the artists of today is none of these things. Theirs is a nude that responds to our age, an age in which the body is the focus for many of the issues that absorb us. Articles about food, weight, fashion, sexuality, health, genetics, pornography, medicine, science, exercise, plastic surgery – the list is infinitely expandable – bombard us online, on TV, in books, newspapers and magazines. Conflicting attitudes battle for our attention. For every article about underweight fashion models and the prevalence of eating disorders in the industry, there is one by a media personality celebrating the curves often proudly announced as synthetic. Information about healthy eating exists alongside reports of increasing obesity in the young. Plastic surgery goes wrong, screams a headline one day, while on the next a lottery winner says she is giving breast augmentations to her sisters. Men are now ridiculed for their imperfections as women have been for centuries. The body is a contemporary obsession.

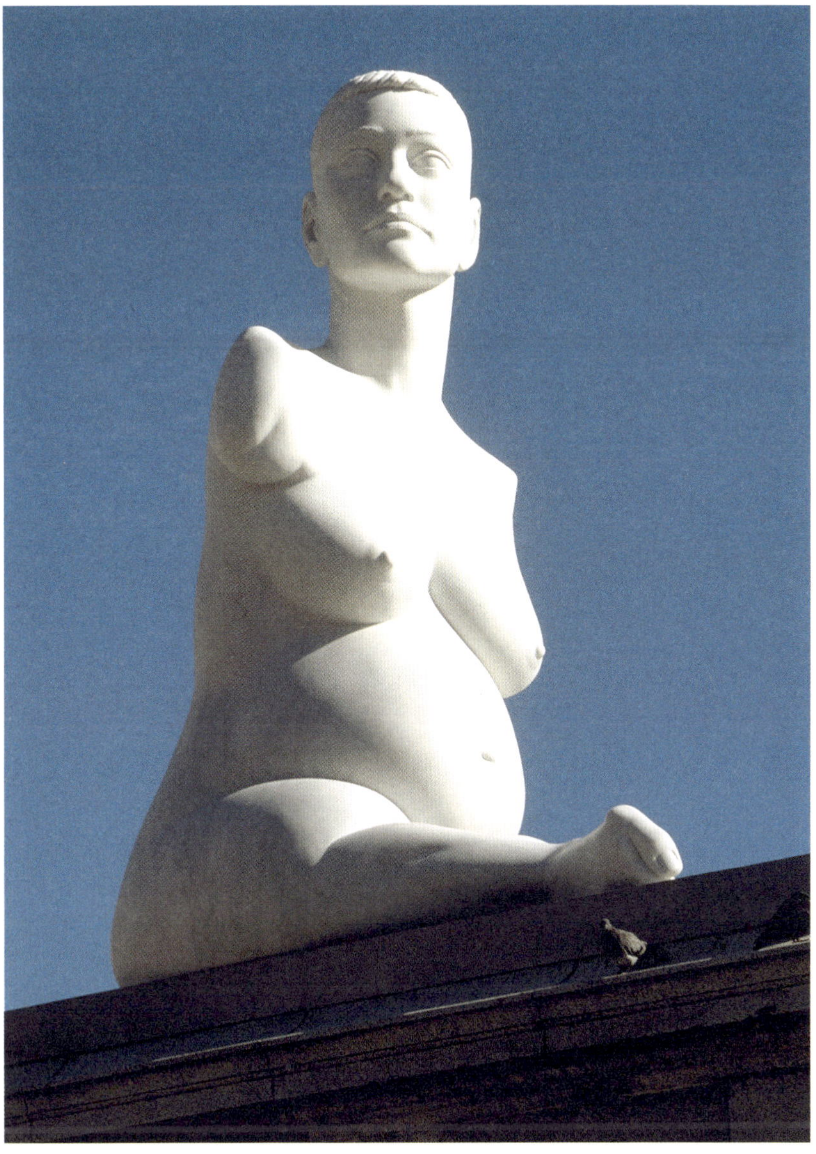

Marc Quinn, *Alison Lapper Pregnant*, 2005, marble. Quinn's portrait of the
pregnant, disabled artist Alison Lapper, which topped a plinth in London's
Trafalgar Square in 2005, epitomizes his investigation of contemporary attitudes
to beauty. Beautiful, 3.6 m (12 ft) high and made from the finest marble,
it questions our devotion to fine art's traditional notion of the ideal.

Today's media bombard us with contrasting sets of images. One set depicts the perfect body, the sexualized body, the young body. Although these are mostly of women, there are an increasing number of masculine bodies beautiful, particularly in the fashion pages of the glossy magazines where they are featured as a kind of glamorous accessory and sometimes as sexual partners of the young models showing off the clothes. These are the modern-day photographic versions of the ideal nude. The young women for whom shaved pubic hair is an aesthetic imperative would be surprised to learn of its origin in the reclining nudes on gallery walls.

An opposing set of images depicts the less than ideal body and takes in everything from distressing photographs of starving people in the newspapers to those, usually women but increasingly men as well, who are so overweight, over-endowed or thin that their depictions border on the freak-shows of the past, making the flaw-free, youthful body seem all the more desirable.

The nudes that are made by today's fine artists reveal an awareness of all these issues and incongruities. They have turned their backs on perfection in order to face up to the concerns and contradictions that surround the 21st-century body. The very things that made the nudes of the past palatable for general consumption – their timelessness, their ideal quality, their pleasure in being part of the great tradition through their link to the chain of nudes preceding them – are precisely the things that do not interest contemporary artists who work with the nude. The new nudes ask awkward questions and behave provocatively. No one calls them nudes, even when there is not a stitch of clothing in sight. In its refusal to edit out the unacceptable, the new nude represents something not seen before in art. It is a very naked nude, created to confront today's attitudes and anxieties. The specificity of the unclothed bodies found in contemporary galleries is rawer than anything that went before. What we have now is a nude that revels in Clark's 'uncomfortable overtones'. It is the naked nude, the nude recycled for our times.

THE NUDE: ITS LIFE, DEATH AND RESURRECTION

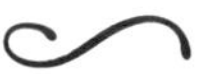

THE FINAL FEW PAGES of Kenneth Clark's *The Nude* are devoted to Henri Matisse, Pablo Picasso and Henry Moore, and conclude with a hope that has more to do with art's past than its future: 'The Greeks perfected the nude in order that man might feel like a god, and in a sense this is still its function, for although we no longer suppose that God is like a beautiful man, we still feel close to divinity in those flashes of self-identification when, through our own bodies, we seem to be aware of a universal order.'[1]

Clark's description of the nude as an earthly suggestion of god-like perfection echoes the attitudes of the classical world where male nudity rarely seems to have raised any eyebrows. Far more important than the female in art, the perfectly proportioned young male body was used as the embodiment of Apollo and the robust proportions of maturity expressed the power of Zeus. Both types were unashamedly naked, with tiny, tidy marble genitals under neat little rows of marble pubic pin curls. The female nude, on the other hand, even when personifying Venus, the goddess of love, revealed her body in a much coyer fashion; whereas male genitalia were displayed, the female hid hers beneath a hand or a piece of marble cloth.

Until the Renaissance, the female nude remained a relatively unimportant player on the stage of fine art. While male nudes in the Renaissance could take the form of Christ or classical heroes, continuing the Greek tradition of expressing god-like qualities through perfect form, there were few roles for the female. Artists and their patrons used Samson, Hercules, even Christ on the cross if they were Italian, as the classical artists did, as the human embodiment of admirable characteristics. Women with no clothes tended to the sinful – Eve, or the beautiful and mischievous Venus – a view of women drawn from the real world in

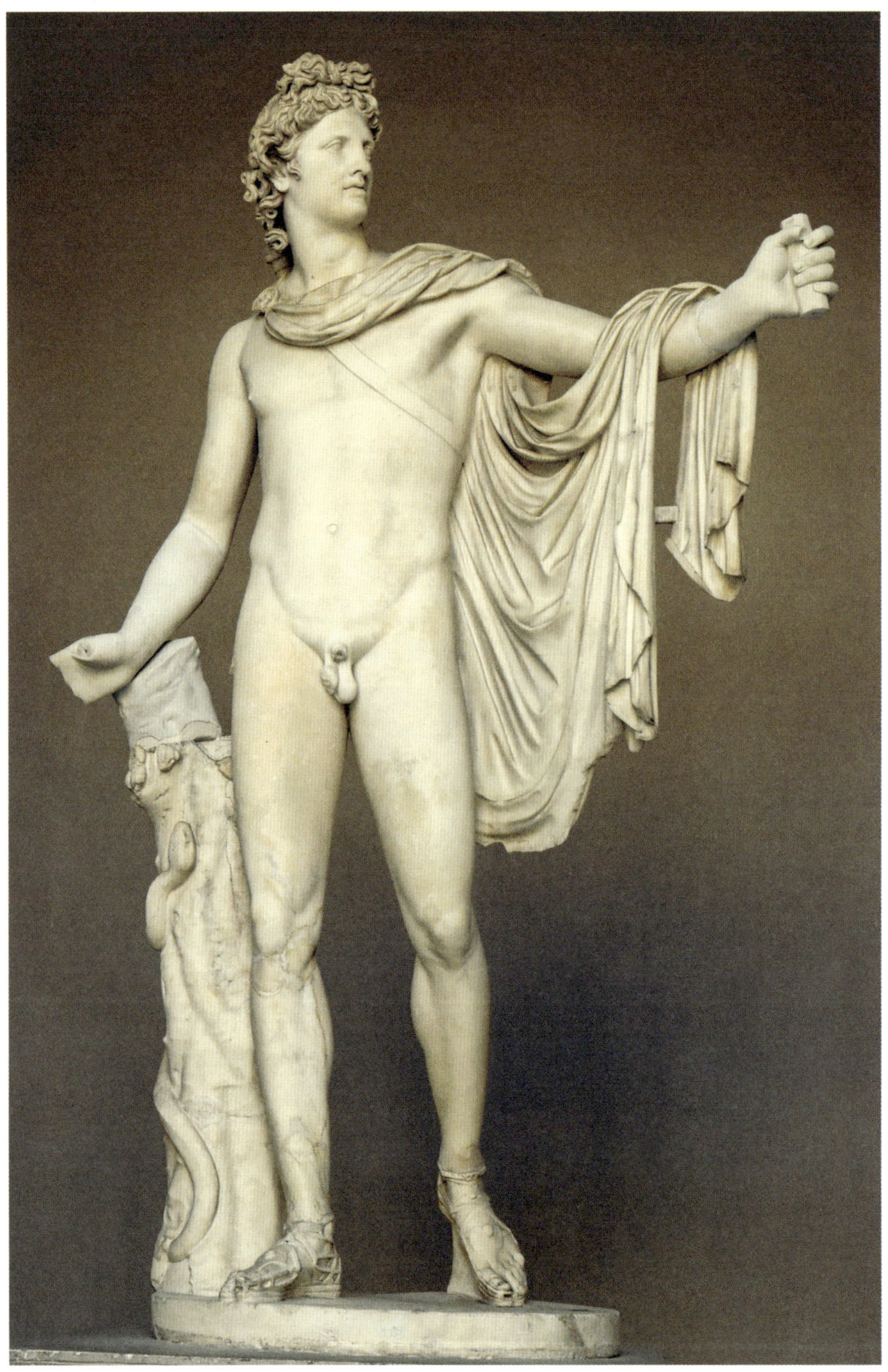

which artists existed, a world imbued with church teachings which unfavourably compared the low, animal nature of women with the intellectuality and spirituality that only men could claim. Venus, goddess of love, could never reach as high a moral ground as Mars, god of war. It was male nudity that represented the ideal.

It was not until the early 16th century that the ideal nude changed sex. In Venice in 1510 Giorgione's glorious invention, the *Sleeping Venus*, opened the door to the unapologetic and ideal female nude, a reclining woman, a beautiful and passive vision of perfection, lying there almost as large as life and needing no moralizing tale beyond the name of Venus to explain her presence. With one arm above her head, the other suggestively shielding her sexuality and her breasts displayed for all to see, she was an amazing newcomer to the world of art who lives on today in a string of painted descendants, in amateur art classes and in everyone's imagination.

Clark's elegant claim that nudes such as these carried no 'uncomfortable overtone' was in fact the triumphant culmination of a campaign that had been waged since a woman first posed naked for an artist. However high minded the resultant image might be, everyone knew it was based on a real woman who had removed her clothes in front of a man and allowed him to stare at her. What fascinated outsiders was the aspect of artists and models that represented the seductive freedom unknown to the average person. From earliest times, the women who were willing to take off their clothes for artists have been surrounded with an aura of sexual availability. Pliny, for example, claimed that the Roman painter Arellius gave goddesses his mistresses' features, thereby introducing sex workers into his paintings.[2]

When London's Royal Academy was founded in the 18th century, it paid a higher fee to its female models in the hope of attracting a better class of sitter – not a sex worker, in other words. Some European academies were so worried about the possible repercussions of young men drawing the female nude that they preferred to do without her. The unedifying speculation aroused by the vision of an unclothed female model getting up to who knew what with a male artist in the studio was a weak spot in the elevated claims of fine art. The situation cried out for legitimization, which took two forms, the practical and the theoretical. In practical terms, the life class became the culmination of academic training, only to be entered once

Apollo Belvedere, plaster cast of a Roman marble copy, *c.* 130 to 140 AD, after the bronze original attributed to the classical Greek sculptor Leochares. The pose and slim male beauty of the *Apollo Belvedere*, discovered in the late 15th century, have influenced a variety of artists, from history painters of the Renaissance to portrait painters of the 18th century.

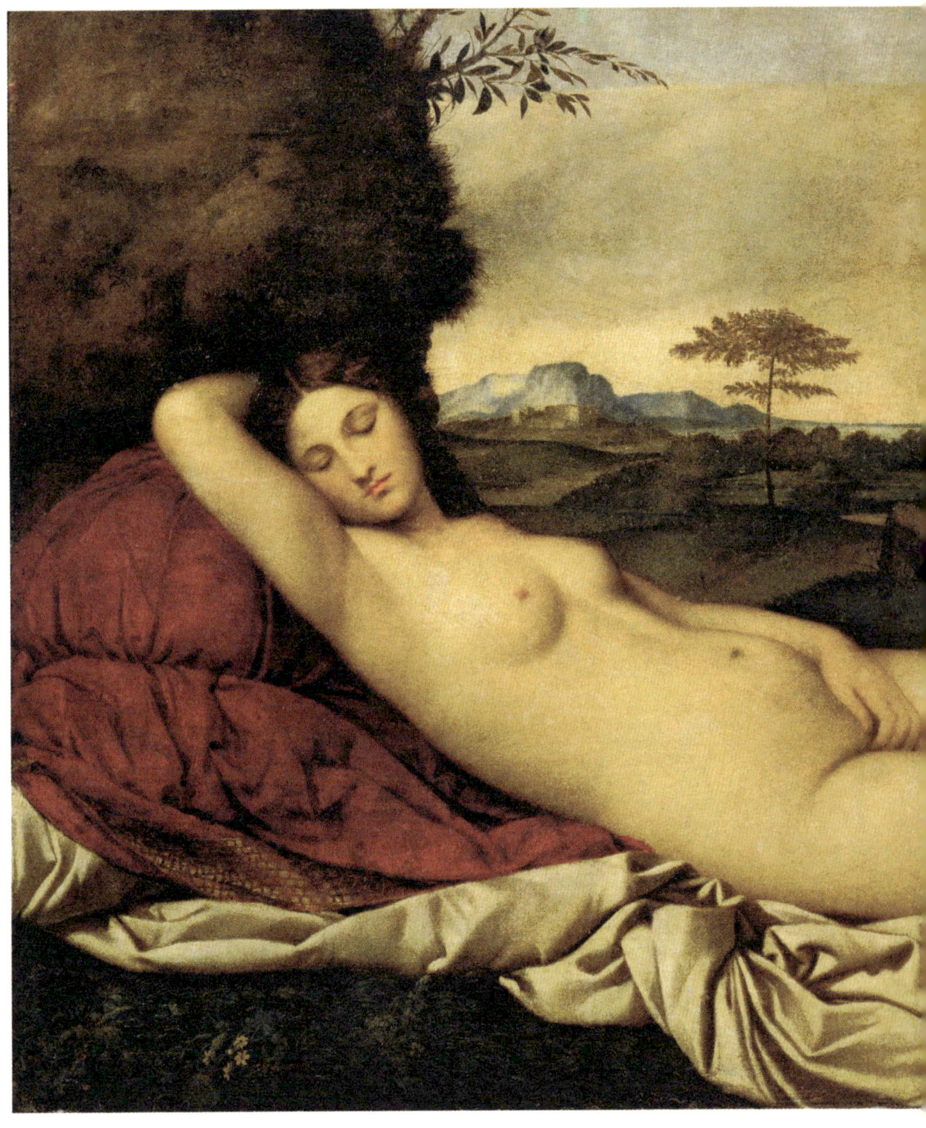

Giorgione, *Sleeping Venus*, c. 1508–10 (background completed by Titian after Giorgione's death), oil on canvas. Passive and perfect, the curves of her body echoing the lines of the soft landscape, Giorgione's *Sleeping Venus* lies at the head of a line of reclining female nudes made respectable for viewing. Her hand both suggests and veils her sexuality, her breasts are displayed, and her closed eyes allow the viewer's eyes to range freely. Her identification as the goddess Venus adds respectability to her nudity.

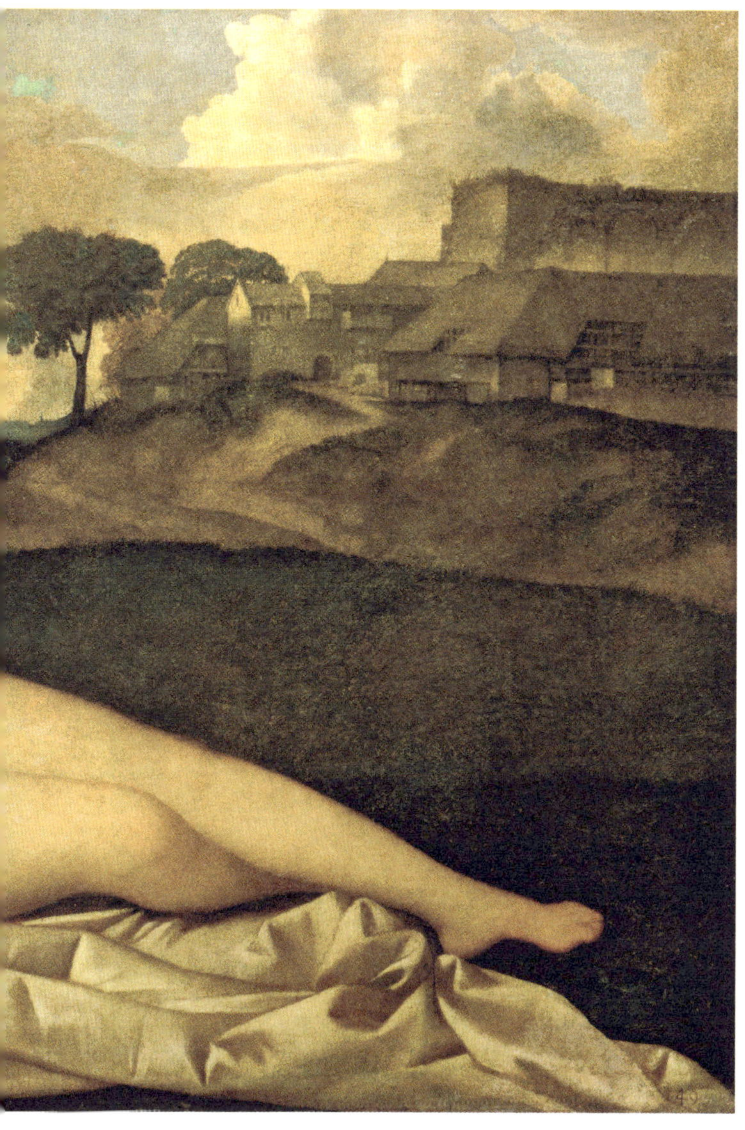

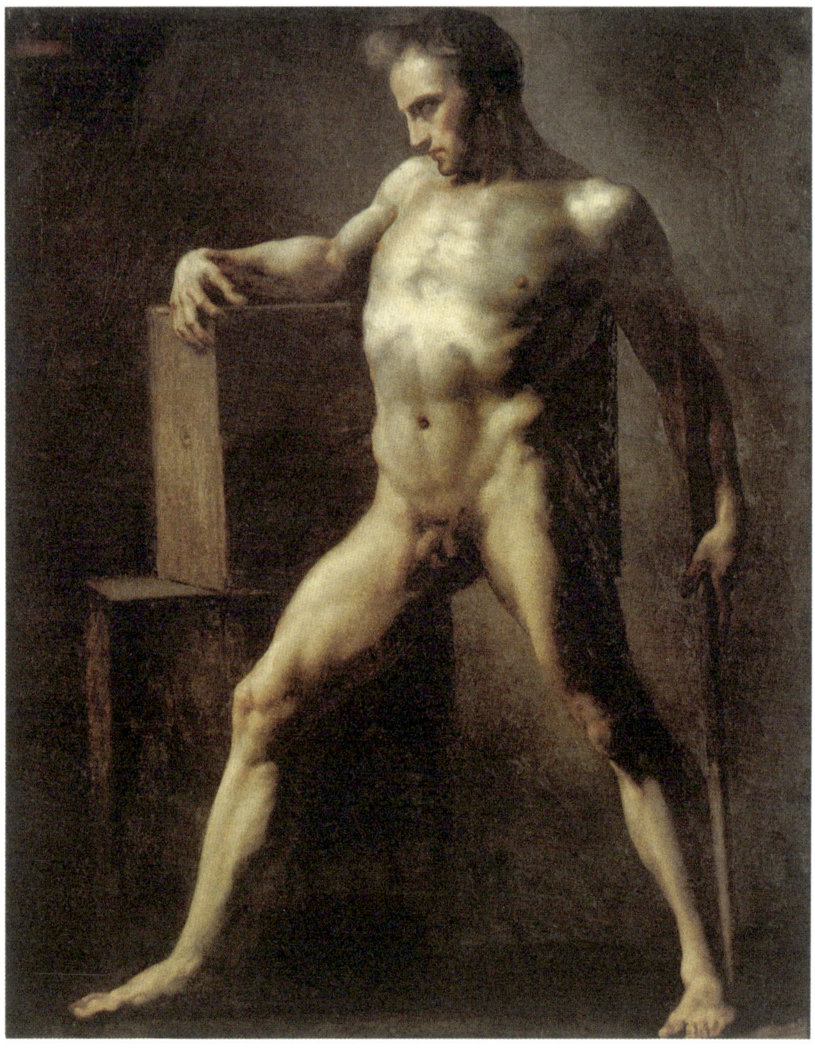

Théodore Géricault, *Nude Study of a Man*, 1816, oil on canvas. Until the 19th century, the male nude was considered superior to the female as a model in the life class. Male models were chosen for the clarity of their musculature and their resemblance to the sculptures of classical Greece. The supports and sticks that helped models hold their pose are visible in this early 19th-century study.

the student had become familiar with the work of earlier masters by copying prints and casts of their work, and the majority of models were female. The ability of graduating students to produce an *académie*, the internationally accepted French term for a painting of a nude male model, was proof that they had learned their skill. The practice of posing became surrounded by ritual: the model approached the podium in a robe and only slipped it off to take the pose; a tutor was always present; talking was forbidden in an attempt to preserve decorum. In some schools, only married men were admitted into the female life class until well into the 19th century, so potentially injurious to young men's morals – and also to the reputation of the academy – was exposure to female nudity considered.

Its theoretical counterpart was the development of justifications for the high morality of art. Commentators and critics did this by ignoring the model, replacing the bothersome fact of drawing from a living naked woman with the more abstract concept of drawing from life. Beginning with Leon Battista Alberti's *De Pictura* in 1435, serious art treatises rarely mention her, even though the whole of art theory and practice was based on working from nature. Not any nature, of course, but the best. And if the best was not available, then an amalgamation of the best from several examples. The knowledge that the living model would have been 'improved' by the artist helped distance her in viewers' eyes from the living female body.

The message was that fine art was superior to life and by extension nudity in art was purer than nudity in life: low thoughts were the result of twisted thinking on the spectator's part. The distancing of the nude from any 'uncomfortable overtone' enabled critics and commentators to take it as seriously as they might a prince's portrait or an uplifting moralizing history painting. It allowed artists to use it as a vehicle of expression that could stand for purity and truth as well as beauty. And it freed the public to admire and aspire to the virtues she personified as she stood in stone with no clothes on in city centres or lay in painted glory inside a picture frame.

This justification became particularly important in the 19th century when an urban entertainment of looking at art developed alongside a complex set of manners designed to protect feminine sensibilities. These developments met over the ideal nude. The growing number of galleries displaying art, the increase in magazines and newspapers to comment on it and the expansion of an educated middle class who wanted to look at it turned viewing the latest offerings of the artists into a spectator sport. The hanging of nudes on gallery walls in front of a public new to art encouraged an elaborate code of art appreciation, which presented art as something superior to life, fit to be viewed by anyone, regardless of gender, and of great benefit in moral terms.

Clark in 1956 was merely updating the views of those of the previous century who had gone to tortuous lengths to differentiate the concept of the nude from the rude. As a sophisticated 20th-century communicator, he had no wish to ally himself with 19th-century puritanism. He delicately alluded to the problem of the body's 'associations' with sexuality, explaining that it 'arouses memories of all the things we wish to do with ourselves; and first of all we wish to perpetuate ourselves'. And he admitted the problem this could cause when faced with the nude in art: 'The desire to grasp and be united with another human body is so fundamental a part of our nature, that our judgment of what is known as "pure form" is inevitably influenced by it; and one of the difficulties of the nude as a subject for art is that these instincts cannot lie hidden, as they do for example in our enjoyment of a piece of pottery, thereby gaining the force of sublimation, but are dragged into the foreground, where they risk upsetting the unity of responses from which a work of art derives its independent life.'[3] In other words, the viewer's sexual arousal risks getting in the way of his (Clark seems to assume the viewer is male) aesthetic appreciation.

Cleverly, Clark factored this problematic area into his new theory. He upturned the Victorian argument that an art that gives rise to inappropriate thoughts is false art and bad morals. Instead, he argued: 'No nude, however abstract, should fail to arouse in the spectator some vestige of erotic feeling, even though it be only the faintest shadow – and if it does not do so, it is bad art and false morals.' And he concludes this defence with a brilliant metaphor: 'The amount of erotic content which a work of art can hold in solution is very high.'[4] Thus, as a modern man of the world, Clark admits to the eroticism implicit in the nude, but in the end, he backs away from dipping his feet in the murky pond of sex. Having disposed of the problem by this discussion in the first chapter of his book, he leaves it behind with relief at having acknowledged and then dealt with a potentially difficult area.

It is ironic that despite his elegant defence, by the time Clark was writing, half a century into modernism, the ideal nude was losing its interest to artists as anything more than a personal inspiration. Personifying virtues and vices through the figure had gone the way of the crinoline, and modernism's disdain of narrative and history painting meant the nude was no longer needed to tell a story from the Bible, mythology or the past.

The birth of modernism signalled the death of the ideal nude. An assortment of linked 19th-century developments began to threaten its position in fine art: photography, Impressionism, the end of narrative, the loosening of artistic rules. And these are just the changes and innovations linked to art's evolution. From other areas came the expansion of education, psychology's interest in the darker corners of the mind, agitation for the emancipation of women and the questioning of the teachings of the church. All are related to the story of the disappearing ideal nude.

The invention of the camera had diverse effects on the world of fine art. Photographers immediately saw the possibilities of the nude as a subject for the new discovery. Louis Daguerre introduced the first practical process of photography in 1839 and by 1840 pornographic images were available, sometimes in stereography for extra realism. The democratization of the production of images brought in by the box camera in 1888 was eventually to make photographers of us all.

When anyone could replicate the world around them with the pressure of one finger, painters were forced to consider what distinguished their own art form. Artists began to fight free of the tight grip of realism which forced their painting arm to reproduce life in the most exact way possible. In 1874 an outraged critic wrote '*mais ce n'est rien qu'une impression* (it's nothing but an impression)' of Monet's painted equivalent of a sunrise, daringly composed of an orange circle and a few orange brush strokes across the blue of the water.

Impressionism's devaluation of the careful preparations needed for the production of what soon came to be seen as the painterly version of the new-fangled photographic realism introduced the stylistic freedom of the 20th century. Critical respect for the avant-garde stress on novelty encouraged innovation. Ambitious artists absorbed the work of the preceding generation and strove to surpass or contradict it, according to their temperament and allegiance. Familiar with the art of the Impressionists, Vincent van Gogh took its freedoms even further: inspired by the sunflowers that so dazzled him, he proceeded to reproduce them in thick, quick strokes that were so energetic and directional they seemed alive, a type of painting that was as interesting for its vigour, its colour, its patterns, its brushstrokes, as for the object it was mimicking.

By 1900 it was clear that the balance between objective reality and the world on the canvas was changing. If in 1905 the Fauves, the 'wild beasts' as they were called, felt their landscape demanded a touch of red in a particular place, then they painted a tree trunk red, and naturalism be damned. By the outbreak of the First World War in 1914, the balance had tipped. Every country in the West had at least one artist who had produced an abstract painting, and some like Russia with

Wassily Kandinsky and the Netherlands with Piet Mondrian, were able to offer major stars of abstraction to the world of art.

Sculpture followed the same path. Its story in the 20th century has little to do with the bodily ideal and much to do with the falling of barriers: the inspiration of pre-existing objects such as anthropomorphic stones or pebbles the Surrealists found on the beaches; the first pierced sculptural shape; the first sculpture to sit on the ground and not on a plinth; the first sculptures built of wood and metal rather than cast or carved. Whereas once the miracle of sculpture was to create the illusion of skin, the fall of flowing drapery, movement, the smoothness of a female body and the musculature of a male torso out of hard, unfriendly stone, now we admired the sculptor's ability to bring out the inner quality of the selected stone or wood and the satisfying elegance of the resulting shapes.

As the importance of realism and naturalism declined, so did art's traditional classifications. For centuries, art had been divided into genres: portraiture, landscape, still life, history painting, and of course the nude. But there was no need for these in an art uninterested in producing a realistic transcription of nature. No longer employed to represent heroic virtues in its male version or goddesses and damsels in distress in its female version, the nude was out of a job. By the early 20th century as the balance shifted from realism to abstraction, terms like colour, tone, design, pattern, brush marks replaced likeness to life as the standard of judgment. All familiar artistic terms, of course, but previously used in the service of realism or naturalism instead of the stand-alone qualities they now became in order to create and assess a work of art.

And as the traditional classifications faded, the materials used by artists multiplied. The age-old materials of paint, clay, stone, metals and wood expanded to include everything from Picasso's bicycle handlebars fashioned to look like the horns of a bull through to Meret Oppenheim's fur-lined teacup to the plaster lobster on top of a Bakelite telephone concocted by Salvador Dalí. Even the idea of what constituted a work of art was up for grabs after Marcel Duchamp signed a urinal 'R. Mutt', and sent it off to the New York Society of Independent Artists in 1917. He coined a name for it, 'readymade', and, despite the outrage, its exhibition ensured that in future gallery doors would open up to whatever sculptors might bring through them. The barriers between painting and sculpture dissolved. In Clark's England in 1929, Ben Nicholson made his *White Relief*. It hung on the wall like a painting, but it was in fact a shallow relief of geometric shapes painted as white as a covering of snow.

All these developments had an effect on the training of artists. As critical interest started to focus solely on the offerings of the avant-garde, the centuries-old educational standards began to seem old fashioned. When the pushing of art's boundaries began to count as much as the ability to faithfully reproduce the world in paint and stone, and when respect grew for the art made by children, the mentally ill, the untrained, the tactlessly named 'primitive' cultures and that which emerged from the subconscious in a form of free expression, it was inevitable that the kind of art training that had held sway for centuries began to seem irrelevant. The life class, that hallowed practice on which fine art training had been based since the Renaissance, was a casualty.

Not only did confidence in the traditional teaching begin to waver, but new educational theories began to flourish. By the 1920s, several ways of training artists had been initiated that gave equal respect to fine art, craft and design by eliminating the divisions between them, symbolized above all by the Bauhaus school in Germany but strong as well in the Nordic countries. When the Nazis' anti-Semitic, anti-intellectual and anti-avant-garde stance against what they called 'degenerate art' led to the closure of the Bauhaus school in 1933, many of its teachers and artists migrated to the United States. One of the art schools to benefit was North Carolina's progressive Black Mountain College, which received a wave of Bauhaus professors.

For the first half of the century, the schools that offered traditional teaching and those whose openness to new ideas or stress on free expression led to a less prescriptive teaching style existed side by side. But after 1960 the balance changed, and traditional teaching no longer impressed the students or their teachers. Life drawing did not die out, but it took on a different form. Artists' willingness to exchange the suave brushstrokes of the past for something rougher encouraged teachers to free their students from pernickety realism, challenging them to get a pose on paper in thirty seconds or paint with a broom in the name of memory or free expression.

This lack of interest in the traditional life class was part of a wider international development: the elevation of art schools into degree-conferring institutions where theory was as important as traditional techniques. Between 1960 and 1980, it was possible for students from important schools of art to graduate without ever drawing from the nude or learning the age-old techniques of painting in oil.[5] In the sixties, 'the new academicism became Conceptual art', says Derek Boshier, who made his name as a Pop artist in 1960s Britain.[6] In 1960s America, according to critic Harold Rosenberg, the upsurge in geometric abstract art resulted from the Bauhaus-influenced university art departments.[7]

The twists and turns of 20th-century art teaching were played out in different ways and at different times in different countries. Around mid-century in France, for example, despite the strength of the atelier system, whereby would-be artists could train in the studios of professionals they respected, the traditional Beaux Arts system based on life drawing kept its status – that is until the revolutionary summer of 1968 prised its fingers off the pen that decreed the national training schemes. When one considers the way the American Abstract Expressionists of the 1950s snatched the crown of the art world from the French, whose century-long domination had begun with the Impressionists and ended with Picasso, it is tempting to look for an educational link. The Master of Fine Arts degree, introduced at four American colleges in the 1920s, was widely recognized by 1960. The idea behind the MFA was that it was staffed by artists teaching artists. It did not offer training on how to make art – that was the job of the undergraduate colleges – but concentrated on producing professional artists. Teaching on the Yale MFA course in the 1950s, Mark Rothko said that everyone wanted to be an Abstract Expressionist.[8]

In Britain in 1956, when Clark's *The Nude* was published, art schools still clung to their conviction that all students should learn to draw from life. Four years later, the devaluation of the idea that fine art was a replication of life made in traditional materials finally reached their doors. It expressed itself in the belief that it was no longer necessary for a student to have either an ability to draw from life or a non-questioning respect for the traditional nudes of the past.

Two government documents, marking the ascent of art education from diploma to degree, illustrate the change. In 1951, the Ministry of Education issued an exiguous leaflet that succinctly dictated the life-drawing exercises required for the National Diploma, Painting.[9] In 1960, the Coldstream Report put the study of fine art at an art school on a par with a university degree. The schools of art were henceforth allowed to decide on the content of their courses and to assess their students' work. Government guidance was so non-prescriptive it qualified as non-existent: 'In the area of fine art the fundamental studies are painting with drawing, and sculpture with drawing...Those who specialize in painting should be given experience of working in three dimensions, and those who specialize in sculpture should conversely be given experience in the use of colour and working on a flat surface.'[10]

Derek Boshier recalls learning to draw from life in the pre-Coldstream decade. His description of the life class at Yeovil School of Art in the mid-1950s would be familiar to a student from the 1850s. To begin with, he was not allowed into the life class for a year and then when he got there, knowledge of anatomy was stressed:

'You drew the model and then you got out your anatomy book and drew in the muscles. And we had to be able to name every bone in the body.' There were two models, but they were not enough for this particular student, already longing for a more modern experience of variety. 'The woman was pretty close to the ideal, not fat, not thin, but she made you long for something different, either very fat or skinny.'[11]

When the life class was made optional or dropped, the nude lost its importance in art education. The revolution that cut the art schools loose from any traditional requirements, and the avant-garde's interest in crashing through barriers and making its own marks, broke the link with the art of the past. The nude was a casualty of this absence of training and tradition and became an irrelevance to contemporary art in the 1960s. The sculptor William Tucker recalls that at art school in London in 1960 he felt 'liberated by the sense that sculpture could be constructed of any material, and its subject need no longer be the human figure'.[12]

By 1960, shut away in a suitcase, packed and ready to be heaved up to the attic, the ideal nude was tidily removed from the world of contemporary art. Except it did not happen quite like that. Even when sat on, the suitcase would not shut. Like a comic illustration to instructions on how to pack, bits of the nude would insist on sticking out. An arm here, a leg there, a curvy thigh that just wouldn't shrink to fit. A trail of nudes was left on the floor and the subject survived, as did realism, as a choice among many that contemporary artists could make.

As always happens, the practice had sabotaged the theory. From the end of the 19th century, the avant-garde artists who set the artistic pace did not so much turn their back on the nude as become interested in new ways of painting and sculpting it. Their position as leaders of the pack was evidence of their desire to shake the status quo. And what better way to do this than by treating the revered ideal nude in their own particular ways? As the traditional nude emigrated to the photographic studios or to amateurs, it left the avant-garde artists free to experiment with the formerly hallowed subject. Loath to give it up entirely, they, in fact, ensured its survival: it kept popping up like an underwater swimmer throughout the following decades, its appearance dictated by whatever version of modernism the artists followed.

Paradoxically, the earliest of the new-style nudes were inspired by photography, that same intervention whose magical, life-mirroring abilities had pushed artists to think differently about their work. In the 1850s, Gustave Courbet used 'artistic'

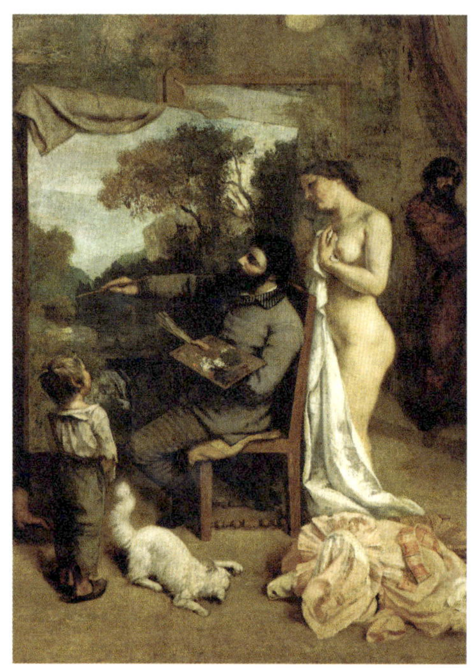

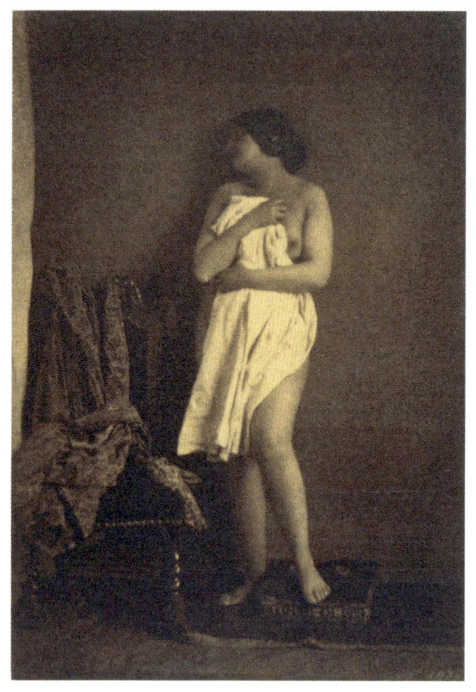

photographic studies as well as live models for paintings of realistically proportioned women whose sturdy nakedness bore no resemblance to the ideal nude.

In 1863, Édouard Manet painted *Olympia* (see page 120), the portrait of a modern, naked sex worker, bringing the nude out of mythology and into the here and now that the camera captured. In the 1880s, Edgar Degas presented a series of women washing, informed by his fascination with the new angles and intimate realism of photographs. They were like animals, said shocked onlookers, a reaction similar to those aroused by Lucian Freud's nudes today. It just was not the way a nude woman was supposed to look when immortalized in a painting.

In the early 20th century, artists looked at the art of other cultures for inspiration. Picasso's *Les Demoiselles d'Avignon* of 1907, one of the first major works of the modern age, is a painting of five women in a brothel whose poses can be traced to the African sculptures in the ethnographic museum in Paris that he haunted at the time, the majority of which were taken from French colonies in the northwest of the continent. In explosively modern Dresden, the artists working before the First World War tried to build a bridge to the future by way of tribal art. Karl Schmidt-Rottluff, Ernst Ludwig Kirchner, Max Pechstein, Erich Heckel and their like-minded colleagues made paintings of naked bathers and studio models whose black outlines and crude colours questioned the whole idea of assessing artists by their ability to produce copycat versions of life.

A surprising example of the many stylistic hats worn by the nude is realism. Although it was standard in sophisticated circles in the first half of the 20th century to put realism down as the work of the amateur, the Sunday painter and the conservative, the Surrealists used it as a strategy to increase the impact of their images. Their fascination with psychoanalysis, sex and the eternal feminine made it inevitable that they would find the female nude helpful in expressing their ideas. The Belgian artist Paul Delvaux inserted bare-breasted women into imagined settings of classical

OPPOSITE ABOVE **Gustave Courbet**, *The Studio of the Painter* (detail), 1855, oil on canvas. In mid-19th-century France, Courbet presented spectators with a new kind of female nude. Less idealized, she played an important role in his commitment to the representation of his view of contemporary French reality. This detail shows the model standing behind Courbet's chair, as a partner in his painting. The full work depicts a room crowded with the people who influenced his ideas.

OPPOSITE BELOW **Julien Vallou de Villeneuve**, *Nude Study*, 1854, print on salted paper from a paper negative. Photography was a huge influence on mid-19th-century artists of the avant-garde, its unexpected angles suggesting realistic poses. Courbet drew on the work of photographers for his seascapes, and was also open to photography's suggestions for his figurative art, as seen in this comparison of his model with Villeneuve's photograph of the previous year.

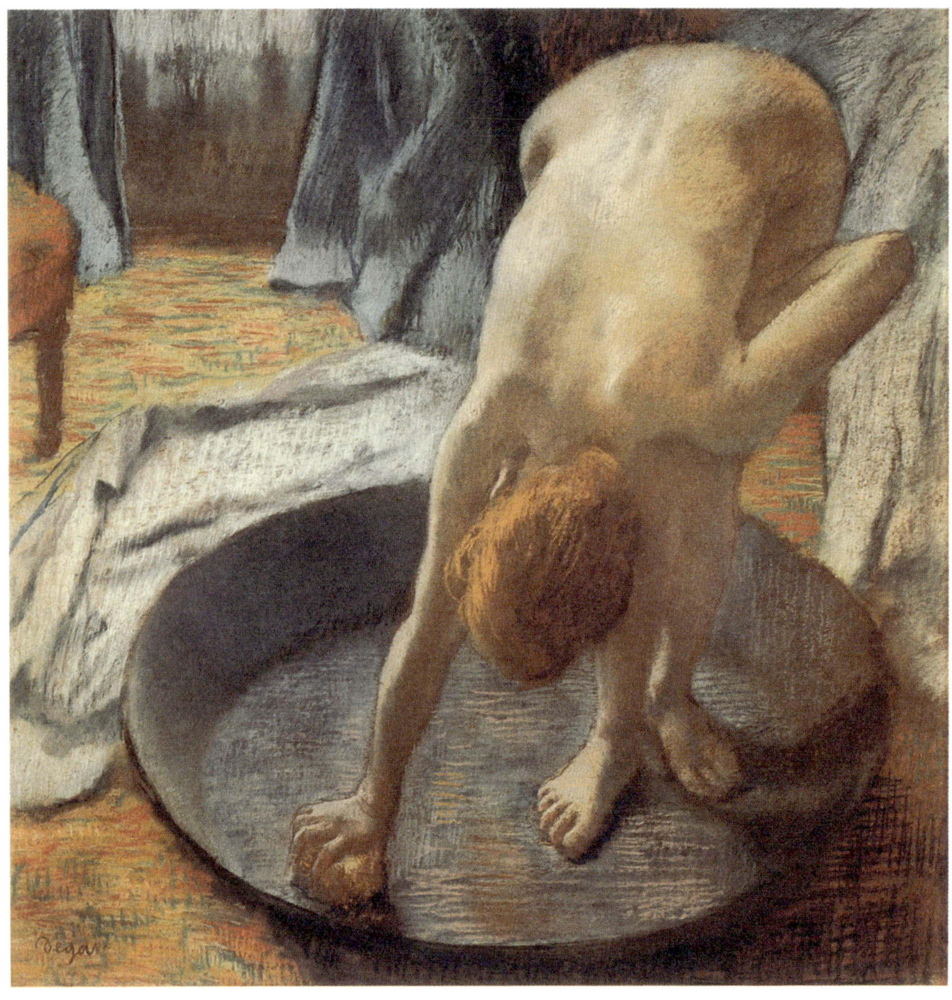

Edgar Degas, *The Tub*, 1886, pastel on paper. Degas was influenced by the new angles and compositions of photography. When applied to his pastels of women washing, the resulting realism scandalized many. The view from above of a stooping, naked female lacked the conventional disposition of limbs arranged to best advantage.

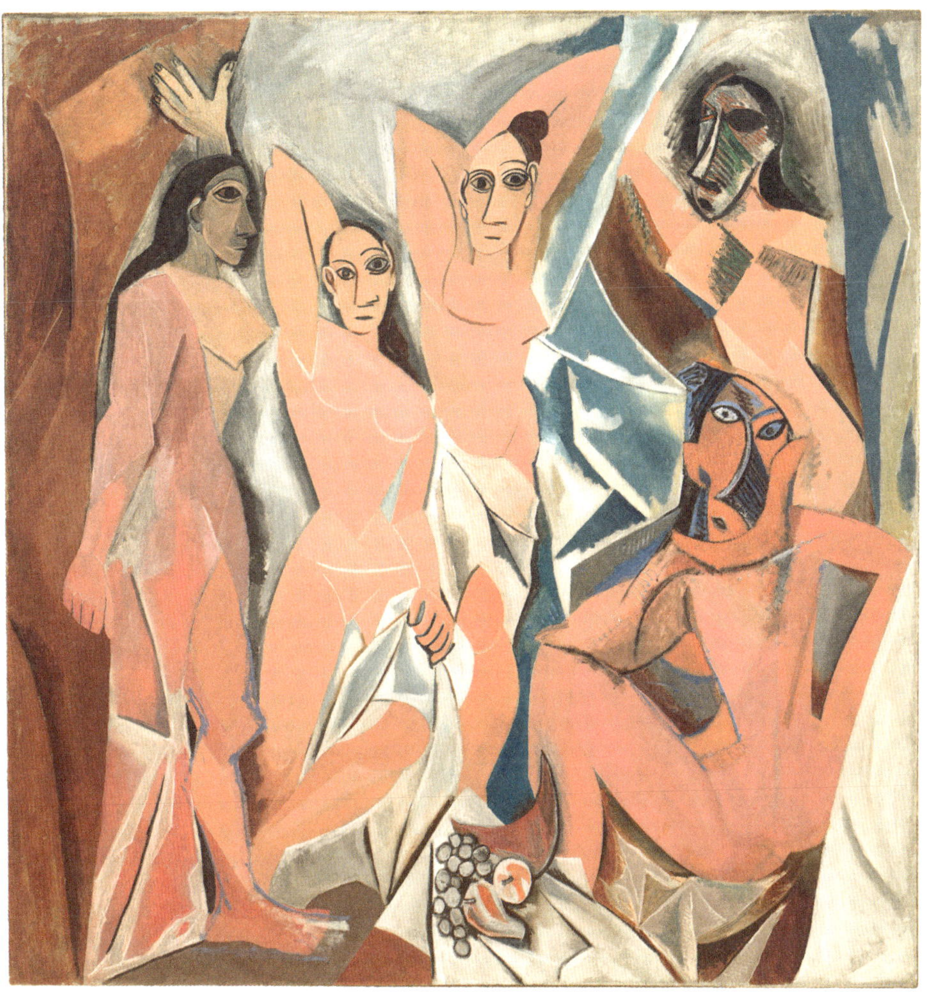

Pablo Picasso, *Les Demoiselles d'Avignon*, 1907, oil on canvas. In the search for new
ways to paint the nude, artists looked outside Western culture. The figures in Picasso's
Les Demoiselles d'Avignon are heavily influenced by the sculptures he admired in
the Paris ethnographic museum. The two faces on the right resemble African masks
and the geometricized poses and bodies owe much to African carvings.

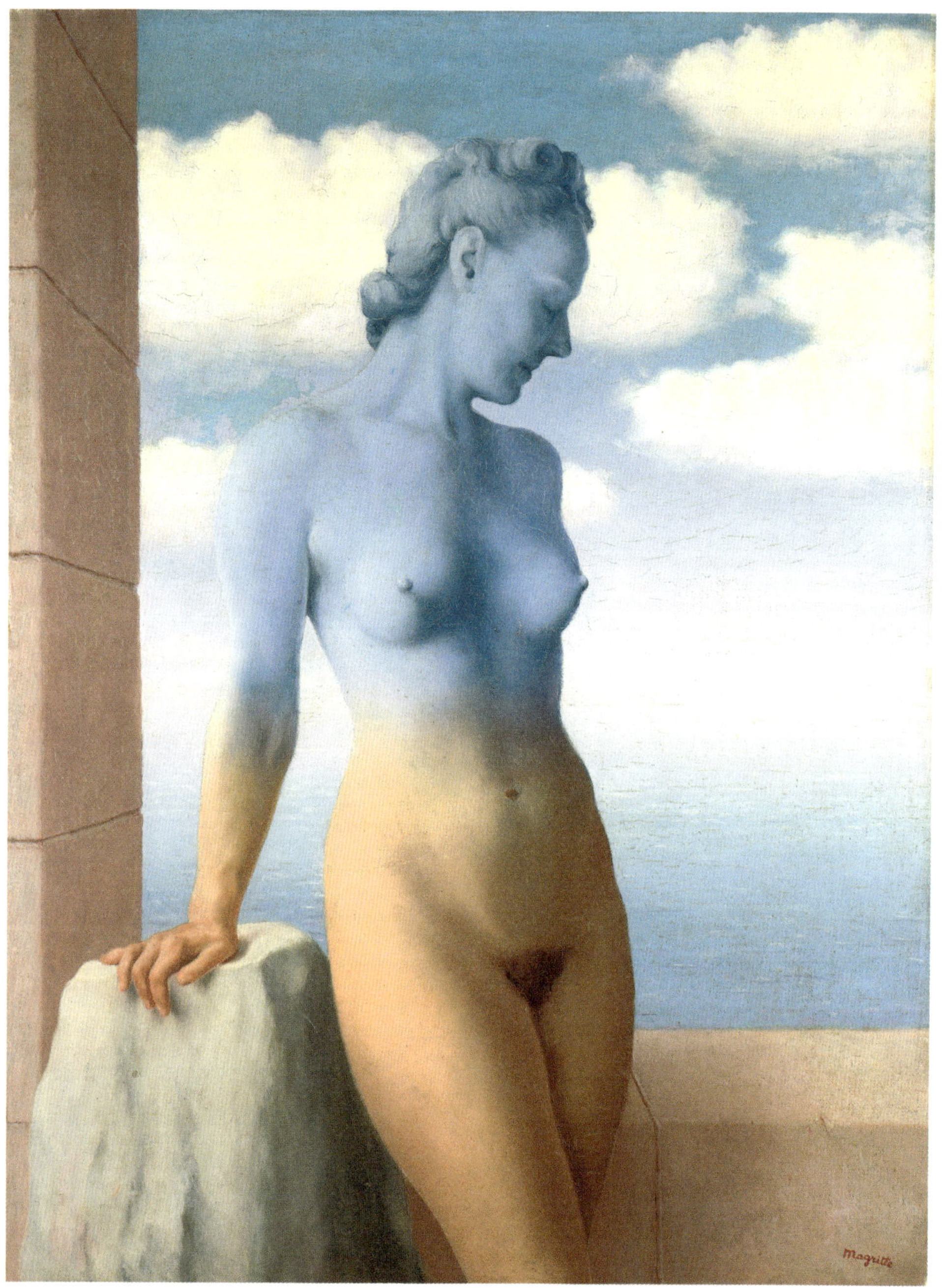

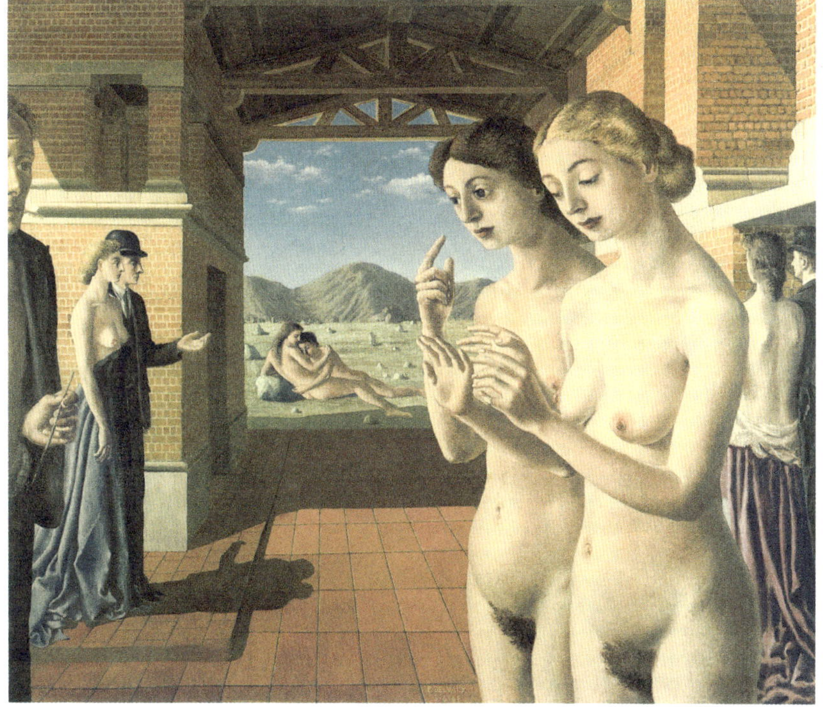

OPPOSITE **René Magritte**, *La Magie noire* (Black Magic), 1945, oil on canvas.

ABOVE **Paul Delvaux**, *Les Mains* (Hands), 1941, oil on canvas. The Surrealists' fascination with women, dreams and sexuality ensured the female nude an important place in their imagery. Magritte plays with ideas of flesh, stone and metamorphosis, while Delvaux paints naked women and bowler-hatted men floating silently through a timeless world of dreams.

architecture that belong to dreams. His countryman René Magritte painted clouds passing behind the torso of a naked woman who stands against a window. Both use reality to question reality.

For three decades from the 1930s, Balthus painted half-dressed adolescent girls in disturbingly sexual situations, which retain their troubling power today. In the 1940s, the iconoclastic Francis Picabia produced a series of colourful nude females that look like luscious pin-ups, an early reclamation of the ideal nude from the popular media to which it had emigrated. Picasso was refreshed throughout his career by new, young female bodies, his painted, drawn and sculpted versions of them distorted as contemporary art demanded, but nonetheless recognizable as women without clothes.

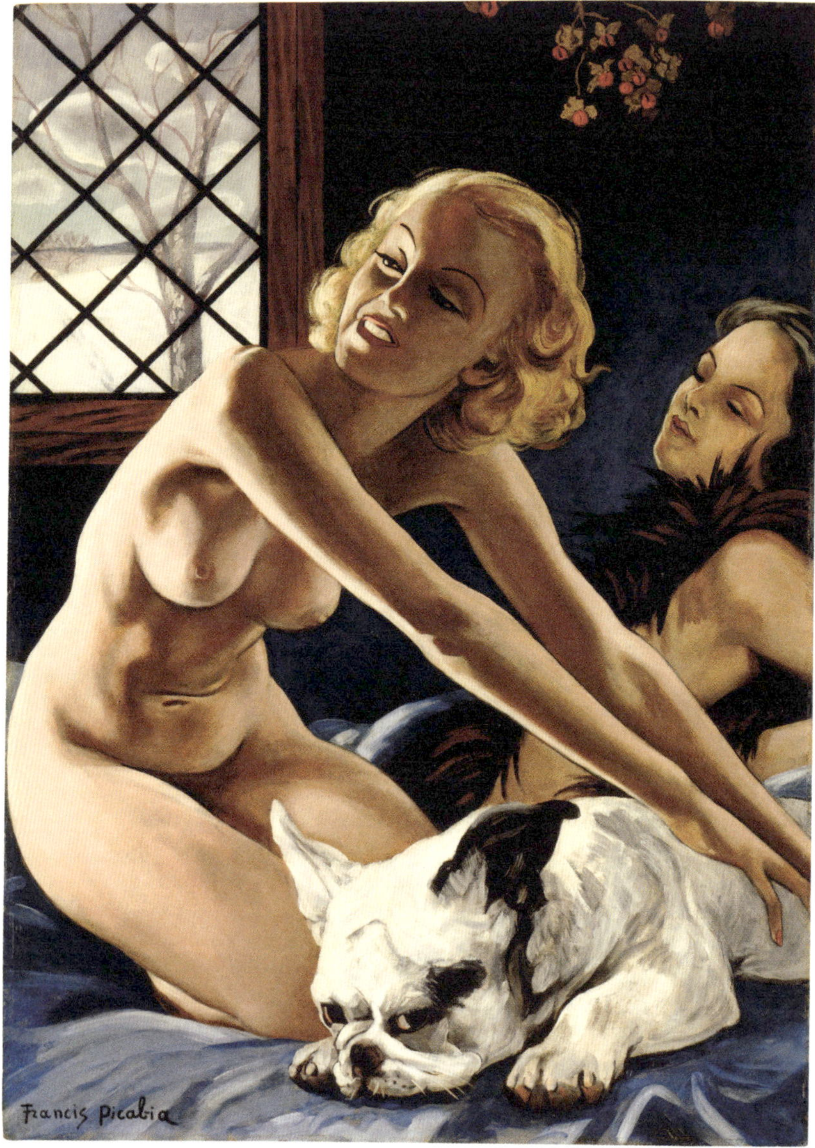

Francis Picabia, *Femmes au bull-dog* (Women with a Bulldog), 1941–2, oil on board.
Towards the end of his life, Picabia, an artist who expressed his Surrealistic sympathies
through abstract art, text-based jokes and found objects, turned to a kind of realism
that foreshadows the Pop art movement two decades later. His sensual, sexy
nudes were inspired by pin-up pictures in girlie magazines.

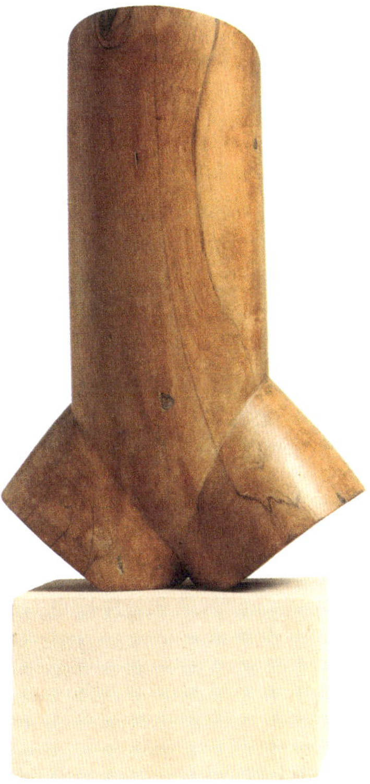

Constantin Brancusi, *Torso of a Young Man II*, 1923, walnut wood.
Abstraction had a huge effect on the presentation of the nude in the 20th century.
Brancusi's pared-down nudes retain only vestigial traces of gender. The apparently
female nature of this torso is counteracted by its phallic upthrust.

Like painters, sculptors never left the nude behind entirely. Although sculptors
interested in the newest developments sneered at realistic representation as suitable only for war memorials, not art galleries, that did not stop the human form
from being an inspirational and exciting starting point for many. An international
array of bodies resulted from the marriage of the nude and modernism in the
first half of the 20th century – from Constantin Brancusi's streamlined bodies to
Aristide Maillol's generously proportioned women, whose emphatic female qualities are closer to fertility goddesses than to their Renaissance forebears. Henry
Moore did not hide the fact that at the heart of many of his great bronze and
stone shapes from the 1940s to the 1970s lay a reclining woman. Some bodies
are geometric, some so pared away they are barely recognizable as bodies, some

refined into smoothly evocative curves, yet all are based on the unclothed human form and many on naked men and women posing in the studio.

The modern nude even began to turn up in the kind of public art that results from discussions by committees intent on bringing culture to our surroundings. Forbidden by its role to offend the taxpayers or shareholders who fund it, or the wide range of people who pass it every day, contemporary public sculpture nonetheless can take forms that, while not as outspoken as those destined for galleries, still speak more of new trends than of the traditional sculptured nude. In 2011, Cornelia Parker, an artist best known for her non-figurative work recycling everyday objects, produced a life-size bronze sculpture of a thirty-eight-year-old mother of two for the British seaside town of Folkestone. Although inspired by Edvard Eriksen's *Little Mermaid*, which welcomes ships to Copenhagen's harbour, Parker's statue of a non-idealized maternal body is an adult version of the girlishly slim original.

For the dedicated follower of the sort of contemporary art that is welcomed by museums and grand galleries and taken seriously by critics, the ideal nude is as hard to find as a realistic still life or an allegory staffed with gods and goddesses. But the nude is still there. It is just that it has changed. The belief in the ideal no longer has a place in art and artists are no longer interested in painting such abstract concepts as beauty. They would rather their audience question the concept, as Jenny Saville does in *Plan*, where contour lines on the belly suggest both hilly regions and surgeons' plastic surgery marks.

Like a rebellious teenager, the well-behaved world of art had developed unruly habits by the time Clark was writing in the mid-1950s. Although he was interested in the changes, there was no way he could guess how things would speed up in the few years after his book was published.

With the helpful hindsight offered by the last half-century, it seems clear that Clark's book occupies a pivotal position between the death of the ideal nude and

OPPOSITE ABOVE **Aristide Maillol**, *La Méditerranée*, 1902–5, bronze. Rounded women rooted to the earth through sturdy legs and feet were Maillol's personal ideal. Although he admired the art of ancient Greece and Rome, the generous proportions of his female forms make them far earthier than the classical ideal.

OPPOSITE BELOW **Henry Moore**, *Recumbent Figure*, 1938, green Hornton stone. Many of Henry Moore's huge sculptures make reference to the hills and hollows of the landscapes in which they sit. At the heart of numerous works is a reclining nude or a nursing mother, subjects that attracted him from the start of his career in the 1920s.

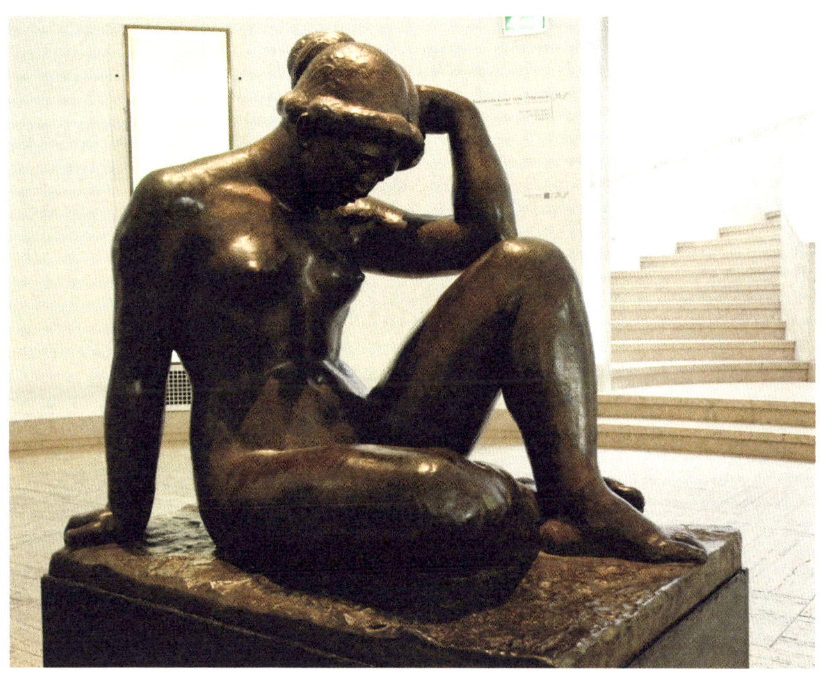

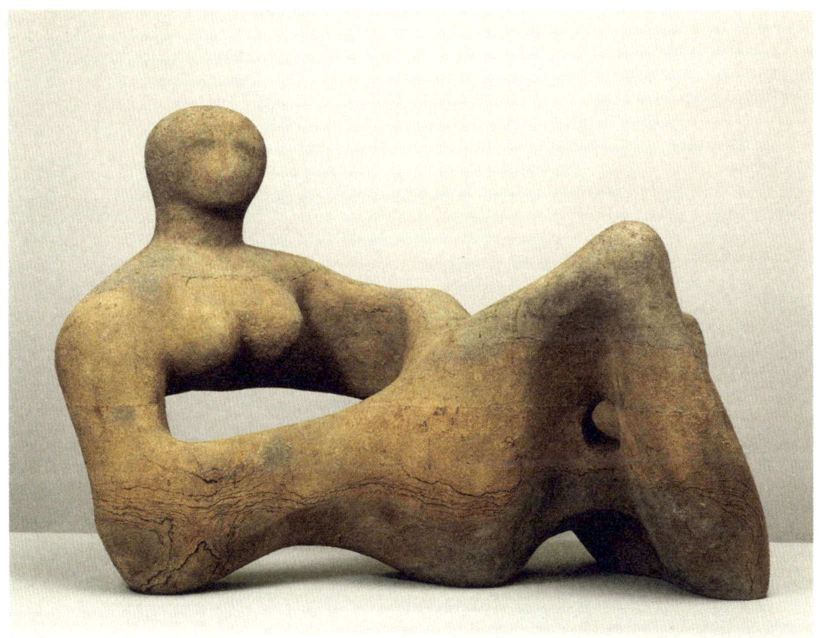

the birth of the naked nude. Clark's ideas remain influential in dealing with historic nudes, but they cannot cope with today's variety. His terms are irrelevant to an art world whose nudity has broken its links to the past, and too blunt as tools to dissect the art based on the body that interests contemporary artists. The successful branding of the nude as untainted by the everyday (of which his book is the final expression), fit to be viewed by men, women and even children in museums and galleries, is a great achievement of post-Renaissance Western art. Its overthrow is what we see on gallery walls today.

2.
BODY ART: THE JOURNEY INTO NAKEDNESS

IN THE SECOND HALF OF THE 20TH CENTURY, the nude became the body. When Clark was writing, 'body art' was a descriptive term for various forms of body decoration – tattoos and piercings, practices such as scarification, beauty by deformation through foot binding or neck elongation with the aid of rings. Ignored by artists, it reached the public through the work of documentary photographers of the weird and wonderful. From the 1960s the creative efforts of photographers who worked for glossy magazines were inspired by the body-painting practices of hippies, whose pleasure in decorating themselves domesticated some of body art's more exotic elements. Readers of *Playboy* for January 1971 were treated to a photograph of the model Veruschka that showed her long, lanky body covered with painted designs and arranged like a leopard along the branch of a tree.

By the time of Clark's death in 1983, Body art, with a revised definition, had been added as a new category to the vocabulary of artistic styles. An art world that had been turned upside down by the canvases of the Abstract Expressionists gave rise to a new kind of art that had a live component, in great part inspired by the gestural painting arm of Jackson Pollock. A sign of how previous certainties were crumbling came in the form of the Happenings of Allan Kaprow in late 1950s New York. In 1960, Kaprow, who had studied with the minimalist composer John Cage and was an art-school graduate, was invited to serve as director of the Judson Memorial Church art gallery in New York. An artistic result of this appointment, what has come to be called an Environment, was *Apple Shrine,* a place of narrow passageways, collage and hanging bits and pieces. It exists today in photographs and through a rave review in the *Village Voice*: 'Its impact is instantaneous and dramatic. It is an art both of high seriousness and of emotional breadth. What does present a problem is its apparent lack of relation to the established cultural tradition ... One cannot comprehend an attitude which bluntly embraces the fleeting. Perishable materials, perishable forms, perishable genius; chance, change – all conspire to damn this work and dissolve our values.'[1] The author, one Theodore Tucker, who described Kaprow as 'an exceptionally original artist' who has 'seen a movement develop around him', turned out to be Kaprow himself.

Kaprow saw his Happenings as a break with the past. 'What we have, then, is art that tends to lose itself out of bounds, tends to fill our world with itself, art that in meaning, looks, impulse seems to break fairly sharply with the traditions of painters back to at least the Greeks,' he wrote in an influential essay in 1958. 'Pollock's near destruction of this tradition may well be a return to the point where art was more actively involved in ritual, magic and life than we have known it in our recent past ... Pollock, as I see him, left us at the point where we must become preoccupied with and even dazzled by the space and objects of our everyday life, either our bodies, clothes, rooms or, if need be, the vastness of 42nd Street ... Young artists of today need no longer say, "I am a painter" or "a poet" or "a dancer". They are simply "artists". All of life will be open to them ... People will be delighted or horrified, critics will be confused or amused, but these, I am certain, will be the alchemies of the 1960s.'[2]

The movement quickly spread. Aside from conventional painting and sculpture, anything was permitted in any combination in the dream of putting new life into art. Singers, dancers, painters, sculptors, musicians and poets collaborated on events that took pride in their unscripted and transitory nature, their evanescence a protest against the power of the art market. In 1962, the painter Robert Rauschenberg and the sculptor Robert Morris became involved with the choreographer Yvonne Rainer's Judson Dance Theater. In 1966–7, Andy Warhol gave the name *Exploding Plastic Inevitable* to a film, a one-issue magazine and a series of multi-media artworks that took place in his New York studio and which were reported with as much excitement in the daily papers as the in art press. The art lay in the performance. Process, the body, transitory, experiment was the vocabulary of the new form.

Although this interdisciplinary moment came out of the New York of the 1950s, the interest in testing boundaries and new ideas was in the air in other places. In the decade of political and social upheavals that was the 1960s, disdain for the establishment and fading respect for conventional art forms were features of the international avant-garde art scene. In Germany in 1968, Valie Export pulled on a pair of crotchless trousers and walked around a cinema in a protest against the

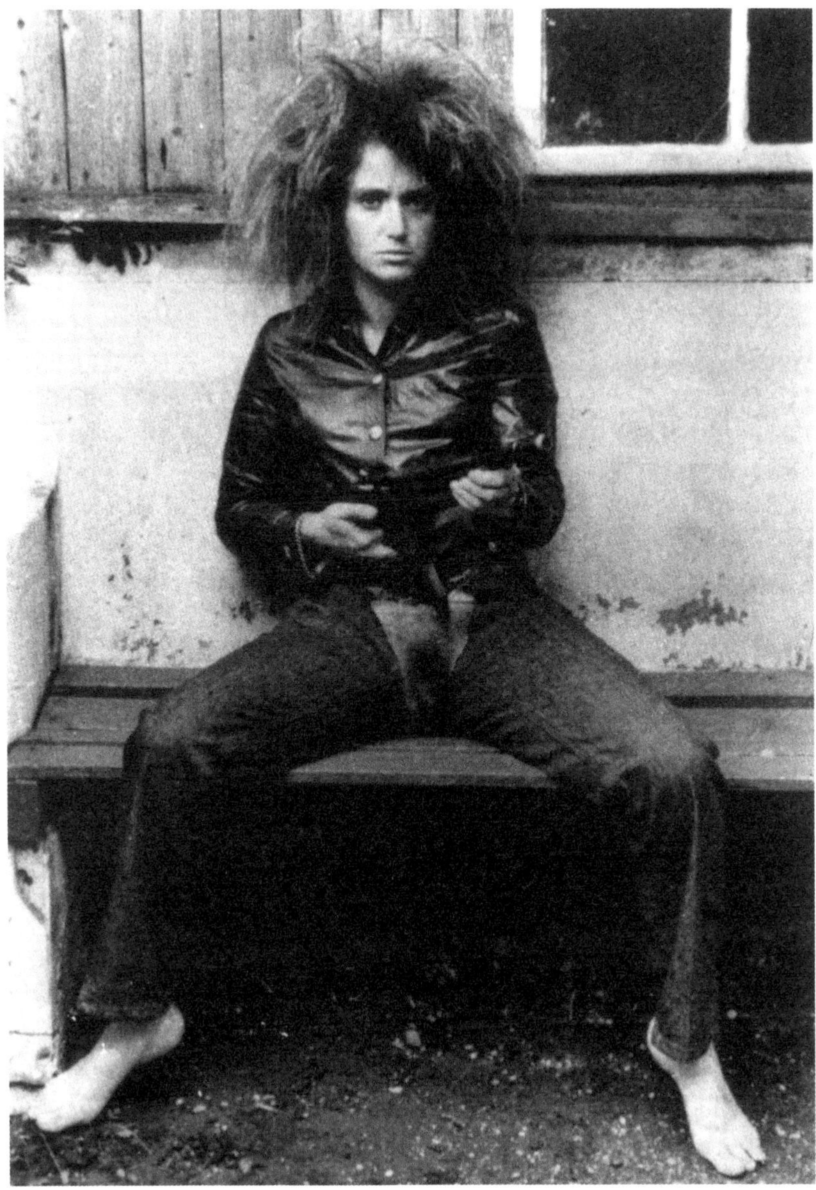

Valie Export, *Action Pants: Genital Panic*, 1968, screenprint on paper. The body, as opposed to the nude, entered art with a fanfare in the 1960s. Valie Export walked round a Munich cinema in crotchless trousers, challenging the audience to face the sexual reality of a real woman as opposed to the sanitized version on the screen.

passive roles of female screen stars. In France, Gina Pane performed a series of actions in which parallels were made between the pain of life and the pain suffered by the body. In *Escalade non-anesthésiée (Unaestheticized Climb)* of 1971 she repeatedly climbed and descended a ladder studded with sharp metal that cut into her bare feet, in the hope that spectators would transfer their recognition of her suffering to the victims of the Vietnam war.

Artists had been making waves outside their studios since the early years of the 20th century. In 1916 poets, dancers and visual artists joined forces under the name Dada at the Cabaret Voltaire in Zurich, declaiming nonsense verses to show their opposition to the First World War and the conventional values that they believed had led to it. At the First International Surrealist Exhibition in London in 1936 Salvador Dalí surprised visitors (and himself when it got stuck) by arriving to deliver his lecture with a diving helmet on his head, to symbolize the dive down to the subconscious. But taking art outside the studio went further during the 1960s, as the visual artists who had been involved in collaborative events from the start increasingly took centre stage. As an audience in 1964 watched Carolee Schneemann intoning instructions to a group of young men and bikini-clad young women losing restraint and their minimal clothing as they writhed on the floor and rubbed themselves with dead fish and bloody pieces of meat in a legendary Performance piece entitled *Meat Joy*, it was clear that a new form of art had arrived.

As the Happenings splintered and metamorphosed with the inventiveness of the artists, new descriptions evolved to make sense of what was on show. Before the decade was half-way through, the label Performance art had emerged followed, in an effort to bring some order to the scene, by a variety of names to identify the assorted new developments: Time-Based art, for example, had currency for some years as a name for video pieces. Not all of them stuck. But one did: Body art.

By the end of the 1960s, Body art had established itself as a branch of visual art that dealt with self, with emotions, with sexuality – the whole experience of existence. The classification was used to cover everything that took as its subject the human body as it related to the world around it in emotional or physical terms. The material was very often the artist's body. It was the perfect art for a period that saw the breaking of social structures and taboos in every area, from the fight to allow black people to sit at the front of the bus in America's southern states to the scene in the musical *Hair* where the cast threw off their clothes and celebrated the age of Aquarius in song, standing there with not a stitch between them and the audience.

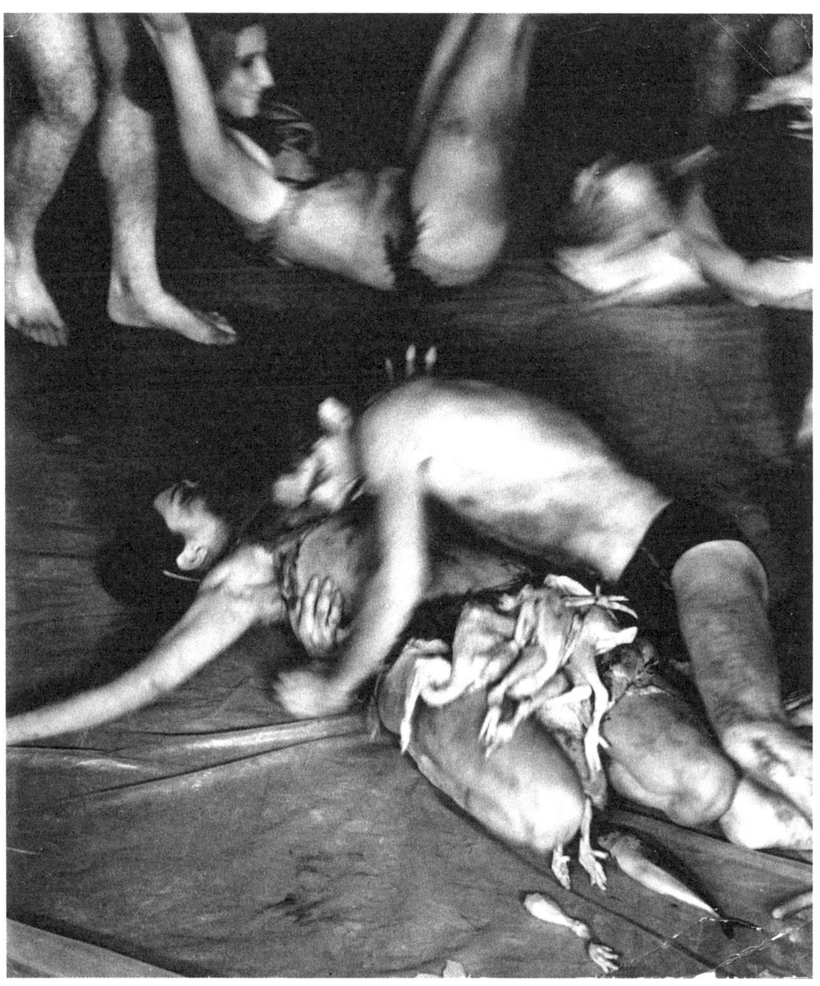

Carolee Schneemann, *Meat Joy*, 1964, performance photograph.
Meat Joy exemplifies Schneemann's interest in sexuality, the body and myth.
First performed in Paris in 1964, its eight performers wriggled and embraced
amid raw fish, chickens, sausages, wet paint and paper scraps.

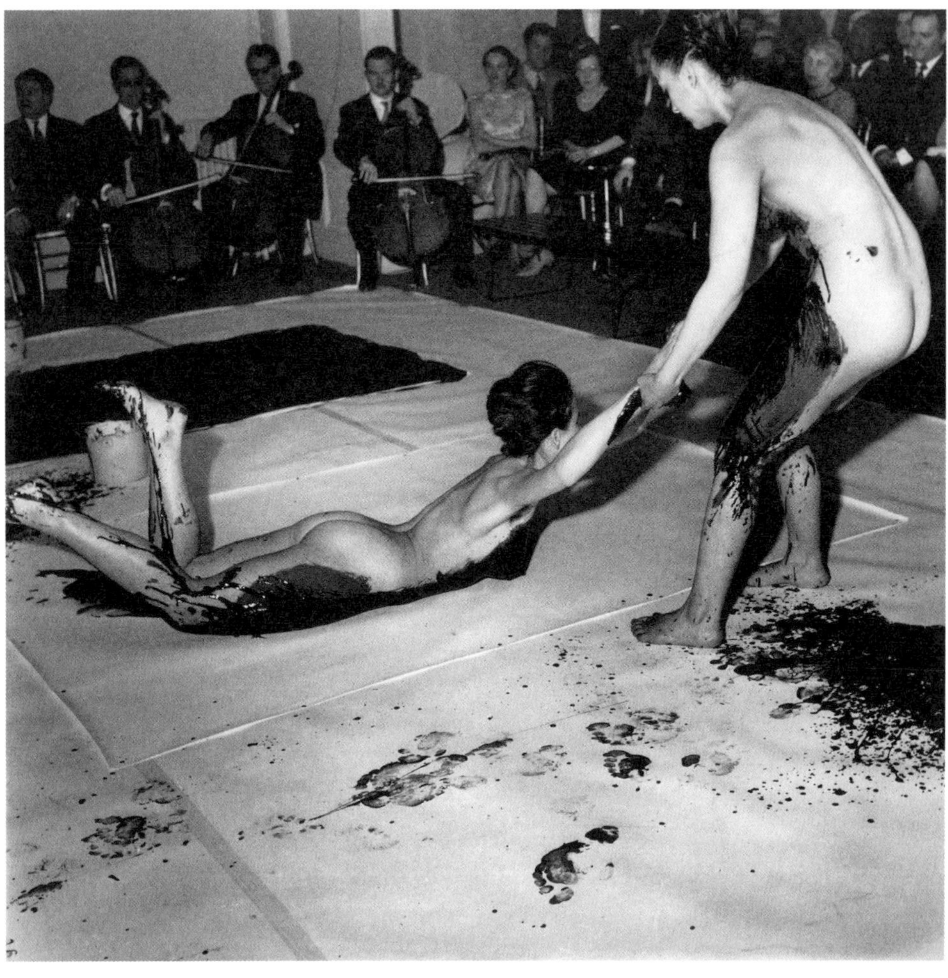

Yves Klein, *Anthropometries of the Blue Period*, 9 March 1960, performance photograph. The influence of abstract art, an interest in the nude and a desire to vivify his fascination with the colour blue fed into the performances dreamed up by Yves Klein at the start of the 1960s in which naked women were used as living paintbrushes. In true performance tradition, the event shown here was accompanied by contemporary music.

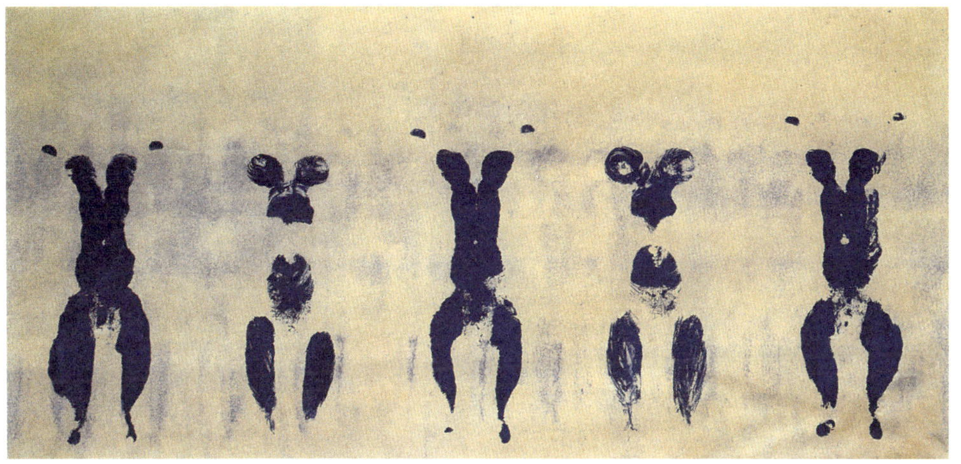

Yves Klein, *Untitled Anthropometry*, 1960, pure pigment and
synthetic resin on paper mounted on canvas. The unexpected result of these
imprints of young and perfect female bodies offers overtones of primitive
wood carvings and ancient European fertility figures.

By 1975, a catalogue for Chicago's Museum of Contemporary Art could
claim: 'Artists using their own bodies as their primary medium of expression is
the most significant artistic development of the 1970s.' The writer considered that
unlike the theatricality of Happenings and the formality of contemporary dance,
and unlike Performance art, this new movement was personal, private and autobiographical: 'It is the artist's physical being which bears the content and is both
subject and means of aesthetic expression.'[3]

Nakedness was an element in the practice of many Body artists, as the nude
had been an element in the art of the past. In Paris in 1960, Yves Klein covered a
group of naked young women in a strong bright blue, now known as International
Klein Blue, and pulled them over sheets of paper on the floor: he called the technique 'living paintbrushes', and the finished product 'Anthropometries'. Labelled
at the time as an event or a Happening, it can with hindsight be seen as a way of
painting the nude that was as random as Jackson Pollock's technique of putting
paint into cans punched with holes and directing them over the canvas on the
floor. As Klein's models pressed themselves on to the paper on the walls or the
floor, or obligingly allowed themselves to be dragged around, a new attitude to
art was being born.

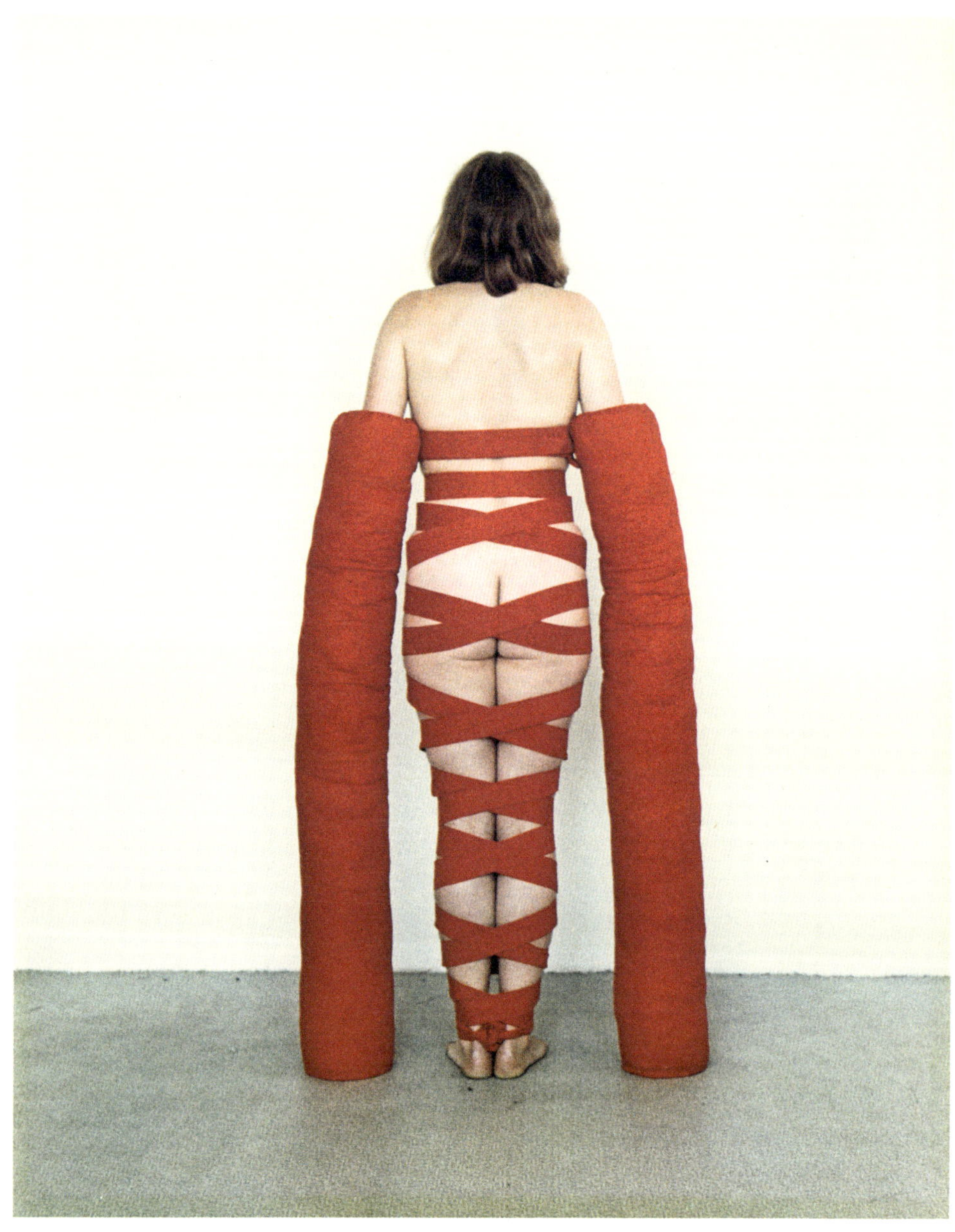

Rebecca Horn, *Arm Extensions*, 1968, fabric, wood and metal. Horn's investigation into the body's need to reach out and touch lies behind this striking work, which shows her at once imprisoned but also with a reach that goes far beyond herself.

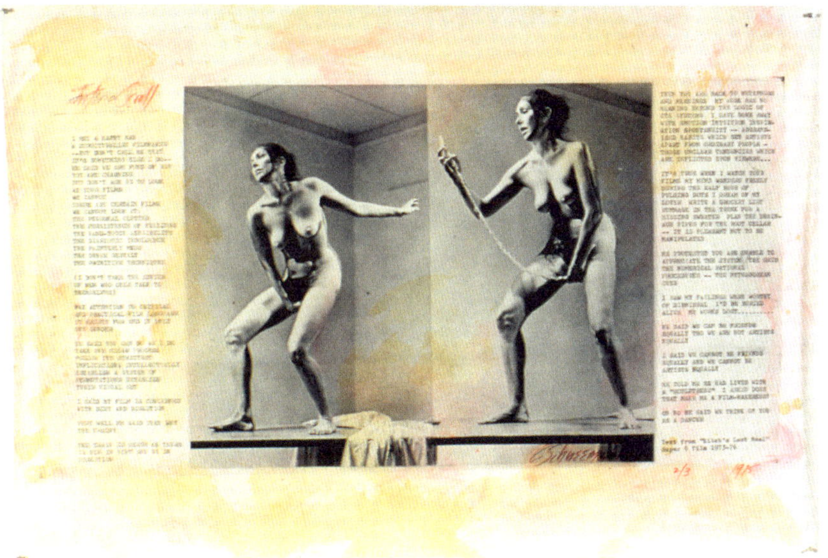

Carolee Schneemann, *Interior Scroll*, 1975, photo collage with beet juice,
urine, coffee, photographic print. In her performance at the exhibition 'Here and Now'
in East Hampton, New York, Schneemann expressed her feminist view of the art
world by reading aloud from a scroll that she withdrew from her vagina.

In 1968, Rebecca Horn wound red straps around her naked body and added padded extensions to her arms. Inspired by the enforced months of bed rest demanded by the lung disease she had contracted from working with fibreglass and polyester at art school, she was attempting to present her desire to touch people and things beyond her reach as she lay in bed. The result was disturbing and new, a bit surrealistic, a bit fetishistic, a bit ethnographic. Sometimes artists got others to remove their clothes for them, as Yoko Ono did in 1964 when she sat on the floor with scissors beside her for the audience to use to cut off her clothes. In 1975, in *Interior Scroll*, Carolee Schneemann stood naked on a table in front of an audience and intoned the words on a scroll drawn out of her vagina: 'I met a happy man / a structuralist filmmaker /… / he said we are fond of you / you are charming / but don't ask us to look at your films / we cannot / there are certain films we cannot look at: / the personal clutter / the persistence of feelings.'

Unlike a performance of *Giselle* or a classic play at the theatre, Body art involves more than familiarity, swooning emotion and appreciative applause from a gratified audience. Because the only choreography is the set-up at the start, it nearly

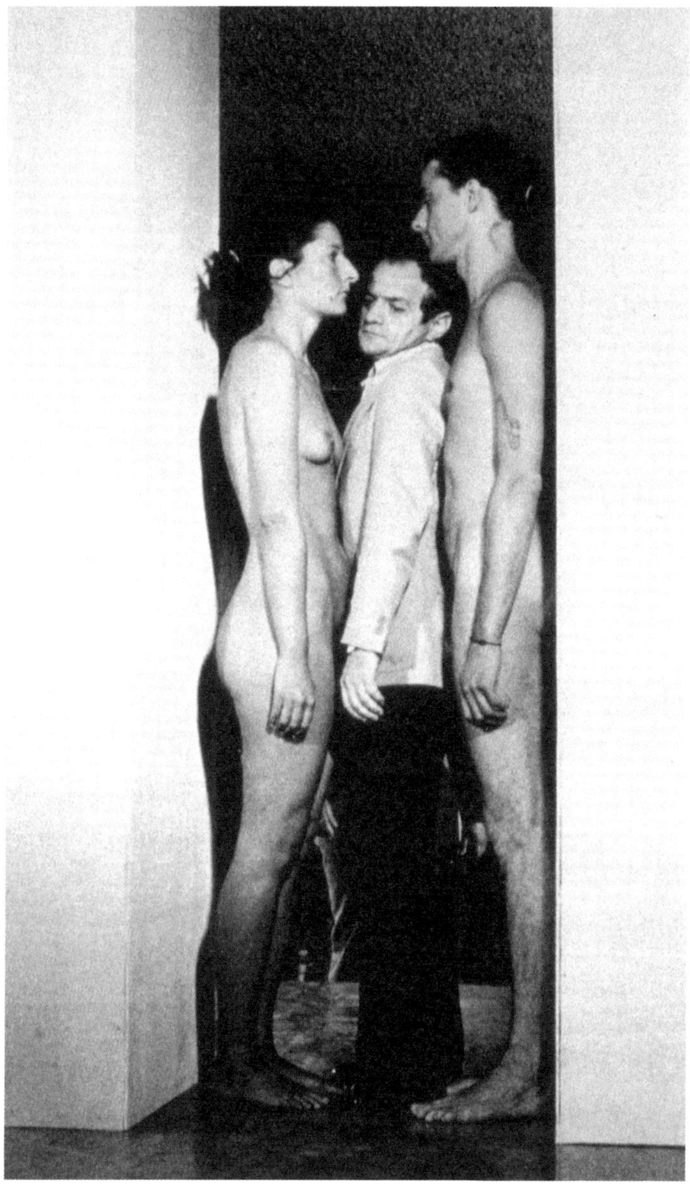

Marina Abramović, *Imponderabilia*, Galleria Communale d'Arte Bologna, 1977, performance photograph. Standing naked with her partner Ulay on either side of the gallery doorway through which the public had to pass, Abramović effortlessly revealed that discomfort with nudity minus the familiar fine-art coating was alive and well.

always incorporates the unexpected, which means the audience can be shaken in uncomfortable ways. Pushing, testing and involving the audience in some kind of reciprocity is a characteristic of much Body art. In 1972, Vito Acconci challenged conventional ideas of what should go on in a gallery by hiding under a false floor and masturbating in a responsive relationship to the sound of those walking above him. Known as *Seedbed*, it is regularly aired today in video form and has become a classic of the genre. In 2005, Marina Abramović re-enacted it in *Seven Easy Pieces*, proof for the sceptical of Body art's acceptance as an art form with its own particular history. (Gina Pane was another of the artists whose work she chose to recreate.)

Abramović, who began her life-long project of testing the limits of her body in 1960s Yugoslavia, has explained that planning the outcome of her events would make it theatre, not performance: audience reaction and involvement, not appreciation, has always been her goal. In *Imponderabilia*, a work from 1977, Abramović and her partner Ulay took off their clothes and stood like two pillars opposite each other in the doorway of a gallery in Bologna, forcing the visitors to decide which way to face as they squeezed through to get in or out. Its re-enactment thirty-five years later at the artist's 2010 retrospective at New York's Museum of Modern Art showed that issues of public discomfort with the naked body were not dead. This is the art of embarrassment, applied to the cause of raising questions.

In 1974 in *Rhythm O*, Abramović, describing herself as the object, endured six hours at the Studio Morra, Naples, while the public chose any of seventy-two objects on a nearby table to use on her as they desired. A disturbing photograph from this performance shows her with tears in her eyes and a thorny rose across her naked body. The audience's guilt and shame at what she had unleashed in them have relevance for an age of brutality disguised as military power. Speaking of art as testing limits, she has said that she agrees with Bruce Nauman that art is a matter of life and death and that if you are there one hundred per cent, then things really happen. Less than one hundred per cent is not good art. It is hard to do it, she acknowledges, but she says it is the only way – and this means no compromises. She has described *Rhythm O* as 'the heaviest piece I ever did because I wasn't in control, the audience was in control'.[4]

It is all a far cry from earlier examples of discomfort in art. Michelangelo on his back painting painfully with his arms above his head or artists' models fainting as they try to hold the crucifixion pose are the traditional examples, not artists conducting experiments on their bodies in the name of art. But although Body artists operate in ways unknown before the 20th century, they resemble the artists

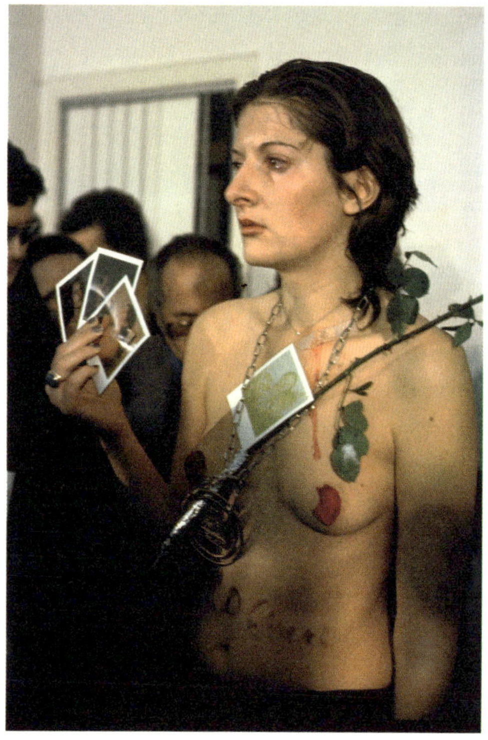

who preceded them in their desire to affect the spectator. Their work lives on in the films, photographs and videos, which nowadays are regarded as part of the art, just as paintings and sculptures resulted from earlier artists' confrontations with naked models.

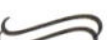

The extremism that fascinated the first generation of Body artists continues to interest their successors. Today there exists a subsection of artists who are willing to submit their bodies to punishment and experimentation in the name of art in a way that can be seen as an updating of the tattoos, decorations and piercings of the traditional forms of Body art. The difference is that instead of putting up with pain for self-adornment, their discomfort references developments outside themselves. They are both scientist and specimen as they undergo their experiments in order to explore ideas about gender, emotions and the body's boundaries.

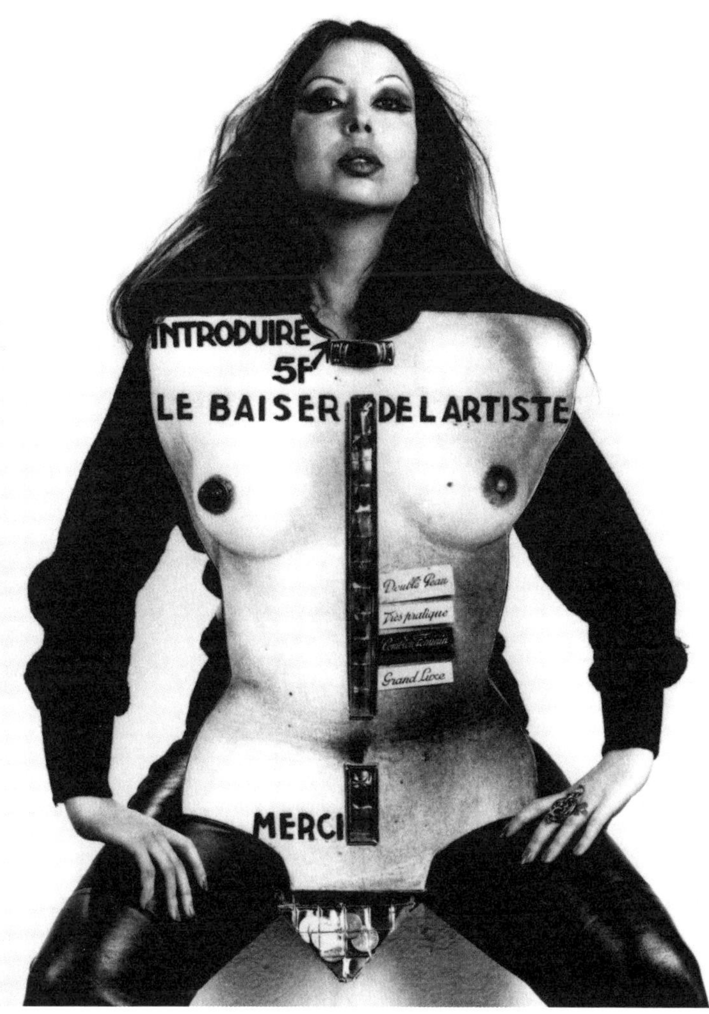

OPPOSITE **Marina Abramović**, *Rhythm O*, Studio Morra, Naples, 1974, performance photograph. Asking questions through testing the limits of the body has been Abramović's artistic objective since the 1960s. In *Rhythm O*, she exposed the relationship between power and cruelty when she stood for hours while the public abused her body using objects on a table next to her.

ABOVE **Orlan**, *The Kiss of the Artist*, FIAC, Grand Palais, Paris, 1977, black-and-white photograph. The implications of the feminine ideal are the target of the French performance artist Orlan's explorations. For *The Kiss of the Artist*, she transformed herself into a vending machine. Five francs inserted into the slot of the life-size torso of herself descended to the crotch to earn a kiss.

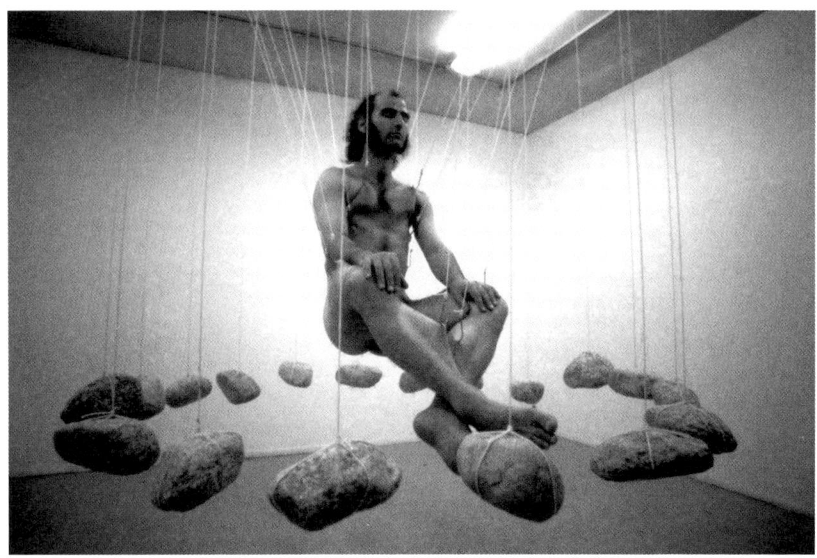

Stelarc, *Sitting/Swaying: Event for Rock Suspension*, Tamura Gallery, Tokyo, 1980,
performance photograph. Stelarc looks at ways to extend the body's powers.
Here he has himself suspended with hooks through his skin, defeating the force of
gravity, an experiment that refers both to gravity-free astronauts and primitive rituals.

Contemporary Body art is as tightly linked to the world around us as was the
ideal nude to the gender assumptions of her time. In a society where plastic surgery
is becoming as common as haircuts, the French artist Orlan's decision to have the
features of legendary beauties grafted on to herself takes the madness of human
attempts to attain the ideal into the artistic arena, the very place that invented it.
In the 1990s, she notoriously underwent nine operations to transform herself into
admired types of femininity, asking, for example, for the chin of Sandro Botticelli's
Venus and the mouth of François Boucher's Europa. The first artist to make plastic surgery her medium, she used pain relief to stay awake during the operations,
which were filmed. Orlan calls her work carnal art, in contrast to Body art, which
she considers the property of men. 'I am all for pleasure and sensuality, not for
endurance and suffering,' she says, and adds that her work is a 'struggle against the
innate, the inexorable, the programmed, nature, DNA – and God.'[5]

In an age of pacemakers, joint replacement and medical interventions to retain
youth and beauty, the Australian artist Stelarc investigates ways to extend the body's

parameters. Like a test pilot of the human body, he designs his performances to push and overcome humanity's biological limits. In the 1970s and 1980s, he made twenty-five works in which he had himself hung from hooks which pierced his skin, forcing the viewer to consider the boundaries of the body, the effects of gravity and the limits of endurance. Although this sort of art can raise questions about the emotional needs of the artist – have they merely found a legitimate way to indulge their masochism? – and of our own voyeurism as we watch in horror, it is legitimized by its own particular history in art and its links to the world we know.

Issues to do with gender are catnip to contemporary artists. By the 1970s, owing in great part to feminist ideas, looking had become politicized. No longer was it possible to regard it as an innocent activity. In a development of John Berger's insight in *Ways of Seeing* that 'Men look at women. Women watch themselves being looked at … The surveyor of woman in herself is male: the surveyed, female',[6] Laura Mulvey theorized that when women looked at female film stars, they saw them through men's eyes.[7] When Jemima Stehli performed a striptease in 1999 in London's Lisson Gallery in front of five men she had gathered from the art world, her work was imbued with an awareness of such ideas.

Stehli's striptease with a difference exists in a series of photographs that show her in the same image as the man who watches her as she gradually removes her clothes. There are two focuses in the photos: the back view of the artist's naked body and the front view of the face and pose of the male viewer sitting looking at her. Stehli's aim was to record the response of a male caught in a position of some vulnerability as he is looked at while he looks. She allowed and wished the men to photograph her, standing in the traditional place of the nude woman as the object of the man's gaze. But at the same time, she also has herself photographed from behind as she performs. By including the faces of the men who are doing the looking, she implicates them in her striptease. More than a simple act of table-turning, it is a way to bring visual life to the theories surrounding women's traditional place in art.

By jettisoning heroic strength in the case of the men and languorous passivity in the case of the women, the involvement of the naked body in Performance art played an important part in modernizing the nude. When Body artists remove their clothes, they remove any notion of the ideal. As they go about producing their art out of themselves, they allow the spectator to see the whole body in poses and activities that dispense with the elegant arrangements of limbs and anodyne facial expressions expected of the ideal female nude and the muscularity demanded of the male.

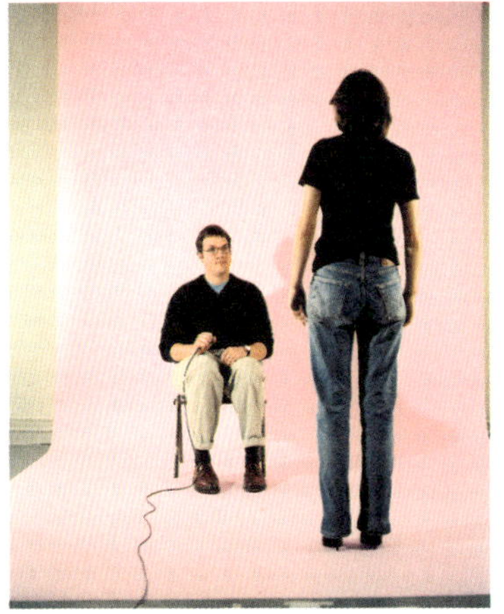 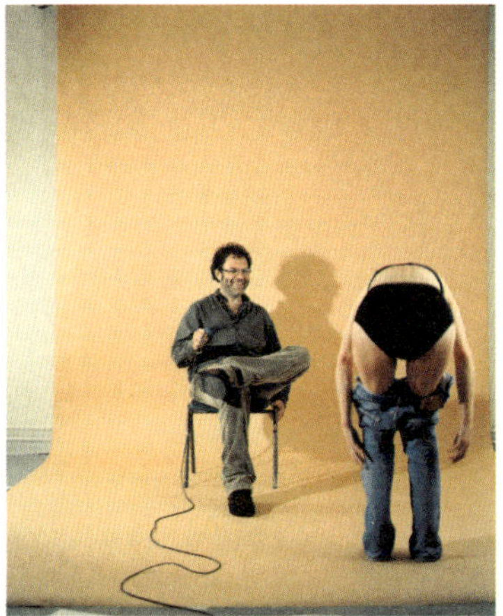

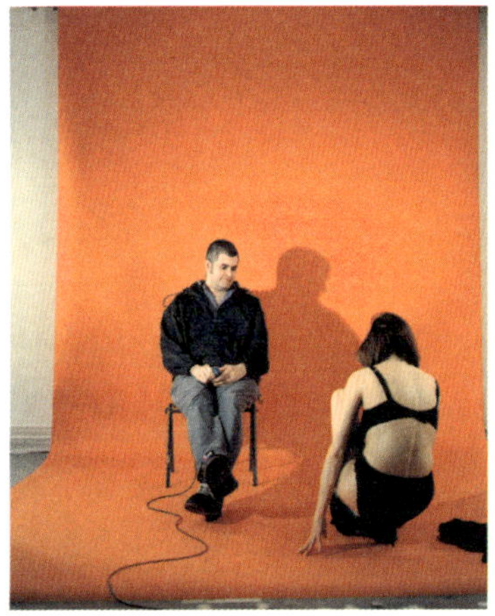 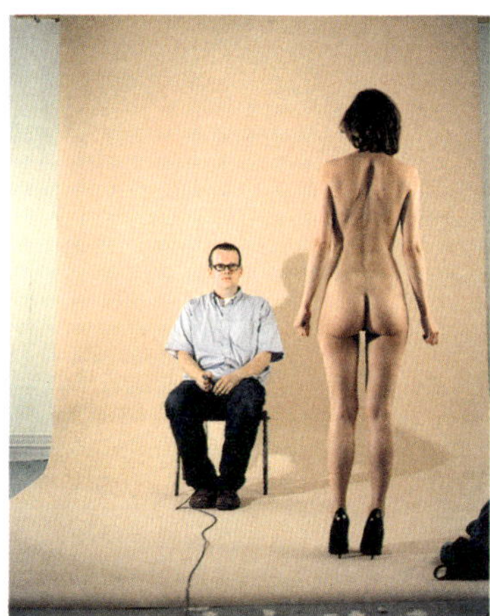

This did not take place in a cultural vacuum. Evidence of the change in attitude that allowed the body to replace the nude can be found in every country after mid-century. In Britain, for example, until the 1950s a version of the ideal nude existed at London's Windmill Theatre, where men went to watch the stationary naked showgirls. By exploiting a legal loophole stating that nude statues could not be banned on moral grounds, the management avoided prosecution as long as the girls stayed still. 'If you move, it's rude' was the catchphrase. In 1967 the variously shaped actors in *Hair* tore off their clothes and danced to the delight and amazement of the audience. It was a theatrical journey that paralleled the ideal nude's journey to nakedness.

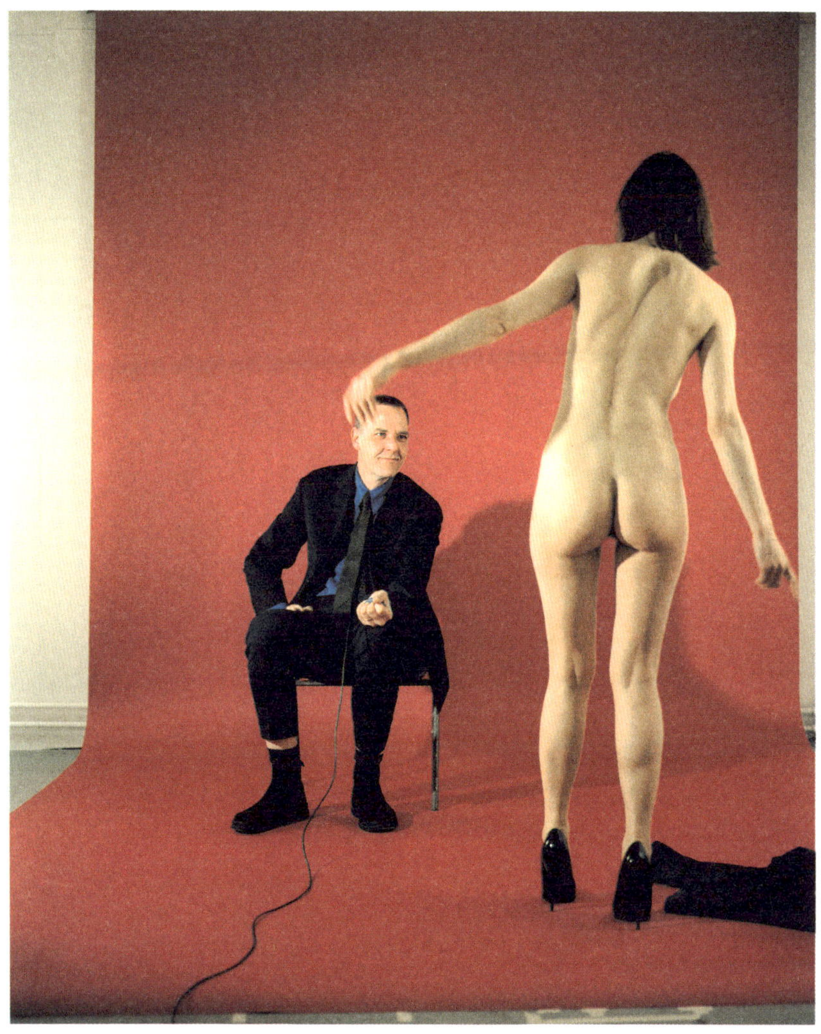

Jemima Stehli, *Strip*, 1999, set of ten chromogenic photographs mounted
on aluminium. [Opposite, l to r, t to b, *Strip No. 1*, *Strip No. 3*, *Strip No. 6*, *Strip No. 7*;
Above, *Strip No. 4*.] In the photographic *Strip* series, Stehli gradually removes
her clothes in front of five men from the art world. She asked each to use a cable shutter-
release to photograph her, capturing themselves as they watched her undress.

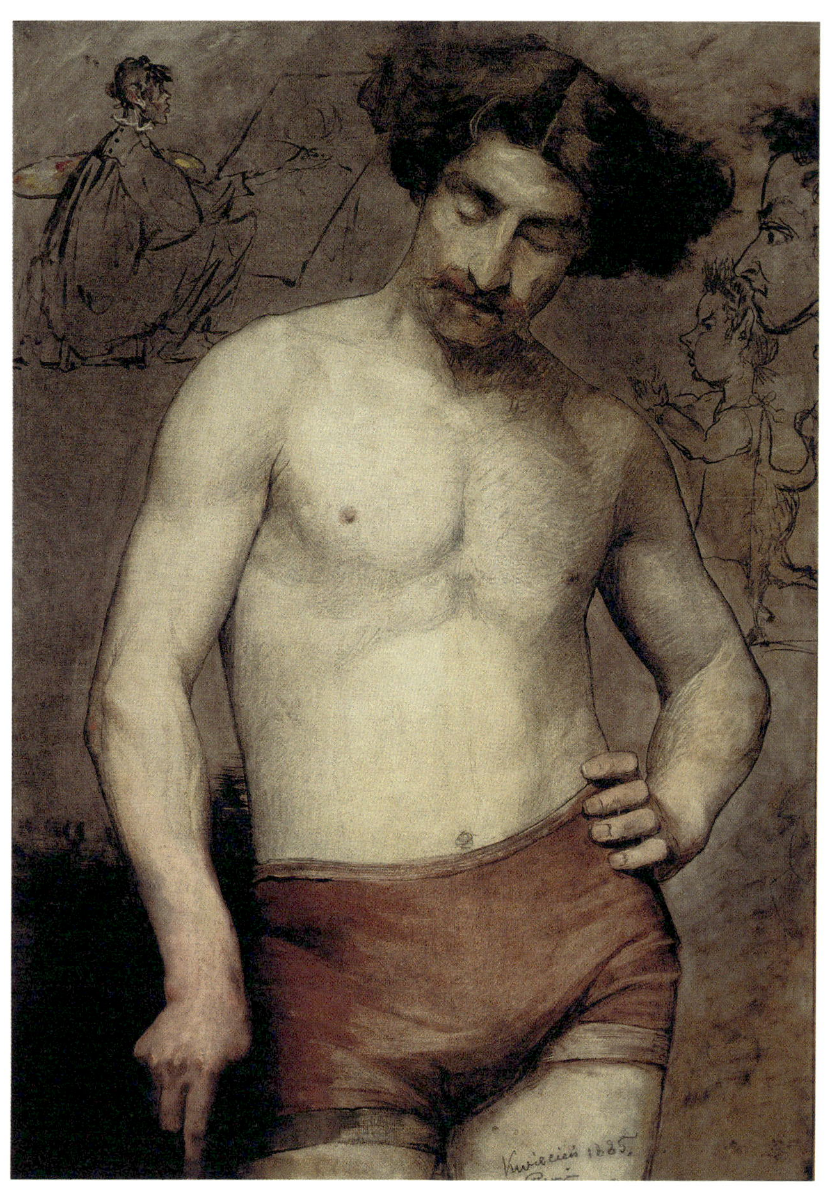

Anna Bilińska-Bohdanowiczowa, *Male Semi-Nude*, 1885,
oil and gouache on canvas. In 1882, the artist travelled from Poland to Paris
where she painted this study of the modestly clad model in the life class for women
at the Académie Julian. The stick he rests on to hold his pose can just be made
out, as can her sketches of the other students hard at work.

THE CHANGING ROOM: FEMALE PERSPECTIVES

IN HIS INFLUENTIAL *WAYS OF SEEING*, first published in 1972, John Berger argued that the ideal nude lived on in academic painting and more widely in the popular media: 'Today the attitudes and values which informed the tradition are expressed through other more widely diffused media – advertising, journalism, television.' 'But', he continued, 'the essential way of seeing women, the essential use to which their images are put, has not changed. Women are depicted in a quite different way from men – not because the feminine is different from the mascu-line – but because the "ideal" spectator is always assumed to be male and the image of the woman is designed to flatter him.'[1]

All true, of course. Although what strikes a modern reader is Berger's accept-ance that things were continuing as they always had. By 1970 new attitudes to women both as makers and subjects of art were infiltrating the art world. He ignores the input of women artists whose numbers had been growing since the end of the 19th century and who in the 1960s had produced some surprising and shocking work. And, oddly for a Marxist who always linked art to social change, he seems to have been deaf to the newly raised voices of women that feminism was encouraging by the time he was writing.

Some of the most exciting changes in the presentation of the female nude in the last hundred years have been introduced by women artists. Their first inter-vention resulted from their entry into the art world as professionals, the recipients for the first time of the academic training that had been denied them until art schools accepted them as students at the end of the 19th century.

The nude body was at the heart of concerns about women's entry into art edu-cation. The authorities saw the female invasion of the formerly all-male art schools as a total upset of the status quo: the world turned upside down. The natural order that was threatened in this case was the masculine ownership of the term 'artist'. Artists were men, women were models, wives and mistresses. In fact, you could go further and say that, even today, one of the great symbols of art is the artist and *his* model. Reproduce it in silhouette on a street sign and every driver would know an art school was nearby.

The authorities' resistance and unease centred on the life class, the place where the bothersome sexual awkwardnesses were unavoidable. They took the women's presence in the female life class in their stride, but their presence in the male life class was a different matter, a mirror image of the situation caused in previous centuries by young male students studying the female life-class model.

Art schools were faced with a replay in reverse of the problem they thought they had solved decades earlier. The envisaged horrors were never named, though one can guess at them by the decision made by the Royal Academy Schools in London to guarantee the male model's fitness for women's eyes. A decree in the byelaws for 1893 stated that when posing for the female students' life class, the model's genital area should be wrapped up protectively in a kind of male chastity belt, first in bathing drawers, then in a nine-foot loincloth, and then, just to be sure, a belt on top of that. Another solution was to segregate the men and women students, in the fear perhaps that the presence of the opposite sex would compound the embarrassment of women studying the naked male body.

At the end of the 19th century, the first female art-school graduates started to work as professionals. What did they do about the nude? As was only to be expected, most women who had the same training as the men produced the same sort of art as the men. Art has its own rules, and it is normal for both men and women to accept those rules. The nude as an artistic category had become firmly female by this time and the fashion of the day decreed that while you studied the nude male in the life class in order to show your mastery of anatomy (thought simpler to see on a curveless male body), when you painted a nude for public consumption, you painted a woman looking lovely.

Laura Knight's subject, she said in her autobiography, was the female nude in sunlight. When she painted herself painting a nude woman in 1913, in the self-portrait which is a top-selling postcard at London's National Portrait Gallery, the image is striking because it is so unexpected, but in truth her visualization of the relationship of artist and model is based on a time-honoured pattern of male self-portraiture. Once you subtract the surprise of seeing a woman artist where one expects to find a man, it is a conventional conception. And why not? Knight

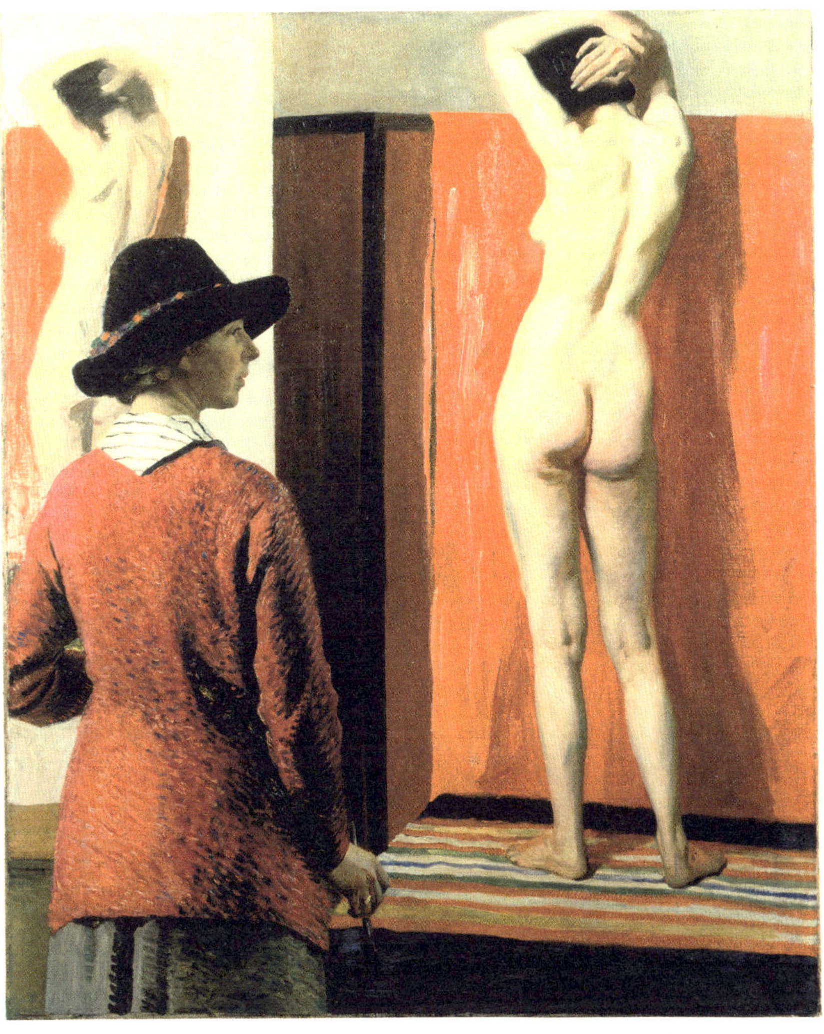

Laura Knight, *Ella Louise Naper (née Champion)*, 1913, oil on canvas. In this life-size work, Knight's pride in her profession is clear. She depicts herself painting, doubling the nudity by showing the model posing, as well as on the canvas in front of her.

wanted recognition from the system which had trained her and that meant meeting its standards. And her strategy worked. She followed establishment rules and she earned establishment approval, becoming a Dame of the British Empire in 1929, a Royal Academician in 1936 and an official war artist during the Second World War.

While most women – like most men – followed a conventional path, there were some women who offered a surprisingly different view of the nude. Surprising because the new nudes came out of the old ways of teaching. And surprising because even in a time of change, women had to be braver than men to go against convention.

In 1906, the German artist Paula Modersohn-Becker produced a startling new way of painting the mother and child. Interested in avant-garde art, she would periodically escape from the German artists' colony where she lived with her husband for a fix of the exciting art life of bohemian Paris. The simplifications in terms of colour and shape of painters like Paul Gauguin and the influences from other cultures that were in the avant-garde air helped her become an important German post-Impressionist.

Sanctified in depictions of the Virgin Mary with Jesus on her lap, the mother and child is an iconic image of art. Men have painted it for centuries, often using their wives and mistresses as models. But Modersohn-Becker's mother and child, with its elemental feel of the primitive carvings that were so influential on the modern artists of the day, offers a new version of the subject. By disdaining to give the young mother the prettiness expected in the conventional presentation, Modersohn-Becker avoids the subject's familiar sentimentality, and by painting the mother's solid nakedness she suggests the animal nature of the relationship. Her image manages to be both monumental in the way it fills the canvas and intimate in the way the mother and child are lost in each other.

At about the same time, the English artist Gwen John made a portrait of her friend Fenella Lovell that is unlike anything that had so far existed in the canon of the female nude. Not the conception of the image, in which Lovell emerges like a classical statue out of a circle of drapery at her hips, but in the type of nude. There are plenty of female bodies like this, but they are rarely shown in art this early, and it is telling that it is a woman who introduces one of them. By 1909, when she painted it, Picasso had already seen off realistic nudes with his proto-Cubist painting *Les Demoiselles d'Avignon* (see page 29). But unlike Picasso, John has chosen a traditional pose and is painting in a conventionally realistic style with consequent expectations of what a female nude should look like, and it is her refusal to satisfy these expectations that makes her nude so unusual. The complete absence of seductive curves must surely make it a candidate for one of the earliest naked nudes. Like Modersohn-Becker, John had brought a new type of female nude into the art of the early 20th century, one imbued, perhaps unconsciously, with a specifically female point of view.

Female puberty was a subject that fascinated male artists at this time, particularly Northern artists who tended to see it in dramatic terms as the fearful end of innocence. In his painting *Puberty*, 1894–5, Edvard Munch paints a Rorschach-like shadow looming beside the tense and naked adolescent seated awkwardly on a single bed with her arms crossed protectively across her lower body. The German Elena Luksch-Makowsky shares this interest in the onset of female puberty, but the result is far less prurient. Her *Adolescentia* ignores the doomy 'what-is-to-come' note of Munch's masculine imaginings of a frightened girl by stressing her graceful subject's indifference to and difference from the male adolescents that form the frieze behind her. By extending the young girl's arms and legs, the artist emphasizes the idea of a body that runs slightly ahead of its owner. There is less stress on sexuality than in the Munch and more on the strange new body changes, which must surely stem from a female insider's point of view.

It has been assumed that in the absence of any opportunity to study the life model, something men took for granted, women in the past who were serious about their art would try to learn about the body by drawing themselves without their clothes on. Gwen John did several watercolours and drawings of herself naked in her Paris apartment. To make money to support herself in Paris, she modelled, and one of the people she modelled for was Auguste Rodin. The inevitable happened but unfortunately, as also tends to happen, her passion outlasted his. A watercolour of herself sitting on a bed naked, painted about 1908–9, is one of a fascinating group of drawings and watercolours done while she waited in her room for her lover to arrive. Fascinating because as a graduate of the Slade School of Art she was not looking at her body in order to learn about the female nude, as women artists of previous centuries may have done. She was looking at it as her lover did. It seems that the fact that Rodin has seen her body makes her see it, too. This is a private image, an image which shows a woman regarding her body through her lover's eyes, perhaps finding it more beautiful than she previously had because of that lover's view. This work could be classed as a private and autobiographical nude.

Gwen John's sketches were probably meant only for herself and perhaps her lover, but at the start of the 20th century a completely new subject appears: the naked female self-portrait. Although several German male artists had been painting

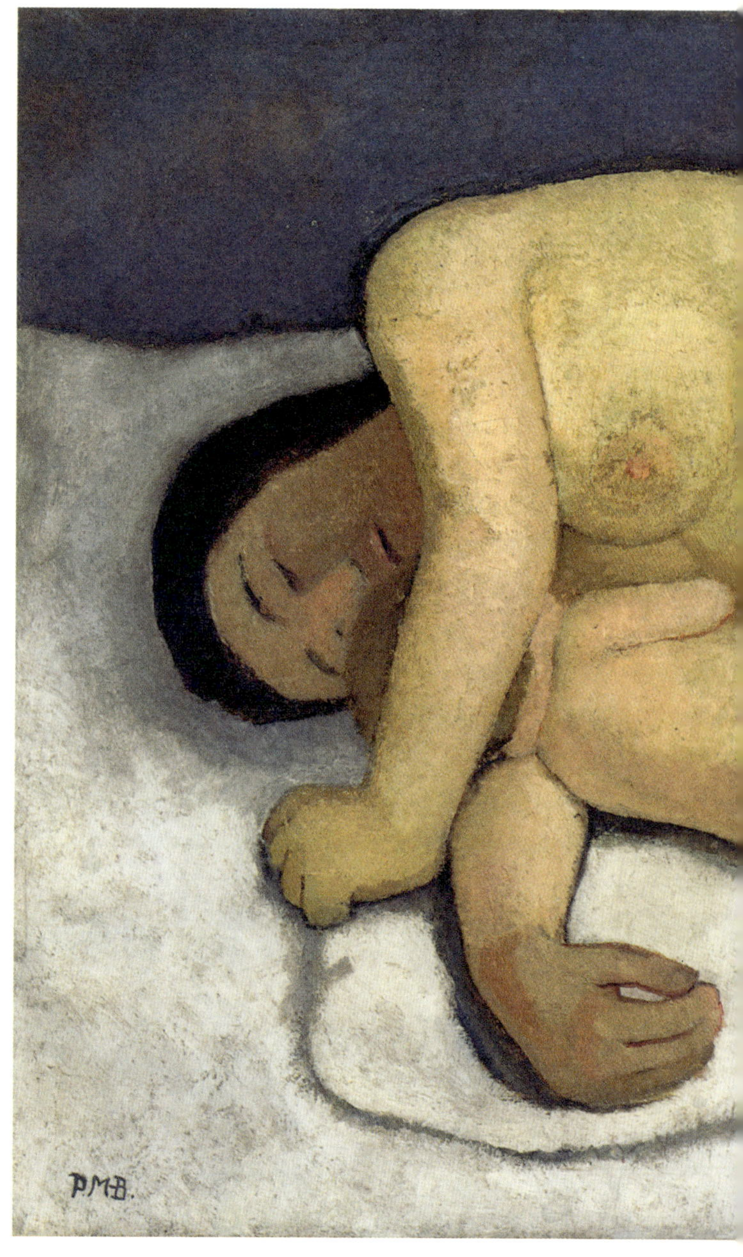

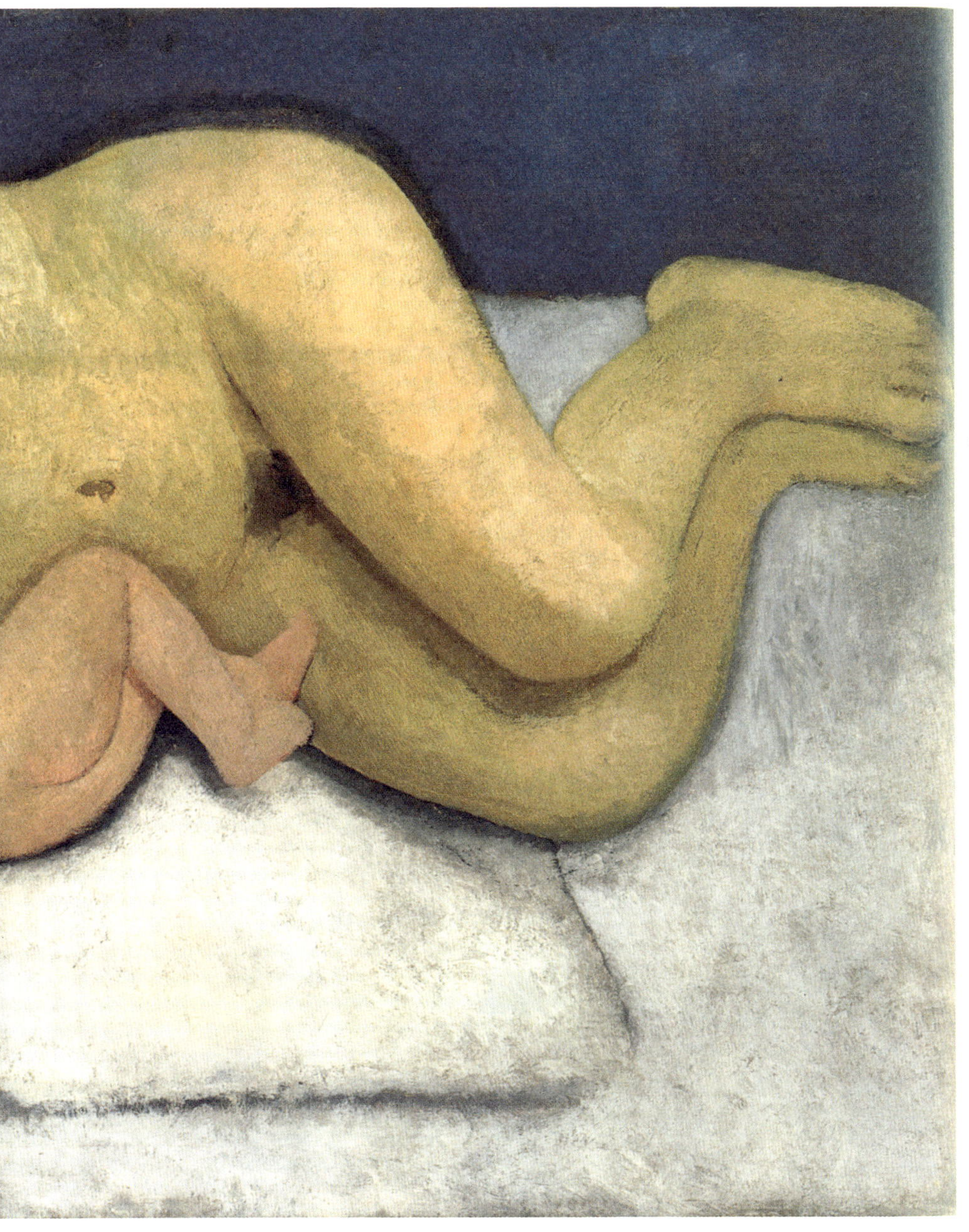

Paula Modersohn-Becker, *Mother and Child*, 1906, oil on canvas. Women artists of the early
20th century brought new kinds of female nudity into art. Paula Modersohn-Becker's nude mother
and child breaks with convention in its depiction of the animality of the relationship.

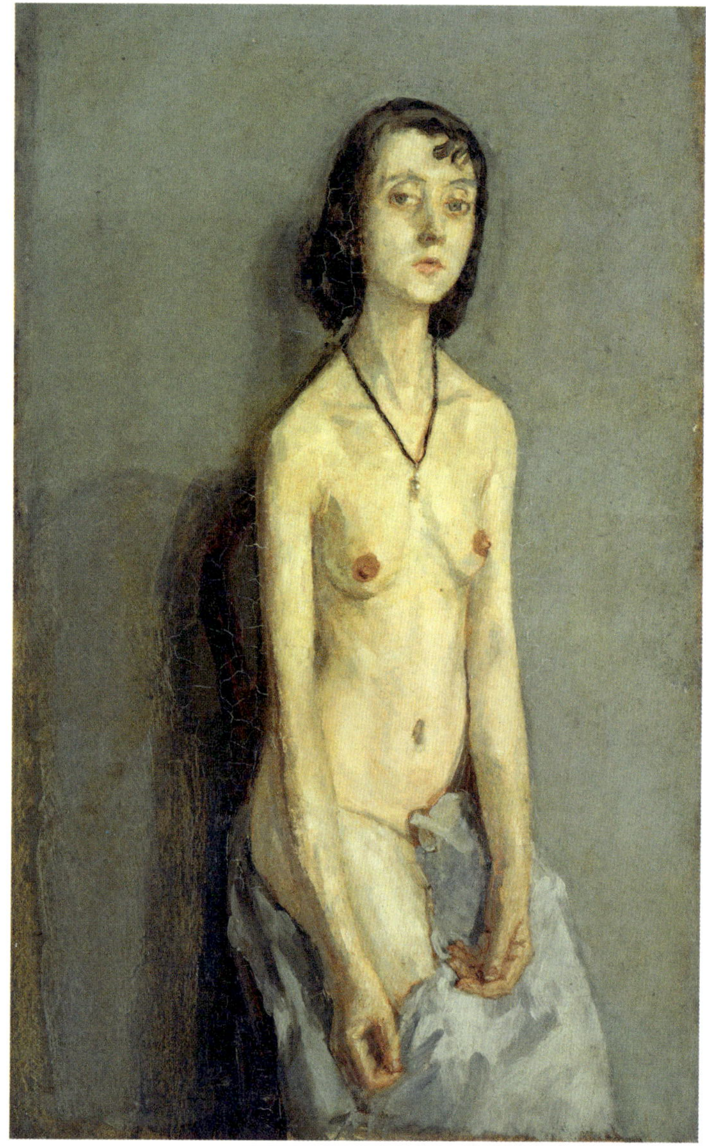

ABOVE **Gwen John**, *Nude Girl*, 1909–10, oil on canvas. John's portrait of her friend Fenella Lovell is traditional in its conception, showing the female nude with hip-encircling drapery. But the honest realism of the model's nakedness has nothing in common with the idealized body types painted by the male artists who preceded her.

OPPOSITE **Elena Luksch-Makowsky**, *Adolescentia*, 1903, oil on canvas. Luksch-Makowsky concentrates on the physical gawkiness of the young woman's arms and legs, which seem to be growing rapidly away from her.

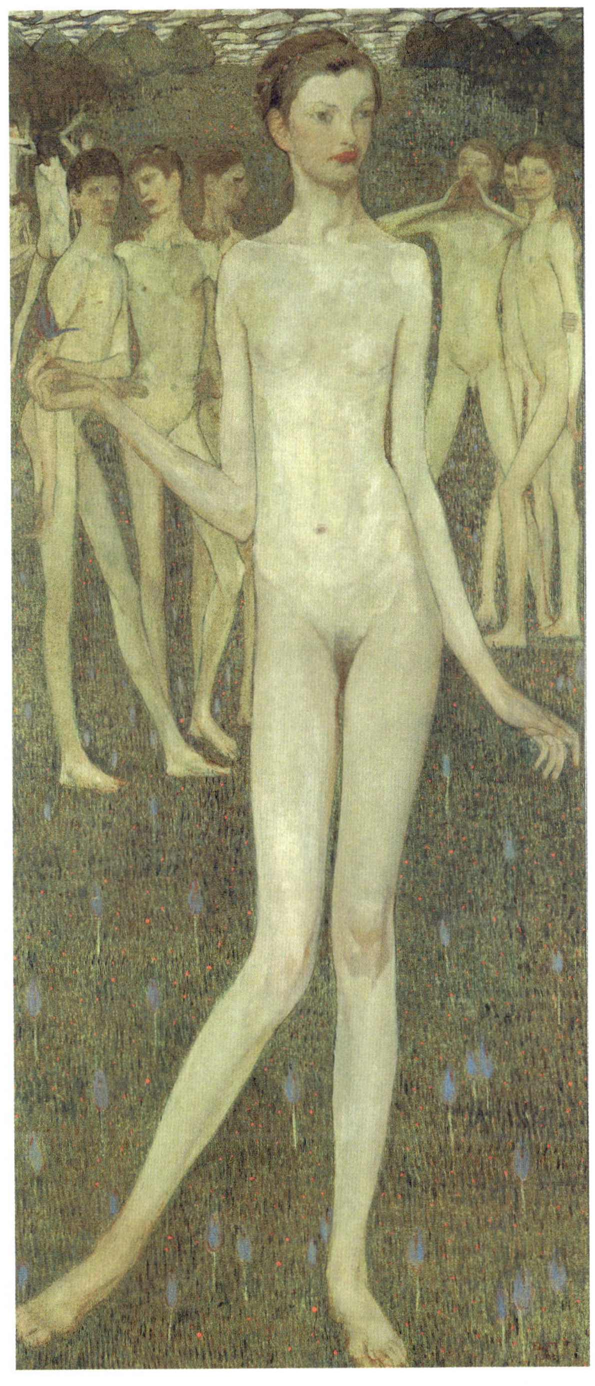

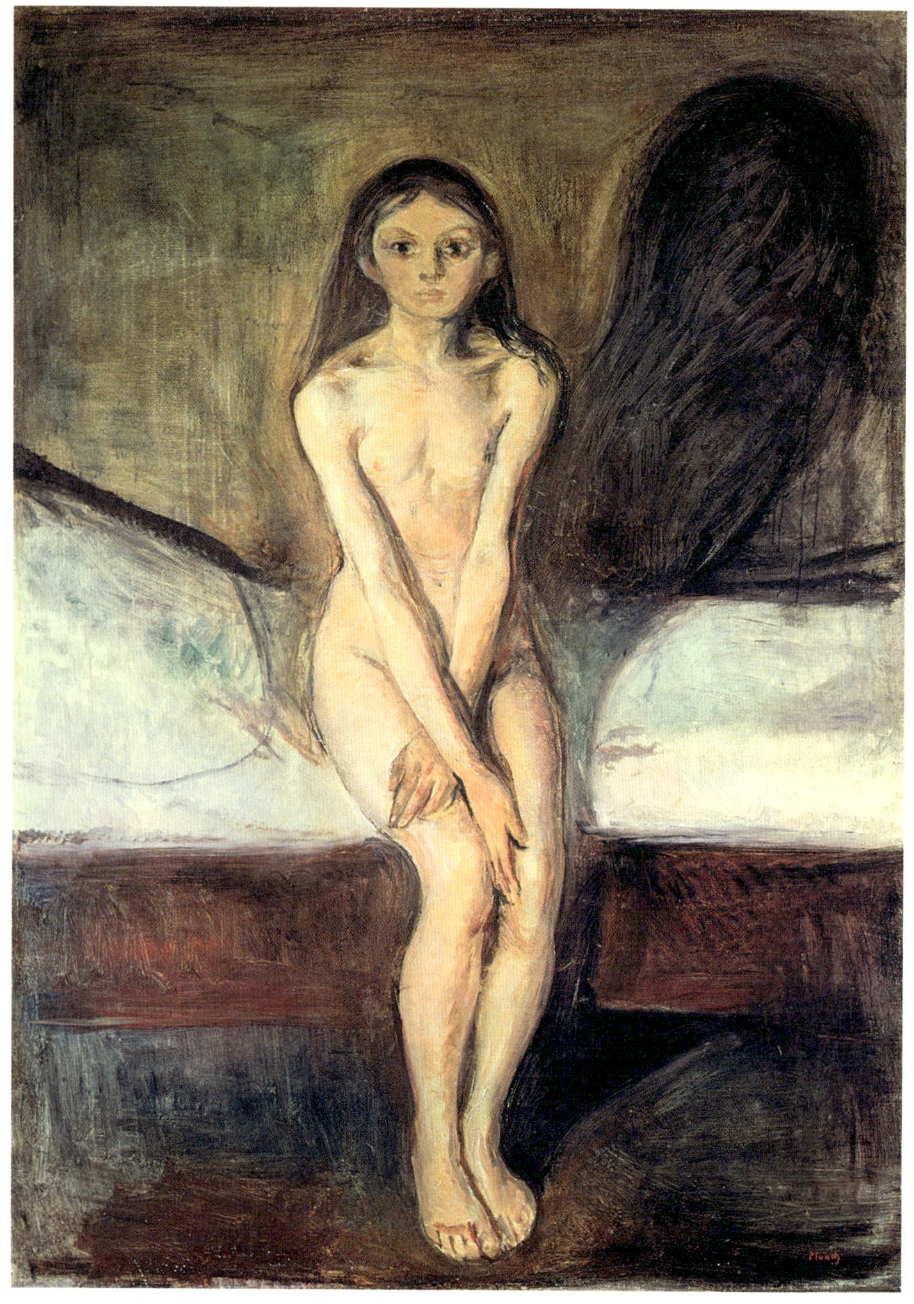

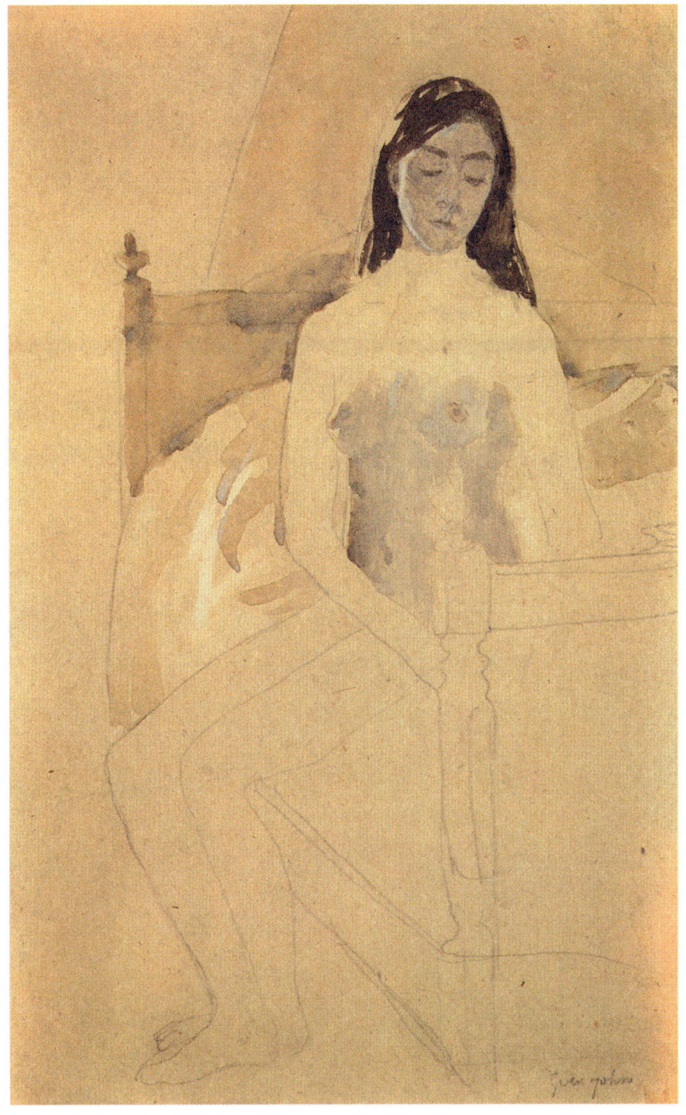

OPPOSITE **Edvard Munch**, *Puberty*, 1894–5, oil on canvas. In contrast
to Luksch-Makowsky (p. 63), Munch seems to emphasize the sexual terrors
of the young girl sitting self-protectively on the bed.

ABOVE **Gwen John**, *Self-Portrait Sitting Naked on Her Bed*, c. 1908–9, gouache
and pencil on paper. John's watercolours and drawings of herself reveal her confidence
in the body that had been brought to life by her lover, the sculptor Rodin.

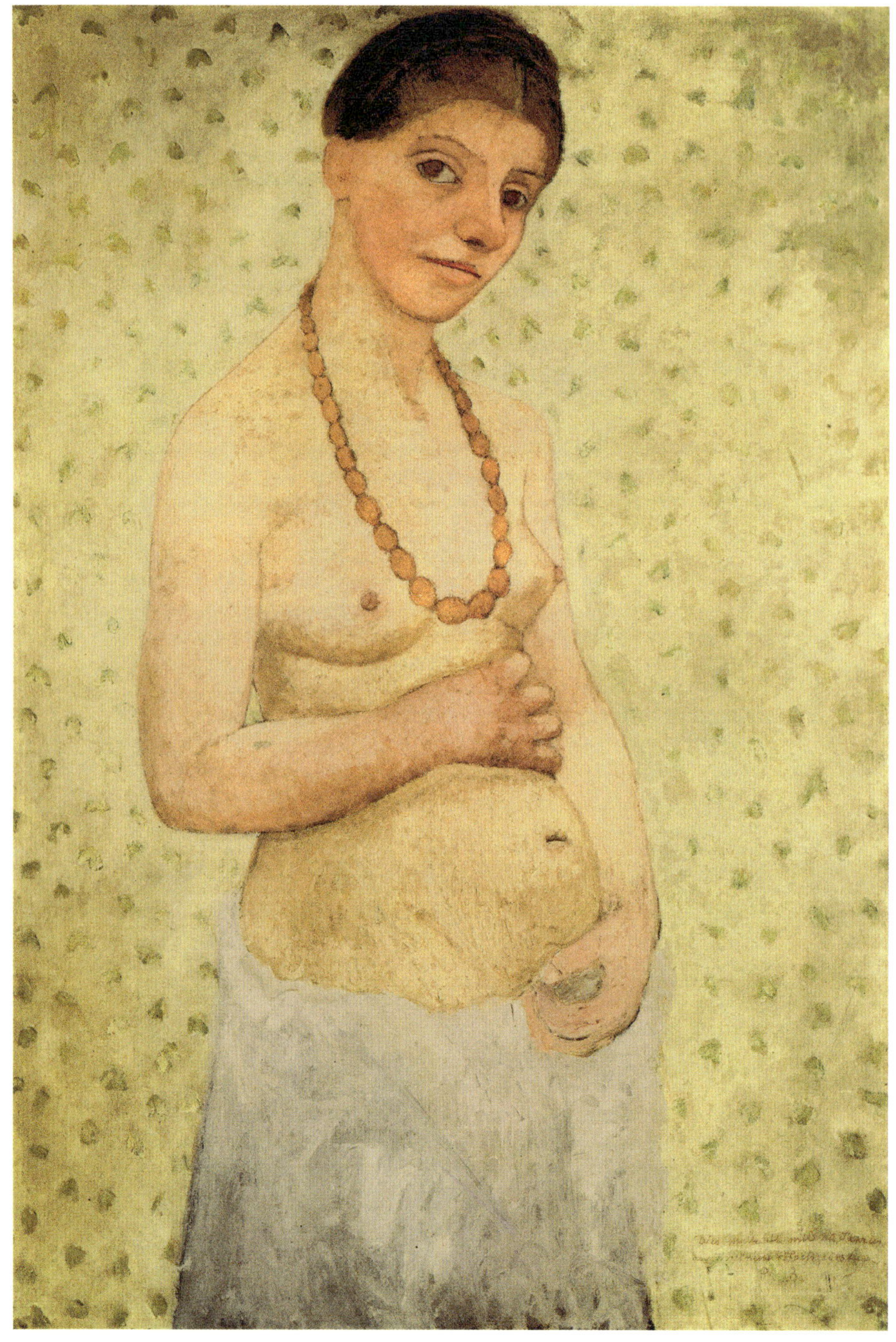

themselves naked for a decade, it took a lot of self-belief and artistic self-confidence for a woman to do so.

Paula Modersohn-Becker's painting of 1906 of herself pregnant is the self-portrait as personal exploration. Male artists had painted clothed pregnant women with one hand resting on the bump in what has become accepted as a classic pose. But a nude pregnant woman is unusual for this date, as is an image with two hands circling the bump. This is arguably the first image of pregnancy from a woman's point of view. What makes it so intriguing is that as far as is known, Modersohn-Becker was not pregnant. Painted on one of her periodic escapes to Paris, it may be – unfortunately her diary gives no clue – that she is thinking about what pregnancy would mean to her painting career: the arms like calipers suggest that she is measuring the effect of motherhood on her life. The following year she became pregnant. An embolism nine days after the birth of her daughter killed her, a death that adds poignancy to the painting.

Over the next few decades, as women became more confident about speaking out in public, these naked nudes painted with a woman's eye, a woman's experience and a woman's point of view pop up in every country. In 1930 Lotte Laserstein depicted her model Traute Rose in a way that is closer to the tradition of a muscled life-class model than the conventional softened female. It is a strong and useful body to add to the autobiographical body, the determinedly non-ideal body, the female body examined from a female point of view.

From the start of her career in New York at the end of the 1920s, Alice Neel was interested in the nude. As well as chronicling in watercolour her life with her partners in uninhibited detail, she also painted oil portraits of her New York circle naked. The honesty of the unruly bodies of the women she knew bears no relationship to the ideal nudes of the past. The breasts of the seated Ethel Ashton, 1930, drooping down to her multi-tyred belly give us one more example of a female painter introducing a new kind of female nudity to art. She repeats it again that year in her portrait of *Rhoda Myers with Blue Hat*, which shows a mature woman with breasts of unequal size and crease lines across her middle. Both of these images of unconfined bodies suggest that conventional feminine behaviour is a stranger to their owners.

Paula Modersohn-Becker, *Self-Portrait*, 1906, oil on card. Surely art's first naked, pregnant self-portrait, the painting was made, according to its inscription, on the occasion of the artist's sixth wedding anniversary. As far as is known, she was not pregnant when she painted it, which suggests that this is a work of personal exploration as she wonders about the effect of pregnancy on her life.

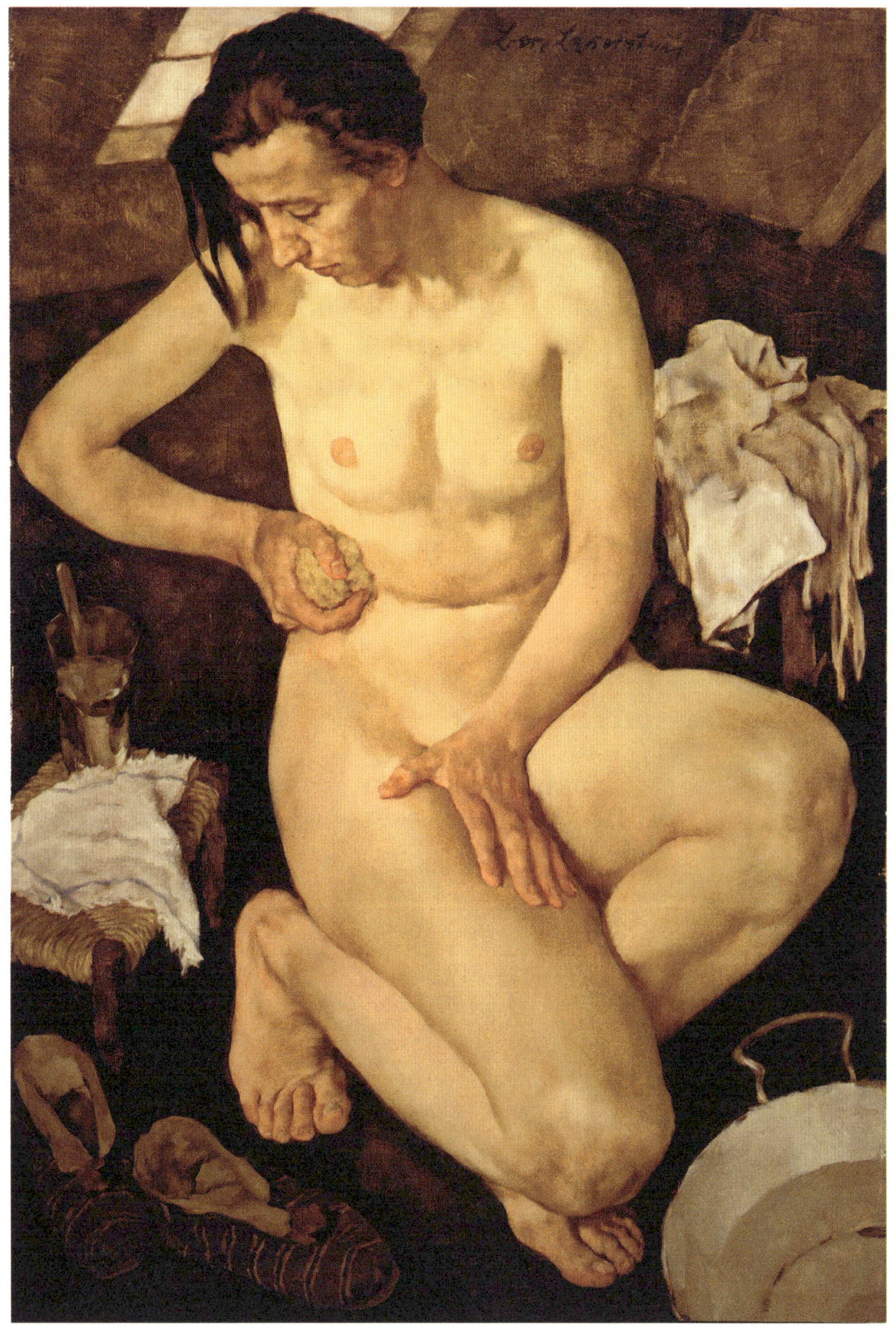

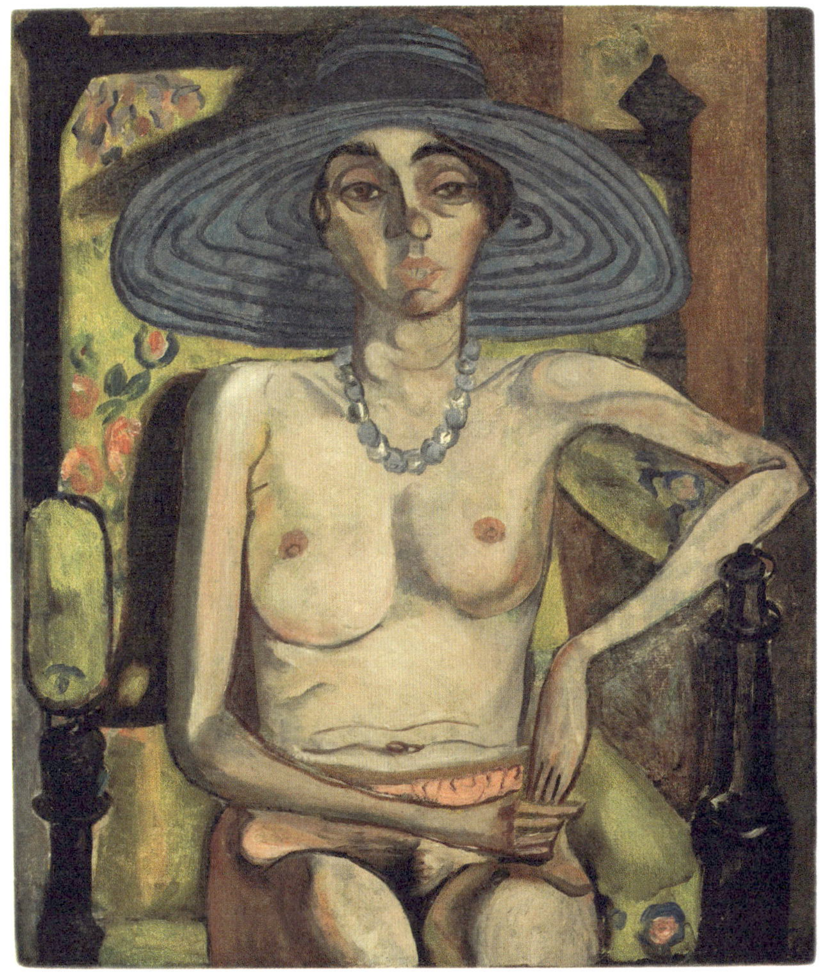

OPPOSITE **Lotte Laserstein**, *Morning Toilette*, 1930, oil on panel.
The large feet, sensible haircut and sturdy legs of Laserstein's depiction
of her model washing suggest strength and purpose and are far from the
passive female body beloved of male artists of the past.

ABOVE **Alice Neel**, *Rhoda Myers with Blue Hat*, 1930, oil on canvas.
Neel was fascinated by the power of nudity to reveal the heart of her subjects.
While shocking in its honesty, this portrait of Rhoda Myers still manages to
express the dignity and individuality of her sitter.

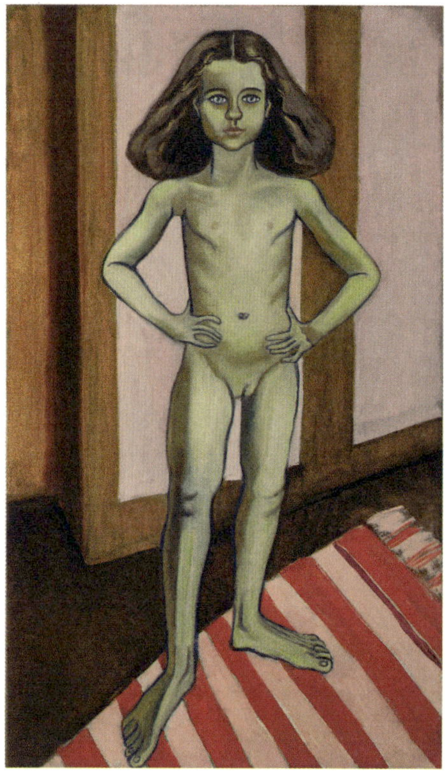

Alice Neel, *Isabetta*, 1934–5, oil on canvas. No one was safe from Neel's unflinching eye, which suggests one reason for the popularity she has today. She painted her daughter Isabetta in a way that forbids escape from the beauty and sexuality of little girls. The portrait gives rise to questions of where that beauty and sexuality reside: in the child or in the eye of the beholder.

A breakdown in 1930, caused by the death of Neel's first baby and the loss of her second to the Cuban father's custody, inspired the distressing *Degenerate Madonna*, a harrowing depiction of a mother and child in which the mother's deflated breasts bear no relation to the bountiful nursing Madonnas of Western art. Painted out of the pain of experience, this image of maternal nudity was far from the sentimentality-soaked paintings of motherhood that were the norm.

Once recovered, Neel continued her interest in nude portraiture. Not even children escaped her stare. In 1934, she painted her beautiful young daughter Isabetta, who was on a visit from Cuba, standing face forward with no clothes on. It is an extremely frank image of a little girl and not one that pleases Isabetta's

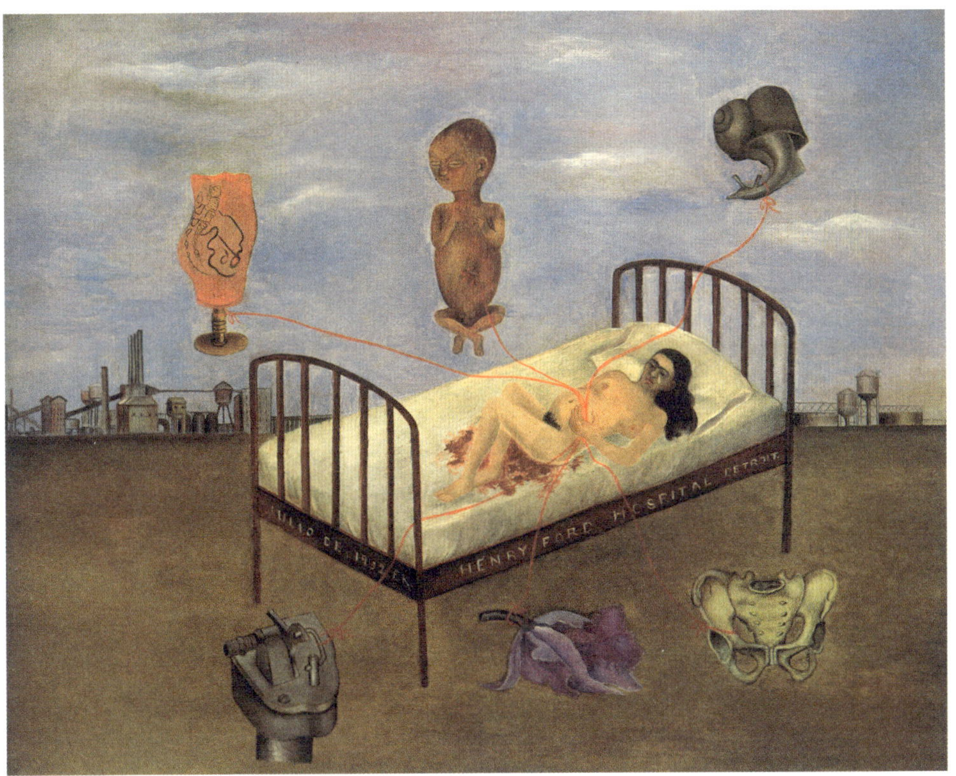

Frida Kahlo, *Henry Ford Hospital*, 1932, oil on metal. Kahlo's imaginative transcription of her miscarriage mixes private symbols with the reality of her blood-stained bed. Set against the background of an alien North America, it records her loss without sentimentality.

own daughter, Cristina Lacella, a mature woman still angry decades later as she asks what kind of mother would paint her daughter in that manner. 'I think it's disgusting,' she says in *Alice Neel*, the film made by Neel's grandson Andrew Neel in 2007. 'I would never have my children naked like that standing for a photo or a painting. I just don't think it's correct … all that genitalia, you know … and it was very pronounced in that picture and I think it's ugly.'

Other women artists also depicted birth and motherhood in this period. Expressing her own point of view – not just about her life and loves but about her political beliefs as well – was the life project from the late 1920s to her death in 1954 of the Mexican artist Frida Kahlo. Her depiction of her miscarriage in

Detroit in 1932 is an image shocking for its blood, its loneliness and its absence of charm, as she lies naked and contorted on blood-soaked sheets, an alien North America in the background.

The second intervention of the female point of view came in the years around 1970 when feminism took art by women in a completely new direction. Feminism can be an uncomfortable word these days. It is used here in the academic sense to describe the wave of artists, critics and historians who used their interest in women's history and current situation to inform their approach to art-world matters past and present. Feminist art historians transformed art history as feminist scholars transformed all the disciplines they touched. Their work shook many of the art world's certainties and they added to its knowledge. In 1971, Linda Nochlin asked her famous question: 'Why Have There Been No Great Women Artists?'[2] The answer, that they had been excluded from professional training until the end of the 19th century, killed off all those opinions about women's creativity going into motherhood and alerted everyone to think more deeply about all aspects of the relationship between women and art. Others surveyed the contemporary situation, explaining how the male art world of curators, directors and teachers had an adverse effect on the career opportunities of women artists. Research into women artists of the past was a major undertaking, which still goes on. In 1976, a landmark exhibition at the Museum of Contemporary Art, Los Angeles, surveyed the work of women of past centuries, its catalogue providing the inspiration for a host of monographs and *catalogues raisonnés* that followed in its wake.

The feminist artists were just as revolutionary, introducing new female subject matter into art. It could hardly have been otherwise with the phrase 'the personal is the political' on every feminist lip. They put forward the feminist point that while they shared an art education with the men, their experience of life was different, and it was this difference they took as their right to express. Just as for centuries the use of 'he' as a generic term for both men and women went unquestioned, so did the belief that a female point of view was slighter than that of a male. Men were convivial in their clubs; women gossiped. Men were rational, women emotional. How could such lesser beings be worth listening to? The feminism of the 1970s gave women a new self-confidence to express their view of the world, and by the end of the decade the world was listening.

Their belief that their concerns were as valid as those of the men meant that a whole new tribe of women turned up in art. A key motivation was to take back control of their nudity from the male artists who had presented them as passive in their paintings and sculptures, paragons to be examined and admired for their beauty. They wanted to replace the dominant way women were presented and viewed in art, by then understood to have been produced by men for men, with a new imagery that told a female truth. This is my body, the feminists said, and I am presenting it to you as I want and as I experience it, not as the male artist or spectator expects to see it.

Although there were people, including some women, who dismissed this presentation of their side of the story as strident, unfeminine and ridiculous, feminists found a huge and sympathetic new audience among men as well as women, with the female nude a particularly electric area of interest. Armed with the latest theories about society's role in forming – or de-forming as some had it – women's roles, they set out to introduce new kinds of nude into art just as their predecessors had at the start of the century. But whereas the earlier artists left no record as to whether their depictions of new female types were intended or unconscious, these 1970s artists articulated exactly what points they were trying to make.

From the mid-1960s, Nancy Spero was obsessed with the idea of presenting female experience: 'I want the idea of a woman's body to transcend that which is a male idea of women in a man-controlled world … But what I suppose must be most subversive about the work is what I am trying to say in depicting the female body – that woman is not the "other" – that the female image is universal. And when I show difference, I want to show differences in women, women's rites of passage, rather than a man's rites of passage. Woman as protagonist. The woman on stage.'[3] And that is precisely what she did until her death in 2009, producing deeply shocking subject matter through delicate marks, traces, archaic drawings and lettering on beautiful paper grounds that were sometimes small and sometimes like huge scrolls that demanded you come close to see her victims, her heroines and her insistence that the world of women was every bit as worthy to be taken seriously as that of men.

Artists decided to tell truths about the female body that had been excised from art. In 1971, in their role as leaders of the Feminist Art Program at CalArts, Miriam Schapiro and Judy Chicago temporarily took over a house in Los Angeles and gave a room to each of seventeen women to do with as they wished. Much of the resulting work related to the reality of women's lives. Sandy Orgel's *Linen Closet*, which exists like all the other works as photographs, sums up the attitudes of the time with her naked female mannequin trapped inside the shelves of neatly folded towels. Judy Chicago's *Menstruation Bathroom* was an installation composed of a pristine white bathroom in which stood a bin overflowing with, in the

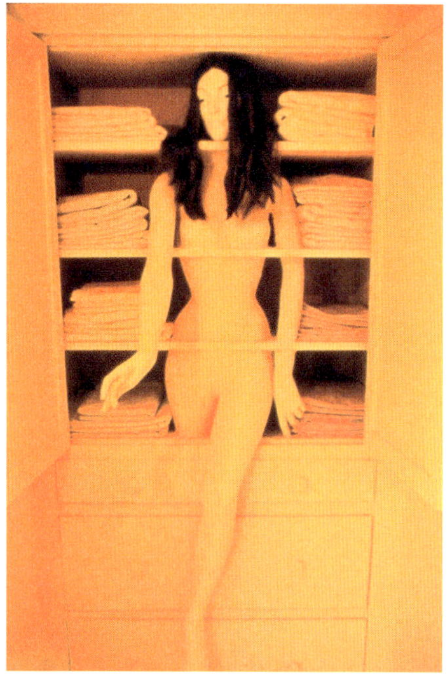

ABOVE **Sandy Orgel**, *Linen Closet*, 1971, mixed media. In an expression of feminist concerns, Orgel's installation made visible women's entrapment in the home.

OPPOSITE **Lynda Benglis**, advertisement, November 1974. Benglis's notorious photo of herself with a dildo in *Artforum* was both an advertisement for her exhibition and a protest against the male bias of the art world.

manufacturers' prim nomenclature, sanitary protection – used, of course. Although not overtly expressed through the nude, its outspokenness was all about the female body. It was a development of her lithograph of the previous year showing a hand withdrawing a used tampon. Its title, *Red Flag*, summed up its revolutionary content and intent. A defiant questioning of gender roles through the naked body typified much feminist art at this time. Readers of *Artforum* in November 1974 found themselves gazing at the artist Lynda Benglis, wearing nothing but sunglasses and holding a giant latex dildo. It was both an advertisement for her forthcoming show and a protest against the male bias of the art world that preferred its women to flatter rather than compete – or mock!

The American Joan Semmel thought about how to reclaim the nude woman from the male gaze and came up with the idea of presenting her own body as only

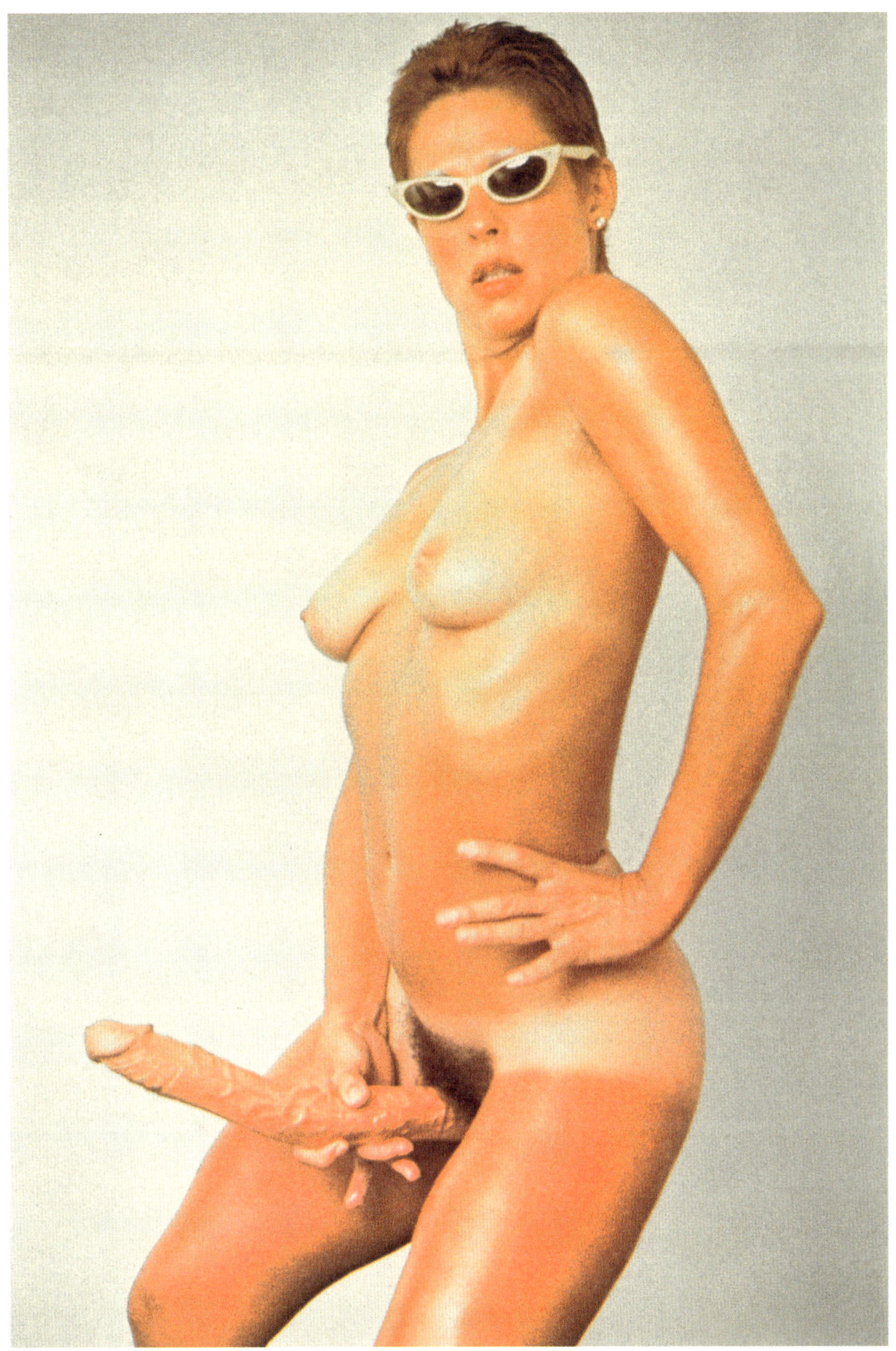

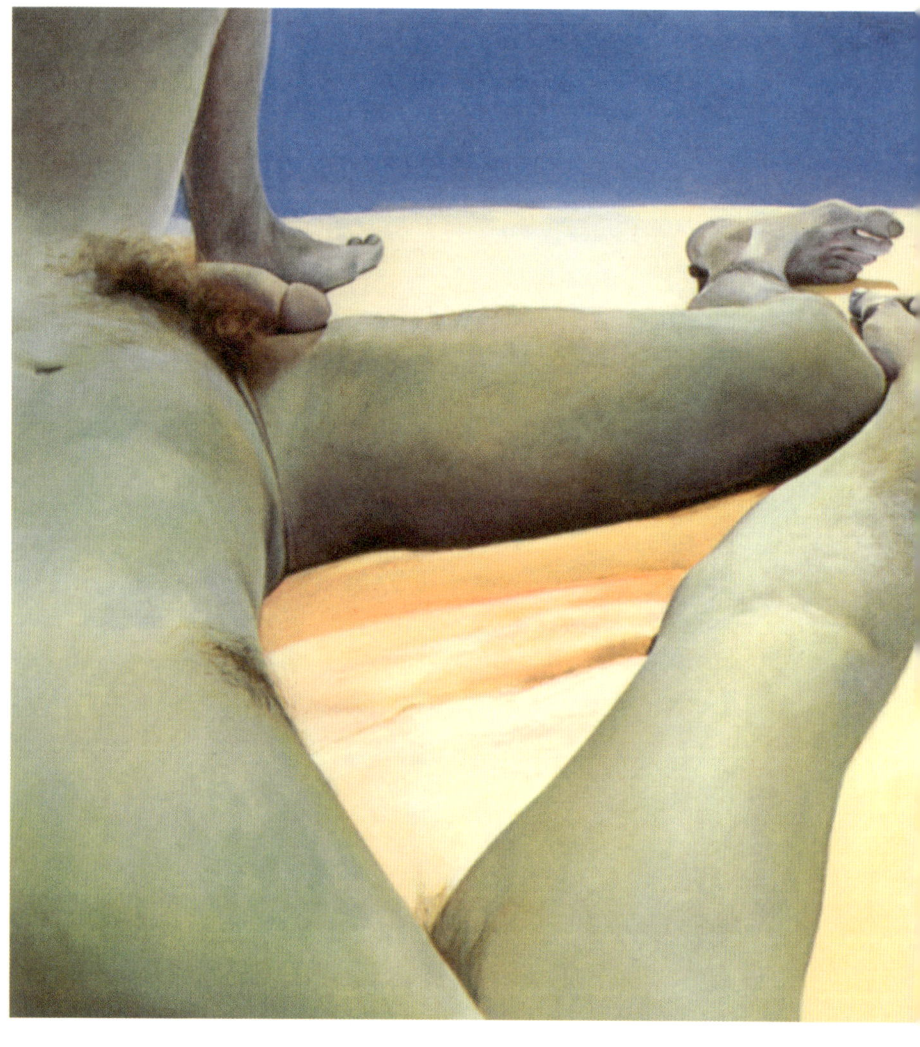

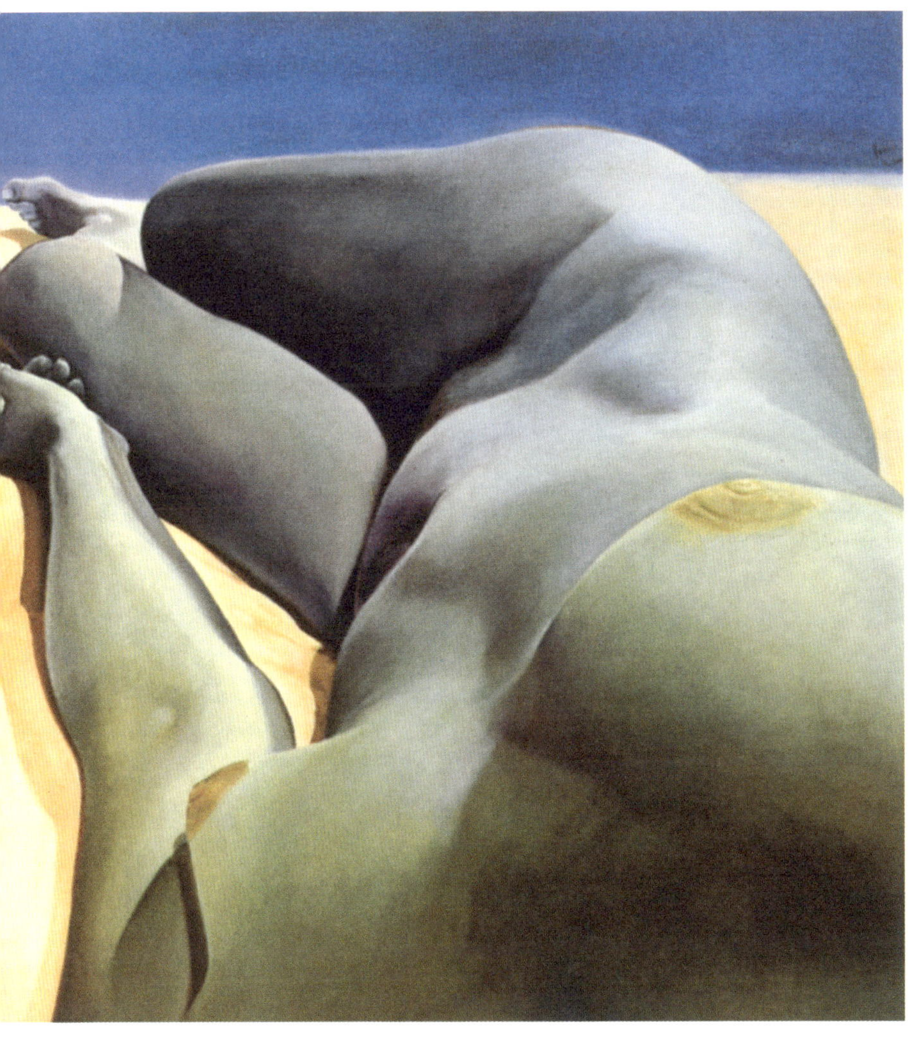

Joan Semmel, *Intimacy-Autonomy*, 1974, oil on canvas. In the 1970s feminists opposed
the objectification of the female body in art for male delectation. Semmel wanted to
paint the nude, and sex, while retaining female ownership of the images. Her solution
was to present the body as only she could see it. The unromantic realism and equality
of the couple leave the painting free to be enjoyed by women as well as men.

she could see it, as if she were looking down at it as she lay in bed. She owned it, in other words. Presenting a female view of sexuality in several life-size paintings, she used her signature hard-edged technique to show her body entwined with a lover in images of intimacy that were completely new. The hope was that the stark corporeality of the bodies, the singularity of her viewpoint and the unromantic clarity of the image would undercut the potential for a sexually arousing reading as well as showing a woman as participant in the sexual act and not a mere recipient.

Women influenced by feminist ideas were particularly fascinated by Body art, discussed in Chapter 2. Although men dominated the field – Yves Klein's *Anthropometries* of 1960 (pages 42–3) had entered legend – the notorious contributions of Carolee Schneemann in the 1960s (pages 41 and 45) made it seem accessible to women artists. A big point in its favour was that unlike the older art forms, it had not been totally colonized by men; the women saw its potential and exploited it. Desperate to have their voices heard, they took the opportunities it offered for exploring through art their belief that the personal was political. Many of them jumped into Body art as into a swimming pool, stark naked, feet first and delighted to immerse themselves in its potential for playing out their thoughts and fantasies.

By making the issues that concerned contemporary women the subject of their performances, the artists took Body art in a completely new direction. Hannah Wilke used her naked body as a kind of living sculpture to investigate the negative ways in which women past and present were regarded. Her performances from the 1970s and 1980s, available to us as videos and photographs, grew out of her concern to liberate the female body from its stereotypes of virgin, mother and whore. In *S.O.S. Starification Object Series*, 1974–82, she attempted to make visible her conviction that women took the reality of their body from a masculine way of viewing it, by studding her naked body with chewing gum taken from the

OPPOSITE ABOVE **Hannah Wilke**, *S.O.S. Starification Object Series*, 1974–82, ten black-and-white gelatin silver prints with fifteen chewing-gum sculptures mounted on board. The feminist belief that the personal is political ultimately led women to create a new kind of issue-based self-portraiture. In this series, Wilke studded her body with vulva-shaped chewing gum, alluding to both the multiple possibilities for women's sexual enjoyment and men's sexual objectification of women in art.

OPPOSITE BELOW **Eleanor Antin**, *Carving: A Traditional Sculpture* (detail), 1972, 144 black-and-white photographs and text panel. Antin documented herself as she lost weight over thirty-six days. The work offers an amusing and telling parody of the macho Michelangelesque idea that the sculptor pares away the marble in order to find the perfect form inside.

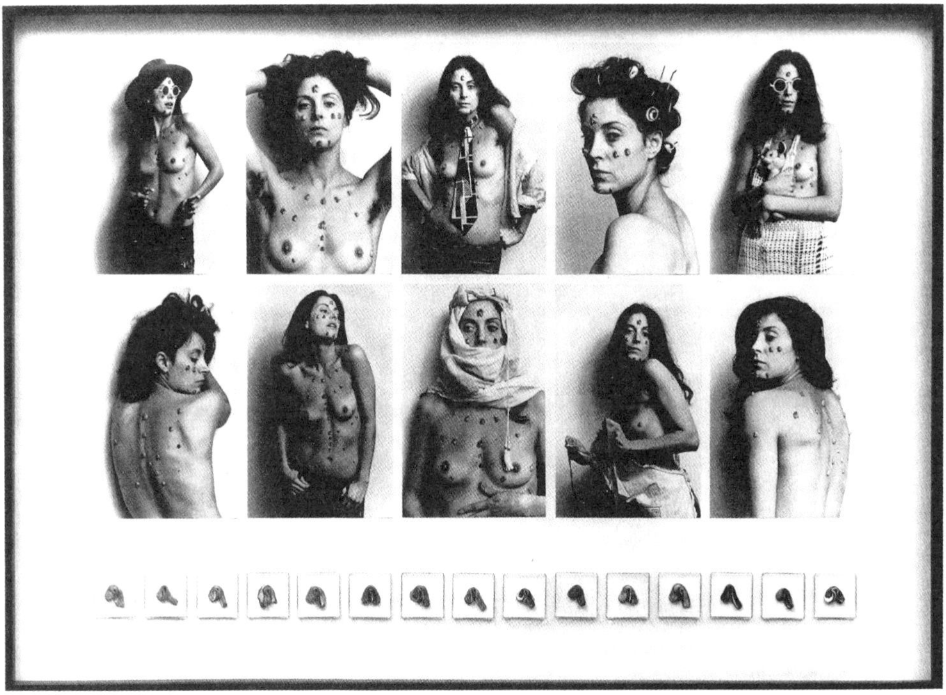

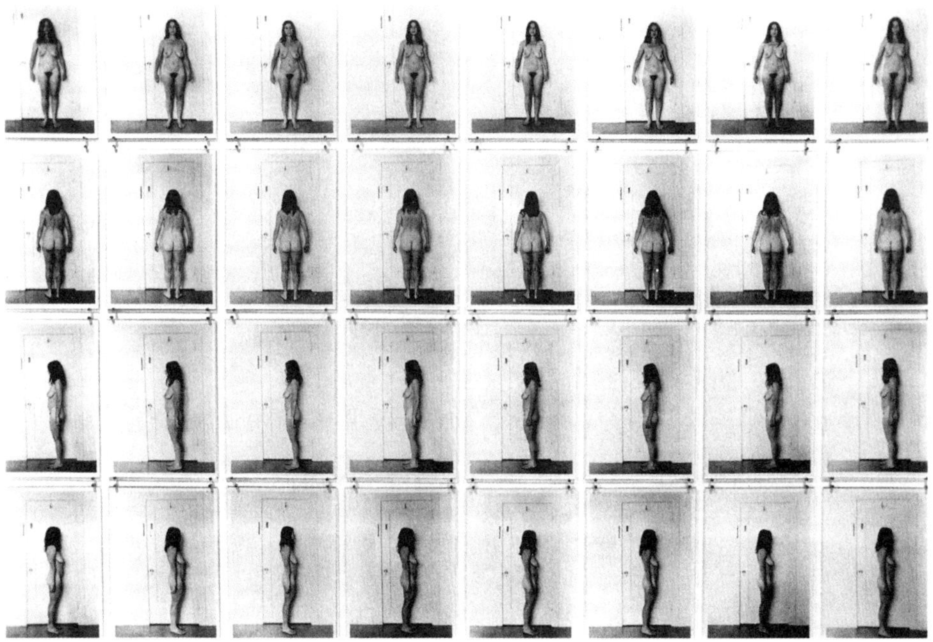

mouths of spectators and fashioned into the shapes of tiny vulvas. She had been struck by the similarity between the genital forms of men and women, and shared with many the new conviction that gender and sexuality were not written in stone and that femininity or masculinity could be learned. 'I have been concerned with the creation of a formal imagery that is specifically female, a new language that fuses mind and body into erotic objects that are nameable and at the same time quite abstract. Its content has always related to my own body and feelings, reflecting pleasure as well as pain, the ambiguity and complexity of emotions.'[4]

Her desire to present the female body as the property of a thinking, active individual, and not as a passive sexual receptacle that needed a man for completion, turned horribly poignant when cancer invaded her body. As she recorded her degeneration in a series of ruthless photographs of her swollen body and tufty hair until her death, aged 43, in 1993, she was still fighting to prove that her body belonged to her and not to the disease or the doctors.

In 1972, Eleanor Antin took dieting, that recurrent female obsession, as her subject and in a huge photographic work pictured herself for thirty-six days as she lost weight. The title, *Carving: A Traditional Sculpture*, is a witty reference to the Michelangelesque idea of the sculptor who chips away at a block of marble to release the beautiful body inside, and prompts thoughts about the ordinary woman's striving for an impossible ideal. It was as if Antin had taken the critique that femininity was a learned behaviour and performed it naked before our eyes. Not only was she in true Body art tradition the scientist who performs experiments on herself, but, in a way open only to a woman, she had also remade the traditional male artist-female model configuration.

Far more than representing personal rituals, the feminist Body artists were doing something more original: they were using Body art to express issues through themselves. Their art starts as personal but applies to many women everywhere, textbook examples of the personal being the political. It was a clever way to personalize the general and it has been used enthusiastically by artists ever since.

These artists were not merely talking about their own bodies through their art, but those of women in general. By speaking in public about the things they spoke about in private to other women, and through their bravery in doing it through their own naked bodies, they took the female nude into a new area on the art map. In doing so, they changed Body art itself by giving it an autobiographical twist, which distinguishes it still today. Their development of the autobiographical arm of Body art can be read as an extension of self-portraiture; these women had invented the issue-based self-portrait.

The female Body artists brought huge changes into the art world by updating the image of the classic female reclining nude to that of the contemporary female body, a completely different matter. The traditional idea of the nude was something offered to the spectator by a male artist: blank and non-threateningly seductive, she knew her place. Standing before this legitimized nudity, a man could allow his imagination to go where it wished, without ever for one moment having to consider what the model was thinking or whether he himself was justified in his activity. Admiring a passive nude – male, too, if that was his taste – was a perfectly acceptable activity, indeed one drenched in culture, good taste and education, rather like appreciating a fine wine.

The female Body artists who performed in the nude may well have attracted their fair share of male gazes from viewers who did not have only art on their mind. But as well as women without clothes, those men saw women who were in control of their art and what they wanted to say with it. Unlike the traditional nude who had nothing to say for herself, the feminist nude had plenty. Their work replaces the silent nudes of the past with the outspoken nakedness of the present.

The liberation felt by the feminist artists of the 1970s radiates from their art. A *Punch* cartoon of 1874 by George du Maurier entitled 'Female School of Art: Useful occupation for idle and decorative young men' shows a group of his serene-browed young women drawing a young man leaning elegantly against a pillar, the sheer ridiculousness of a male model posing for women artists no doubt causing laughter in homes all over Victorian Britain. Just under one hundred years later, Sylvia Sleigh created a self-portrait in which she is painting a nude – a male nude. She is the upright active artist who cares not a jot how she looks, while he is the model, pretty and passive as he lies across the sofa in a pose intentionally reminiscent of Diego Velázquez's *The Toilet of Venus* (see page 119). The date, 1971, tells you the reversal was inspired by the first wave of passionate female research into the position of women in the art of the past as muses, mistresses and models. It may not be subtle, and you could argue that she has merely substituted a male ideal nude for a female, but nonetheless it makes its point that the entrance of the feminists into art changed our ways of thinking about the nude forever.

During the succeeding four decades, women – and not all of them would call themselves feminists – have used the nude to investigate a variety of female concerns. In many cases, these concerns were touched on by the first wave of feminist artists, but just as the early theories have been tested and rethought, so the work of women artists has expanded to become more subtle and more complex. A questioning air often dilutes the certainties of the 1970s.

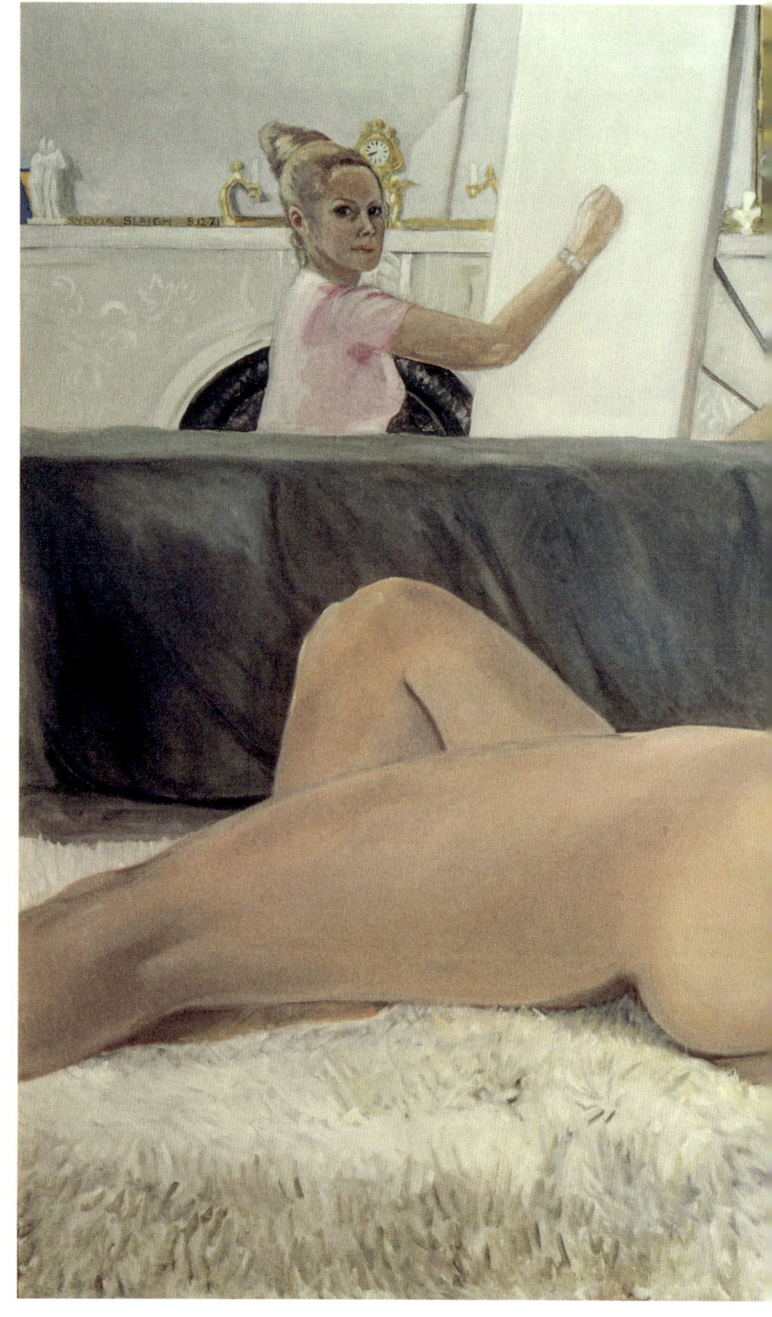

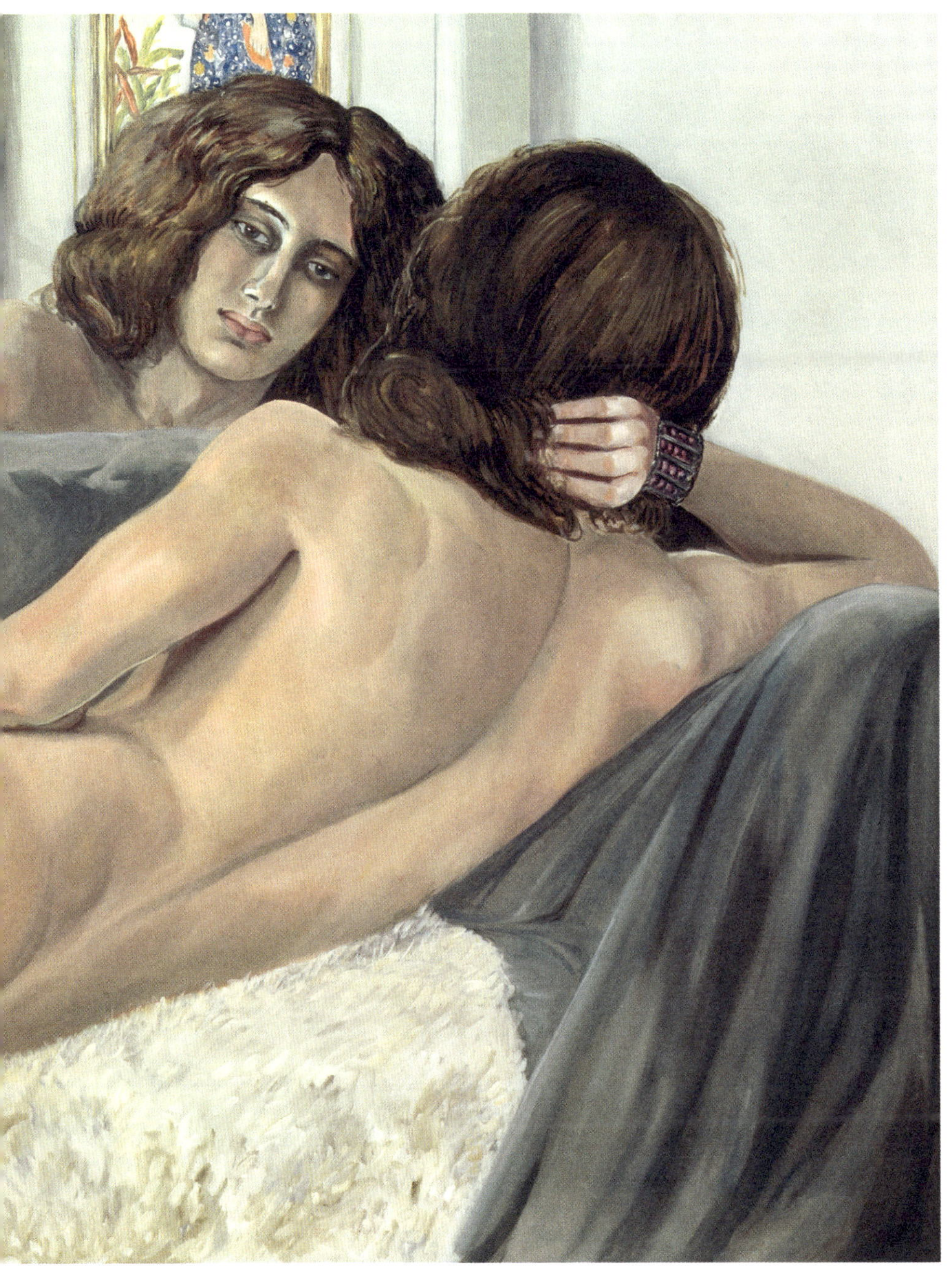

Sylvia Sleigh, *Philip Golub Reclining*, 1971, oil on canvas. Sleigh devoted
herself to reversing the traditional male artist and female model paradigm.
Here the young man takes his languorous pose from Velázquez's 'Rokeby Venus'
while the female painter sits alert, upright and at work.

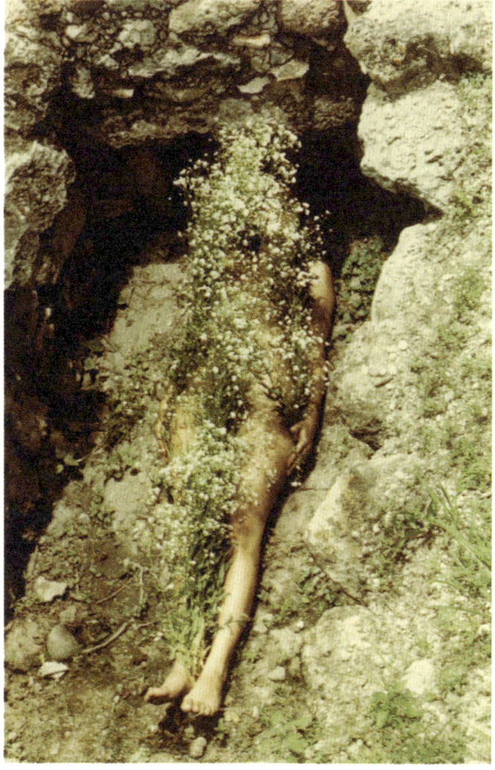

Ana Mendieta, *Imagen de Yagul* (Image of Yagul), 1973, Lifetime colour photograph. In the poetic works of the *Silueta* series, Mendieta fused her body with the land. Here flowers spring from her torso and legs as she lies stretched out on rocky ground.

The issue-based self-portrait continued in the work of the young Cuban exile Ana Mendieta who in 1973, shocked by a rape on her American college campus, smeared herself with blood and had herself tied down in order to personalize the horror of the event. Her subsequent work is as passionate but more romantically expressed. In the *Silueta* series she used her naked body to leave traces of her shape in leaves, flowers and grasses of the landscape, poetic works that suggest the memories and losses of emigration. The photographs which record her insertions into nature are themselves a kind of trace and show her particular fusion of Body art, Performance and Land art to express her need, a very human need, for roots.

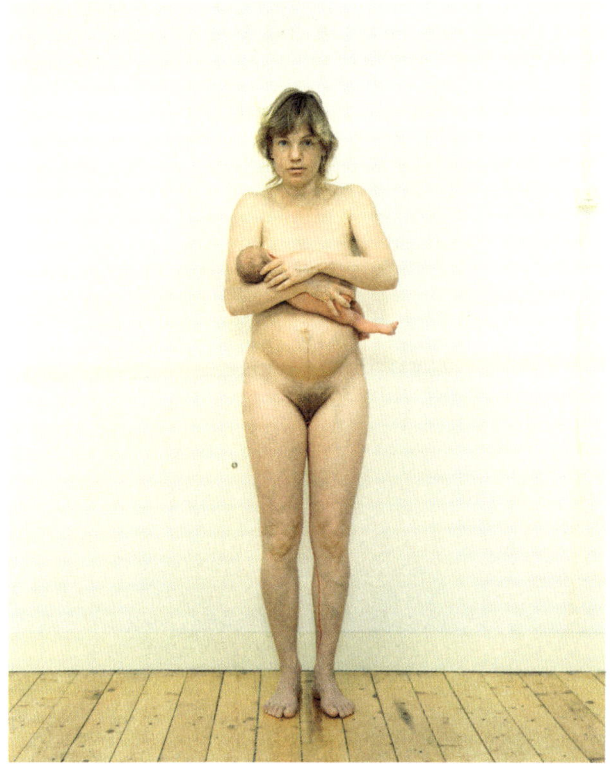

Rineke Dijkstra, *Tecla, Amsterdam, Netherlands, May 16 1994*, photograph on paper.
Dijkstra's image of a woman with her day-old baby evokes all the traditional emotion
of mother and child imagery. But the line of blood curving round the mother's
calf adds a physical detail of intimacy and realism foreign to earlier art.

The interest in birth was taken into a completely new direction in 1994 when
Dutch artist Rineke Dijkstra made three large images of women standing holding
their babies one hour, one day and one week after having them. She successfully introduces the physical reality of the process, for example showing Julie wearing a sanitary
pad one hour after the birth, while at the same time revealing the immense dignity of
the women. The photograph of Tecla, taken a day after birth, manages to suggest
that the vulnerability of the new mother is as great as that of her baby. Protecting
her newborn close to her body, she looks at the viewer, the tilt of her head and shoul-
der revealing that she has just raised her eyes from looking down at her baby. It takes
a moment to see the thin line of blood that trickles down the inside of her calf.

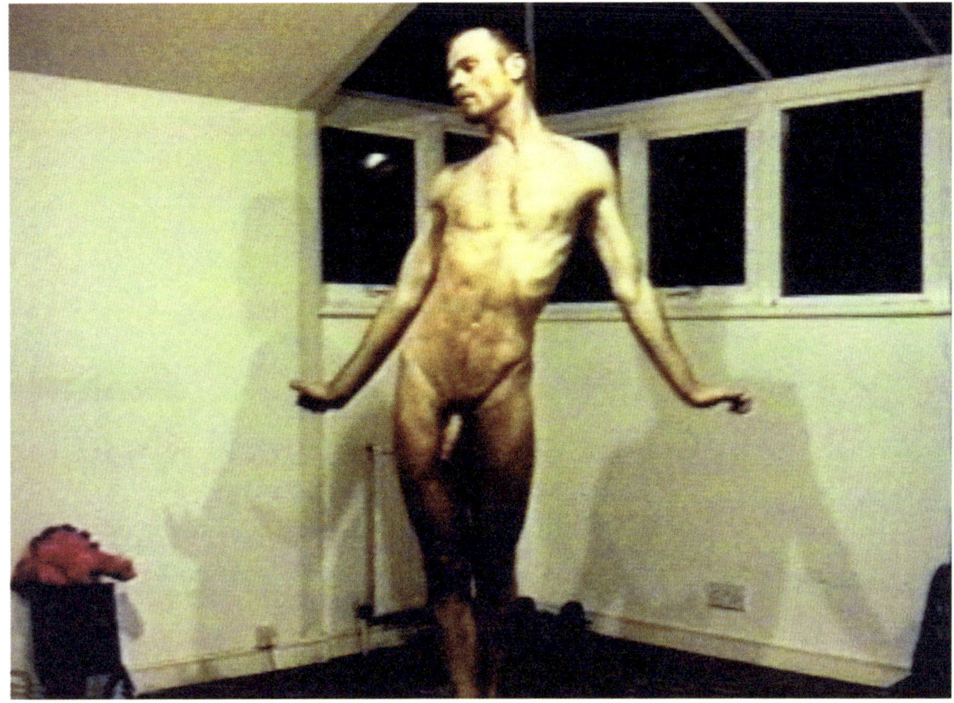

Sam Taylor-Wood, *Brontosaurus*, 1995, video still. In recent decades, women artists have considered how to represent male nudity in art. This ten-minute video shows a man dancing in slow motion, set to Barber's *Adagio for Strings*. The oddly vulnerable and thought-provoking result is far from the heroic masculinity of past art and contemporary films.

Joan Semmel's inclusion of her lover in her paintings and the portraits of nude men by Sylvia Sleigh, which resulted from women's role change from model to maker of art, opened the gate to more works with men as the subject – though perhaps not as many as might be expected. Sensitive to the way they had themselves been objectified in imagery for centuries, women thought seriously about how to represent the male in art. In the 1980s, some women artists attempted to paint or photograph men in playful, non-threatening or erotic ways. The possibility of creating images of erotically appealing men was also in the commercial air at the time. *Playgirl* magazine, complete with hunky centrefold nude, was founded in America in 1973 in response to the feminist-instigated but widely shared interest in previously silent female views about their sexual needs. Writer Sarah Kent's verdict on this was that while art history was full of beautiful homoerotic male bodies that women could appreciate on the sly, the exploration of women's erotic fantasies was meanwhile in its infancy.[5] Ten years after Kent wrote this, Sam Taylor-Wood filmed a nude man dancing frenziedly to techno-music. *Brontosaurus*, the ten-minute video that resulted, is a projection of that film in slow motion set to a soundtrack of Samuel Barber's *Adagio for Strings*. A mystery emanates from this naked slender man as he leaps and stretches in a strange but oddly graceful manner to the familiar plangent music. A tiny pink dinosaur in the corner of the room refers playfully to the title of the work, which manages to suggest the primitive, the ecstatic and the vulnerable.

Today women take the right to be heard, won for them by preceding generations, for granted. And they let their art go wherever it wants. In 1992 the American artist Cindy Sherman, partly in a defiant response to attacks on freedom of artistic expression at the time, produced a series of *Sex Pictures*, huge photographs of sexually active mannequins that were eye-avertingly horrible to look at, not just in terms of subject matter but also in terms of their unappetizingly glossy coloured surfaces. No. 255 is particularly crude with its jointed woman-facsimile naked on her knees. The use of a mannequin with moulded plastic genitals that face the viewer and glass eyes that stare vacantly to one side subtracts the personal from the sex act and degrades the woman. A frequently cited predecessor is

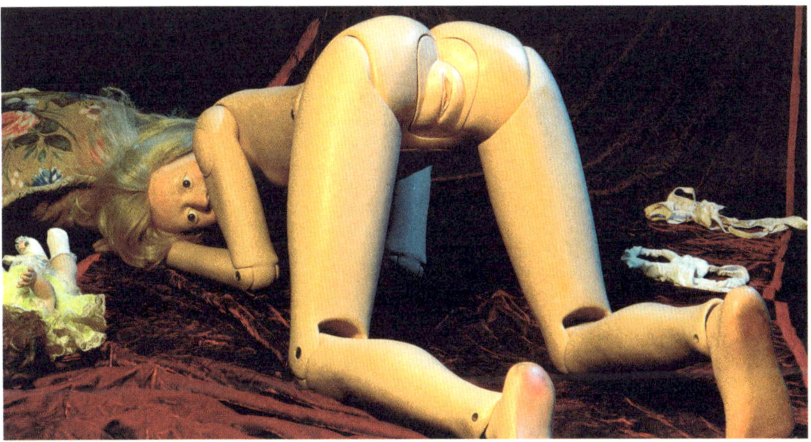

Cindy Sherman, *Untitled* (No. 255), 1992, colour photograph. Sherman's work centres on the roles of women, not just how they are seen, but how they act. In the series *Sex Pictures*, she moved away from photographing her own body to using mannequins and prosthetics to explore the terrible. In this image the mirror and discarded clothes question the nature of the woman's complicity. Free will or nurture?

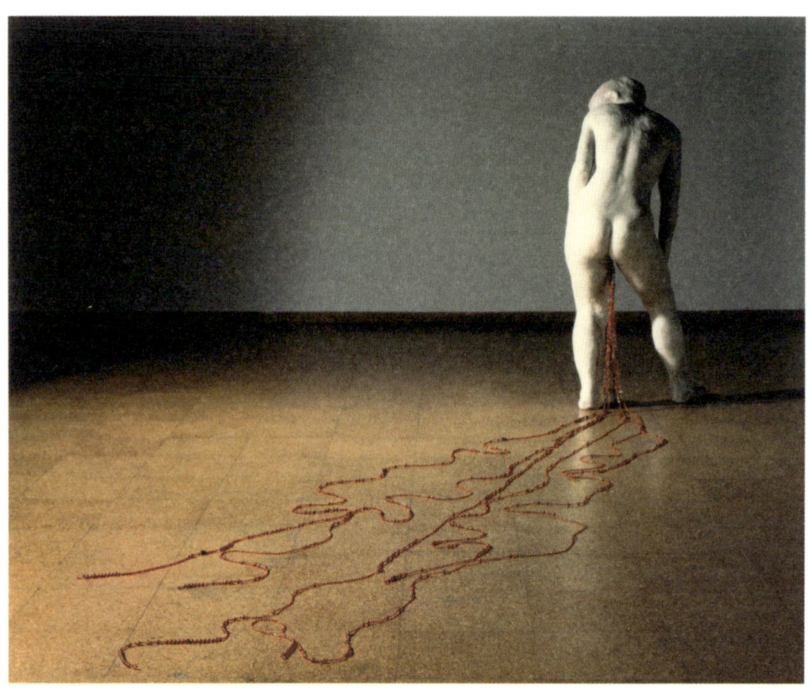

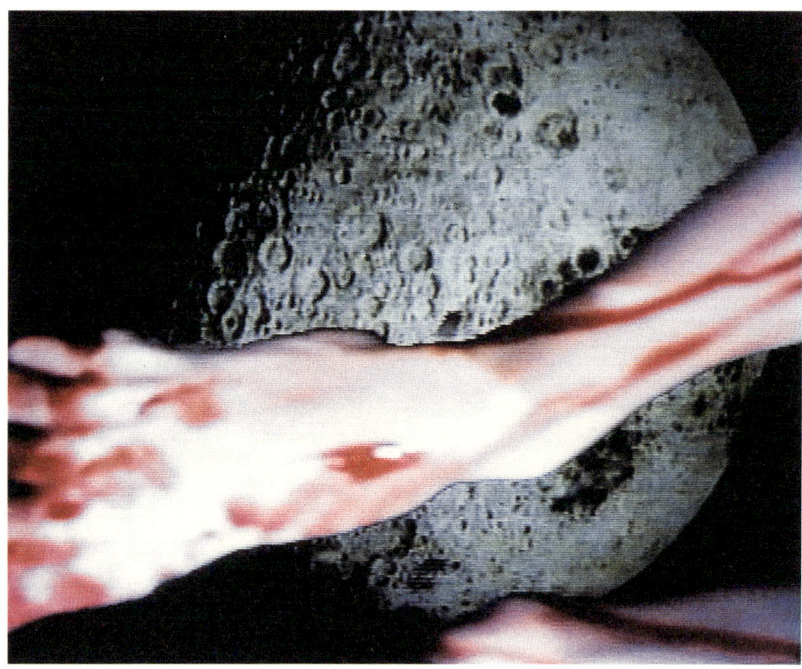

the German Hans Bellmer, whose models of distorted, tortured dolls represent a violent version of the Surrealist fascination with female sexuality. But the misogynistic fear and dislike of women revealed by his bound and broken female bodies are replaced in Sherman's work by something much more complicated. Sherman's imagery reflects the way the passionate certainty of seventies feminism developed into a feminism with the confidence to admit to awkward questions. Her decision to use female-facsimiles as subjects gives her double powers: its artificiality not only allows her to present a scenario too terrible to depict through realistic means, but also gives the viewer a space in which to think and not merely react. Does the 'girliness' symbolized by the doll, hairbrush and discarded underwear inevitably lead to the abject situation pictured? Does the horror Sherman visualizes beset women with or without their complicity? These are not comfortable thoughts.

The introduction into art by the 1970s feminist artists of hitherto hidden aspects of the female body continues, although in new and allusive ways. Bodily functions, the turning away from which is what the traditional nude is all about, were dealt with by Kiki Smith in 1992 with *Pee`Body*, a sculpture of a crouching female relieving herself of a stream of yellow beads, and *Tale*, a crawling woman depositing a long tail of faeces on the gallery floor. Menstruation followed in 1993 with *Train*, expressed metaphorically through red beads that flow from between the legs of the sculptured female nude. On paper, the subjects of the Swiss artist Pipilotti Rist sound taboo-breaking, but the results are often ravishing. The short video *Blutclip* (Blood Clip) of 1993 is about menstruation and is a visual poem to what she calls 'this wonderful sap'. But then to talk of subjects in connection with her video works gives quite the wrong impression. Her films are full of colour, floating changing movement, sensation, surprise. 'Handbags', she calls them, because with video there is room for everything: painting, technology, languages, music, poetry, commotion, premonitions of death, sex and friendliness. 'The term subject matter is something I've never understood,' she says. 'My subjects are amorphous and overlapping … It's the subjects that choose me, not the other

OPPOSITE ABOVE **Kiki Smith**, *Train*, 1993, wax and glass beads. Whereas the ideal nude was cleansed of the body's physical processes, Smith is keen to introduce them in her art, as here in her red-beaded metaphor for menstruation.

OPPOSITE BELOW **Pipilotti Rist**, *Blutclip* (Blood Clip), 1993, video still. Rist uses video to examine subjects conventionally taboo in art. *Blutclip* eschews realism by showing her body covered with gemstones or floating through space in a colourful, flowing river of a poem to what she calls 'this wonderful sap'.

way round. We marry, the subject and I, and every now and then I'm being hurled out of the whirl of time and catapulted to my editing suite.'[6] One of her works, *Closet Circuit*, 'came out of a discussion after lunch, when I expressed my desire to visualize what, where and how my body produced every day. I made a joke that we set a camera in the toilet and play the real time images back to the seated person on a screen in front of them.' The 'joke' was taken seriously.[7]

Artists who use photography are particularly drawn to the ageing woman, that same ageing body that in the past was used to represent the wickedness of witches and the tragic decline of beauty. Melanie Manchot wants to convince us of the acceptability of the tabooed older female nude body. In *Time Orders Old Age to Destroy Beauty* of 1746, the worst horror for a woman that the painter Pompeo Batoni can imagine is the loss of youthful beauty. As Time holds his hourglass, Old Age, a hideous crone, scratches the face of the rosy beauty. But Manchot's photographs of her mother show a beautiful and dignified woman. She makes

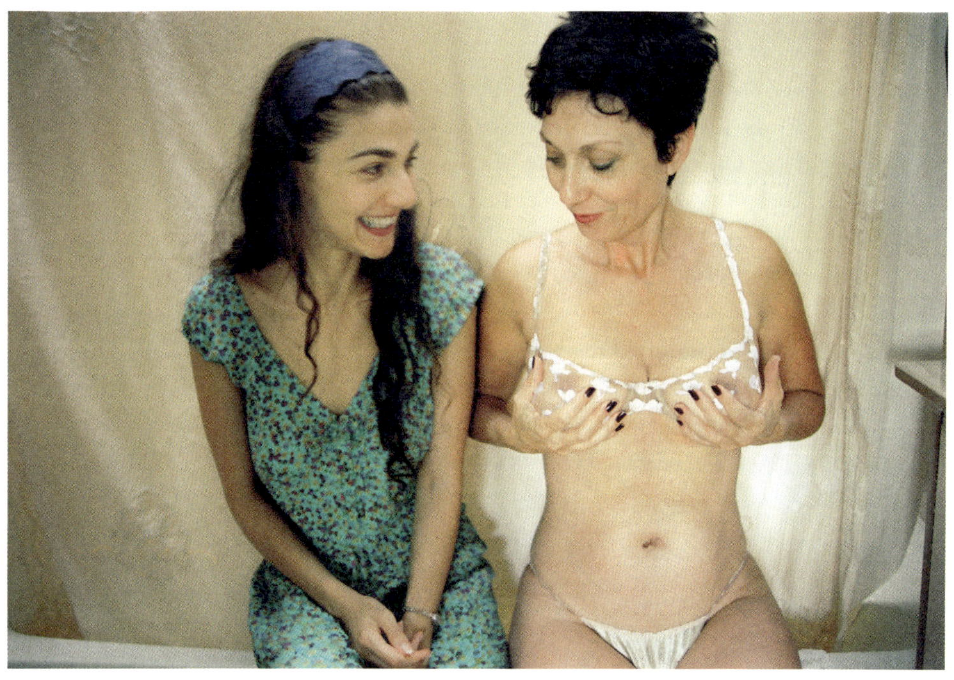

Elinor Carucci, *My Mother and I*, 2002, chromogenic print. Carucci set out to show the wit, wisdom and sense of fun of the older woman as she shows her daughter the power of the push-up bra.

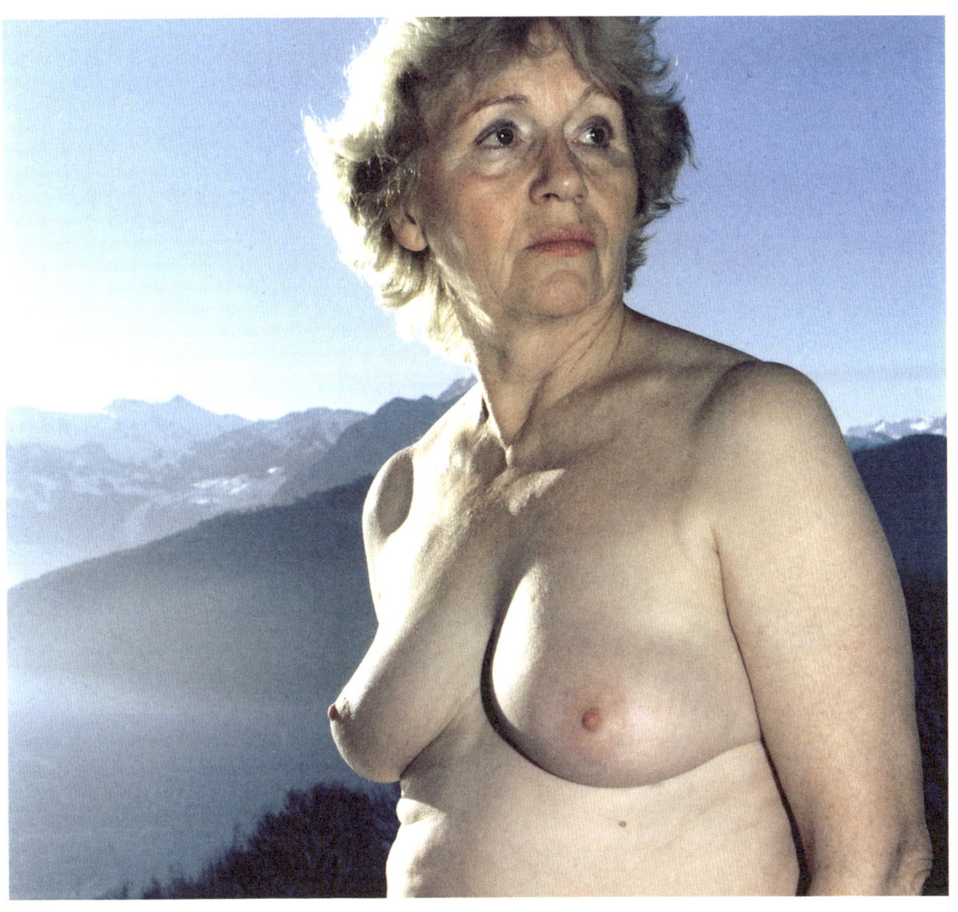

Melanie Manchot, *Liminal Portraits 1999–2000: With Mountains 1*, 1999, C-print. Naked old women
have been portrayed in art without compassion, their bodies repellent for their lack of youth.
Manchot's series of photos of her handsome mother forces a rethinking of this traditional view.

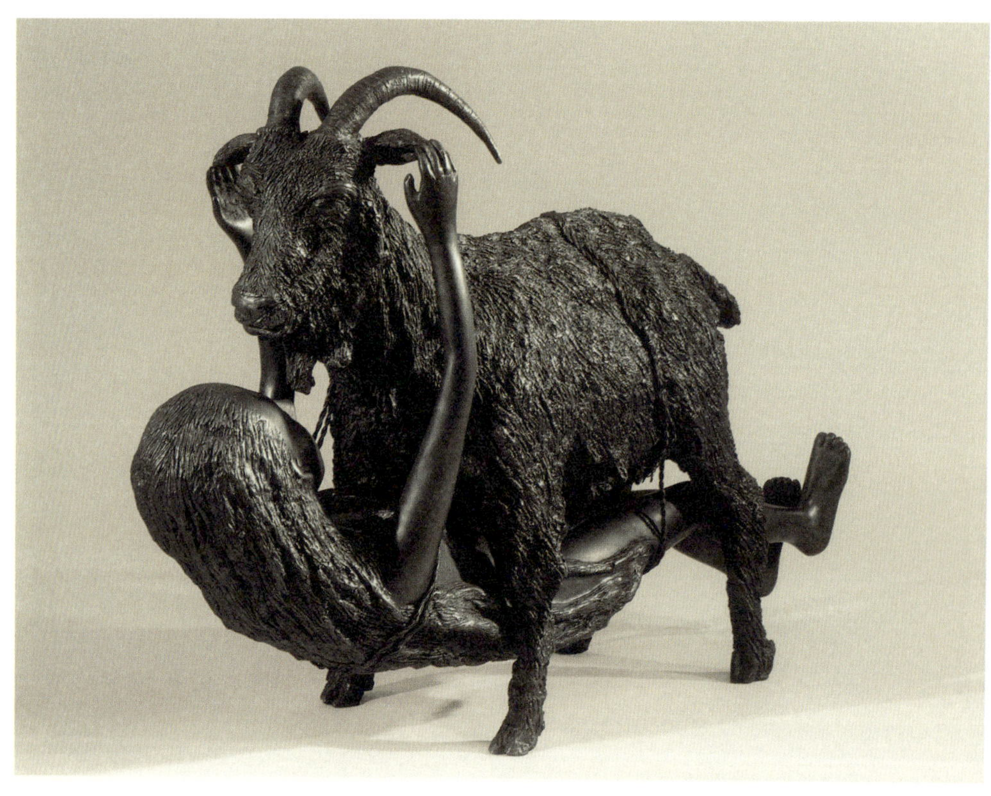

Kiki Smith, *Tied to Her Nature*, 2002, bronze. Smith explores the animal side of women. Far from a passive victim, this is woman embracing her physical desires.

no attempt to prettify her or make her younger in that TV-makeover sort of way. Instead, you see the skin of an older woman, the facial lines of an older woman and the unfamiliar, handsome bosom of an older woman. In short, Manchot makes her mother look as attractive as any of the younger women who have traditionally starred in art. The Israeli artist Elinor Carucci uses the richness of the mother-daughter relationship to rethink the presentation of the older woman as someone full of life and fun. She used a self-timer for the series of photographs *My Mother and I*. In one sequence: 'My mother was going on about how to get guys, how all they want is sex – and how to wear a push-up bra.'[8]

The issue-based self-portrait developed by the seventies feminists has proved a gift to contemporary artists, though in its journey down the decades it has changed. While some, like Ana Mendieta, used it to explore ideas of nationality and rootedness, others, like British artist Tracey Emin, put the personal in place of political and social concerns. Producing images of female sexuality and desire in graphic works and watercolours of the greatest delicacy, Emin makes her private life the subject of her art, but seems to feel no need to yoke her personal experience to contemporary issues affecting women. Though one helped pave the way for the other, there is a world of political difference between Emin's self-expression and the vaginal plates commemorating great women of Judy Chicago's *Dinner Party* of 1979 inspired by Chicago's awareness of sexism in the art world.

Never one to shirk the unsayable, Kiki Smith has produced a group of works in various materials that explores the relationship between women and animals. Some, like the bronze sculpture *Tied to Her Nature* of 2002, depicting a young woman tied to the goat on top of her, face up to the theme of submission to an uncontrollable nature, and arouse disturbing thoughts that would have struck the 1970s feminists as politically incorrect. A strong admirer of what he calls Smith's visceral quality, perhaps surprisingly given the hardness and sameness of the casts he makes of his body, is Antony Gormley, although he adds, 'I have never wanted to deal with the body in pieces or use *Gray's Anatomy* as a blueprint for analysing gender politics.'[9]

The women's success in introducing new female types and points of view into art has been an inspiration to men. In the 1980s, the photographer, curator and one-time *Artforum* editor John Coplans made photographs of his ageing body, minus his head but not hiding the fact that it was his own body and no one else's, each sag, crease and hair trapped cruelly by the camera. *Self-Portrait (Torso, Front)*, 1984, is a close-up from breastbone to pubis, the wrinkles and body hairs suggesting a face and the sagging skin recalling the flayed skin held to be Michelangelo's self-portrait on the altar wall of the Sistine Chapel's *Last Judgment*. In its stress on age and the non-ideal, it takes feminist questioning of the ideal body into masculine territory.

Women have sensitized men to the old certainties about masculinity and femininity, showing the unsuitability of these notions for a modern age. In 1996, Antony Gormley explained that 'Part of the reason that so much of the work tries to lay the verticality of the body down, or re-present it by putting it on the wall, is that I am aware that even when a body case is directly on the floor, because I am tall there is a sense of dominance.' He called this way of displaying his sculptures 'modified maleness' and he did it to help protect women from the male gaze which sees the female body as 'the object of desire, or the object of idealization'.[10] It is a very polite intention, and one that had no existence before women changed art forever.

John Coplans, *Self-Portrait (Torso, Front)*, 1984, photograph on paper. The women's daring uses of their naked bodies in self-portraiture seems to have inspired male artists, such as art journalist and photographer John Coplans, who made a number of photos of his ageing body in the 1980s. Here, arms raised, his chest and stomach evoke a landscape – or a face.

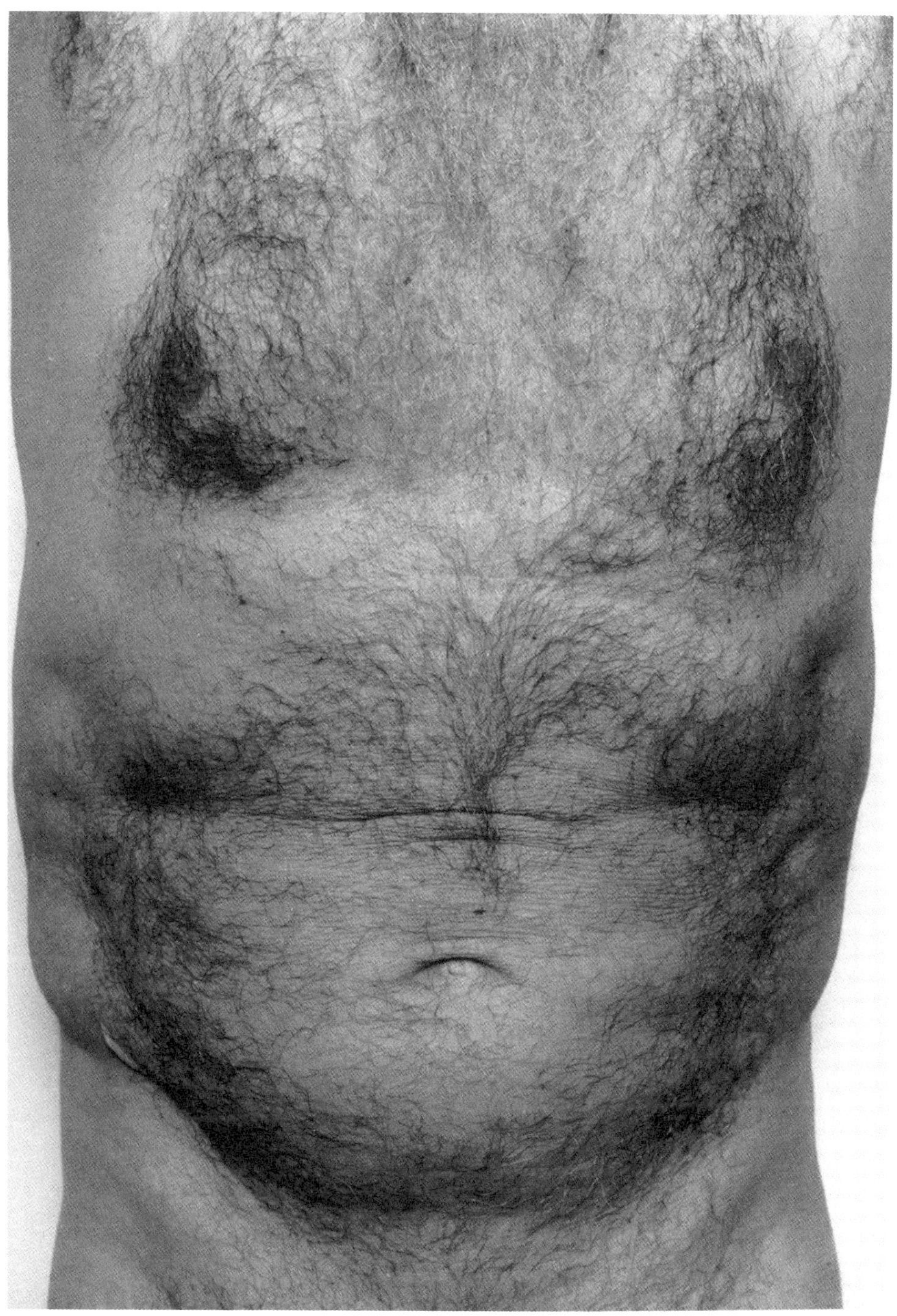

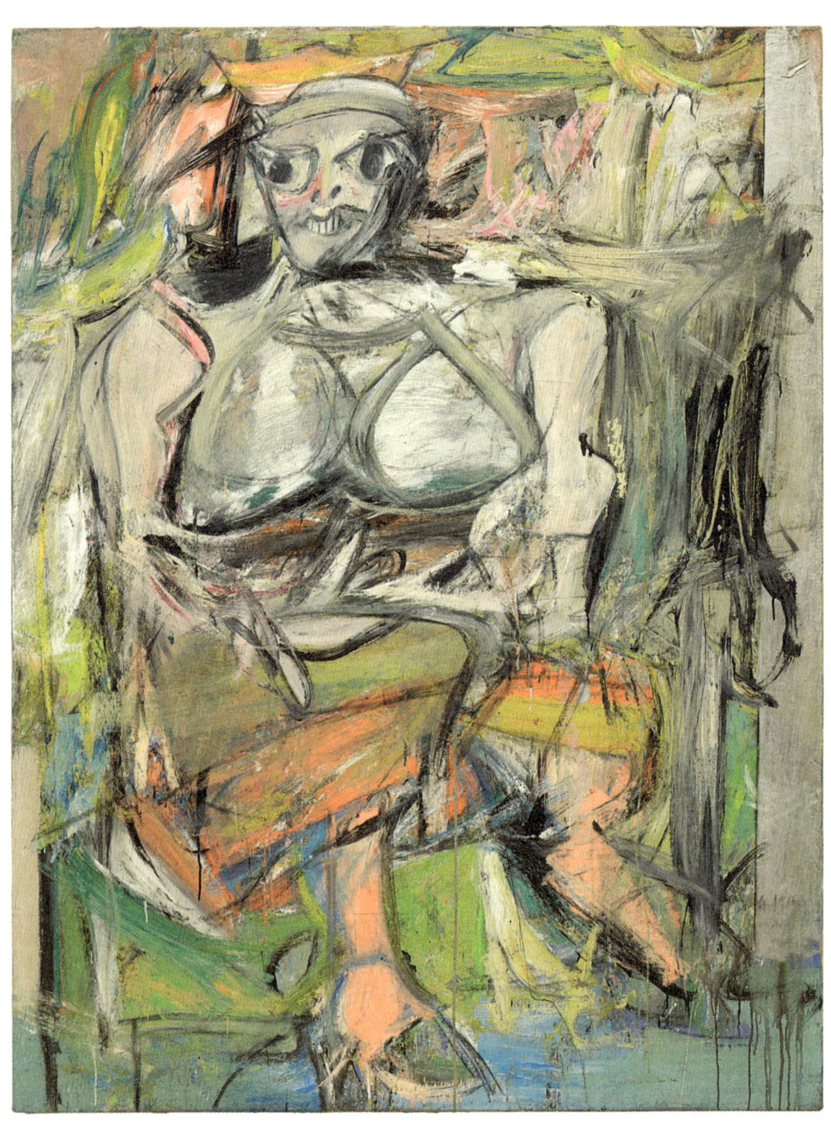

Willem de Kooning, *Woman I*, 1950–2, oil on canvas. With his *Woman* paintings, leading Abstract Expressionist Willem de Kooning gave permission to painters to bring the nude back into art. His personal vision, unrelated to the nudes of the past, horrified many, but its influence is still felt today.

4.
FORGIVE ME, I'M A PAINTER

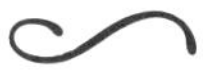

THE NUDE AS A SUBJECT FOR ARTISTS had one of its periodic 20th-century boosts in 1953 when Willem de Kooning exhibited his *Woman* paintings at the Sidney Janis Gallery in New York. Grotesque conglomerations of staring eyes, breasts and crazy hair emerging out of a mass of brushstrokes and wonderful wild colour, they were definitely of a woman with no clothes. They were also by a museum-standard artist who was one of the group of revered New York Abstract Expressionists, and it was for this reason that they attracted so much attention. The nude had reappeared in yet another of its 20th-century reincarnations, this time as a crude personal vision with no relation to the ideal.

Realism at mid-century had been weakened by the dazzling glamour of the American Abstract Expressionists and the formidable critic Clement Greenberg's argument that art was about form and colour and not narrative. When de Kooning, a man from the non-figurative side, produced the *Woman* paintings, it gave ammunition to painters interested in figurative art. Asked a decade later whether he had felt 'out on a limb' when he returned to the figure, de Kooning revealed that he had reached an impasse with his non-figurative work: '[Forms] ought to have the emotion of a concrete experience … I am very happy to see that grass is green. At one time it was very daring to make a figure red or blue: I think now that it is just as daring to make it flesh-coloured.'[1]

Philip Pearlstein recalls de Kooning dropping in to the Tanager Gallery in New York in the mid-1950s. As well as a painting of a group of nude men inspired by a newspaper photograph of a football tackle, Pearlstein, then a young man in his twenties, was exhibiting a group of paintings done in a geometric form of Abstract Expressionism. Most people advised Pearlstein to drop the sportsmen; de Kooning told him to continue. Although there is no sign of any influence of de Kooning's wildly gestural and controversially male-centred vision in the precisely delineated bodies that have absorbed Pearlstein since the beginning of the 1960s, de Kooning's advice typified the way the nudity baton has been handed on from one artist to another throughout the 20th century. In terms of keeping the nude alive in art, their stylistic difference is irrelevant.

A revealing aspect of Pearlstein's decision to take the naked body as his subject is the need he felt to justify it. Despite de Kooning's venture into figuration, the world of avant-garde art was in thrall to abstraction of various kinds, and it was a brave decision for an ambitious artist to choose to work in a figurative style. Pearlstein, justifying his choice in order to be taken seriously by the critics, laid out his rationale in his teaching and in articles in art journals. In 1962, at the height of abstraction and minimalism, he acknowledged the problem in *Art News*: 'It seems madness on the part of any painter educated in the 20th-century modes of picture-making to take as his subject the naked human figure, conceived as a self-contained entity possessed of its own dignity, existing in an inhabitable space, viewed from a single vantage point.'[2]

Art as an expression of something in the world around us was an unfashionable idea in the America of the 1960s when the art world saw meaning residing in the qualities of art itself: colour and form were the content of art, not any representation of the life outside. Pearlstein's artistic way through this was to ensure that his everyday nudes of men and women, sometimes pictured apart, sometimes together, betrayed little of his or his models' feelings. He set up his studio with covered windows and three floodlights in order to banish any moodiness and atmospheric overtones that might come from fluctuating light. And he explained that his nudes were different from the discredited life-class nudes because he was not copying heroic poses or correcting flaws, but trying for a clinical approach. They are models with workaday bodies posed in odd positions in the studio and painted with the same hyperrealistic detail as the rugs and chairs around them, just one more component of the domestic world. In this detachment lies their novelty; they are neither young nor old, neither plain nor beautiful. 'Once I decided that the models and those objects in my paintings just added up to a kind of big still life, I felt that had dispensed with the problem.'[3]

But inevitably when the human body is the subject, readings follow. Questions have already been asked about the apparent innocence of his spectacular decorative accessories, the native American Indian rugs, the fairground paraphernalia. The models' bodies may remain neutral but some of the props – the black 19th-century carnival puppets, for example – invite an attempt to provide a context. Pearlstein responds to this by saying: 'I don't go out of my way to set up stories.

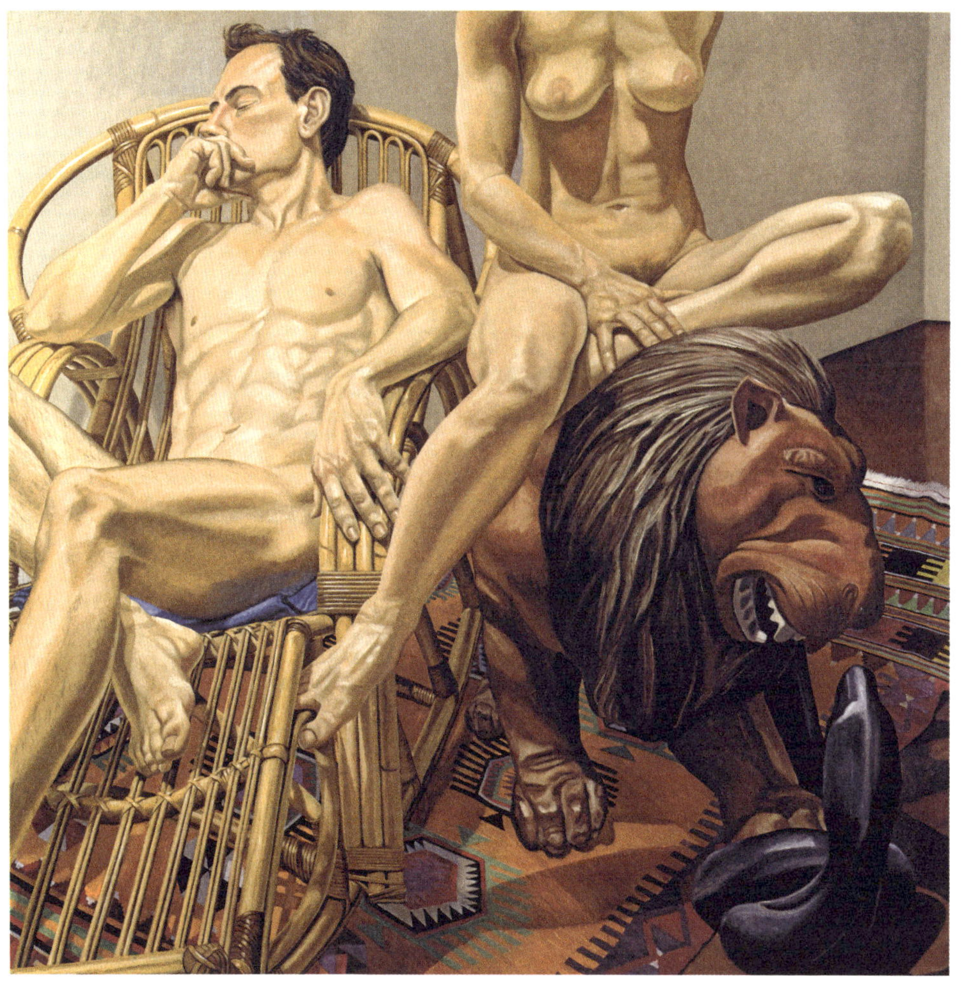

Philip Pearlstein, *Male and Female Nudes with Luna Park Lion and Bamboo Chair*, 1991, oil on canvas. Pearlstein's clinical treatment of the workaday bodies of his models displays the same detachment as his handling of the objects in his paintings, here a fairground lion, bamboo chair and Native American rug.

My paintings are about painting. Painting problems, period. Whatever meaning there might be attached, I mean what people might attach, is almost accidental.'[4]

The bodies painted by the British artist Lucian Freud seem to come from a different planet from the ideal nudes of the past. It is not just that his models and manner of painting them would strike earlier generations as brutal; they remain so for many today. Freud is famous for casting a non-idealizing eye upon the naked body. Every lump and bump and wobble, every shade of yellow, pink, blue and brown that make up the overall skin colour, is captured on his canvas in nudes that exude the reality of a doctor's examination table. Hard to categorize, their size, technique and absence of idealization explain why they are considered paintings rather than portraits. As realistic portrayals of bodies, they have no artistic category to fit in to, neither traditional nude nor portrait. Although the names of many of his naked sitters are no secret, and although he likes to work with them over several canvases, the physical qualities of their bodies and not their faces are what fascinates him: 'I'm really interested in people as animals. Part of my liking to work from them naked is for that reason.'[5] His description of Sue Tilley's body in *Benefits Supervisor Resting*, 1994, indicates his interests: 'It's flesh without muscle and it has developed a different kind of texture through being such a weight-bearing thing.'[6] The attempt to express the essential qualities of flesh is shared with Rubens, say, or Rembrandt, but unlike their paintings it comes without the sweetened coating of the artist's admiration for the beauty of his sitters. 'Initially being very aware of all kinds of spectacular things to do with her size, like amazing craters and things one's never seen before, my eye was naturally drawn to the sores and chafes made by weight and heat.'[7]

As a modern painter, Freud stressed his distance from anything as simple as the conventional conversion of live model to painted image. This specialist in ruthless transcriptions of unclothed bodies says that his work is about art rather than the models who are its ostensible subject: 'The picture, in order to move us, must never remind us of life, but must acquire a life of its own precisely in order to reflect life.' He said he needed the model as 'the starting point of his excitement'. But they drop away and 'the picture is all he feels about it, all he thinks worth preserving of it, all he invests it with'.[8]

Like Pearlstein, he aspires to a kind of painterly neutrality. 'One thing I have never got used to, is never feeling the same from one day to the next, although I try to control it as much as possible by working absolutely all the time. I just feel so different every day that it is a wonder that any of my pictures ever work out at all. …When I was painting a picture of my mother years ago I was feeling sadder

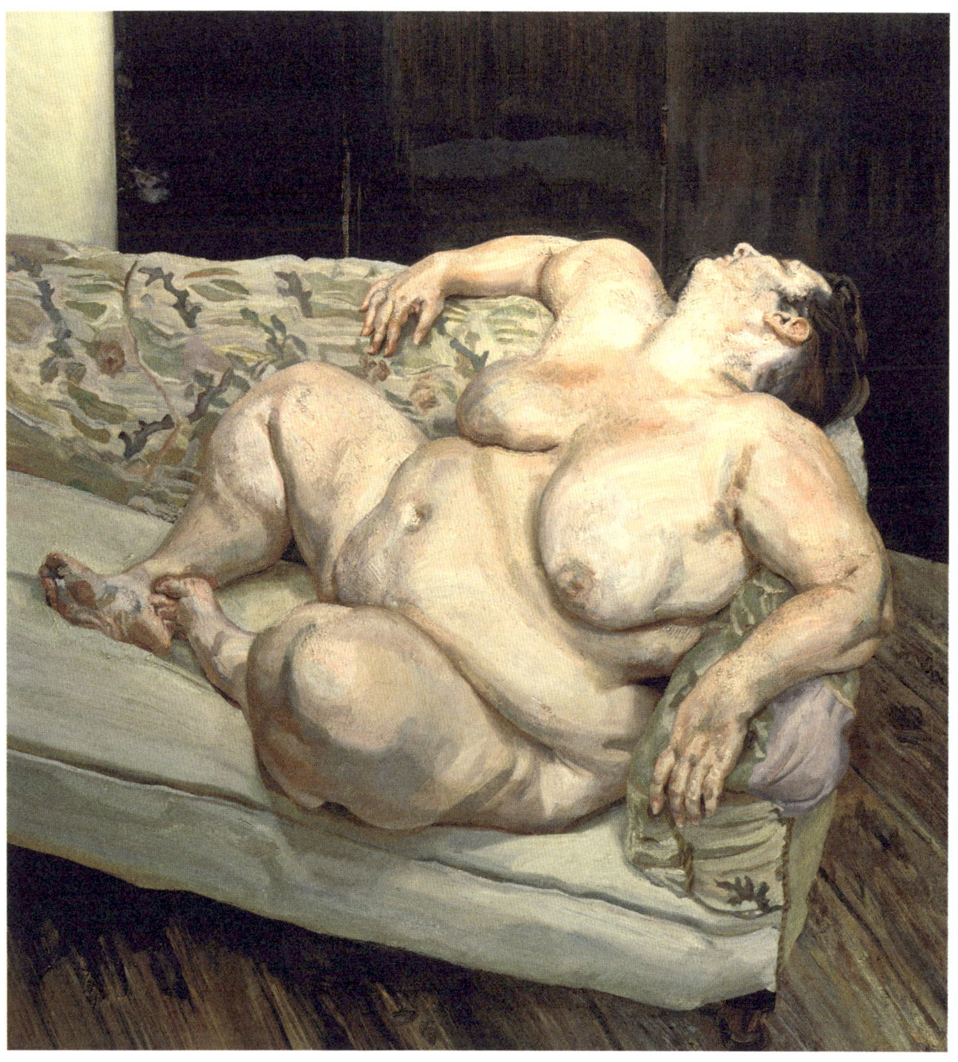

Lucian Freud, *Benefits Supervisor Resting*, 1994, oil on canvas. Freud said he was 'really interested in people as animals'. Their bodies and not their faces were what fascinated him. With Sue Tilley, pictured here, it was 'all kinds of spectacular things to do with her size'.

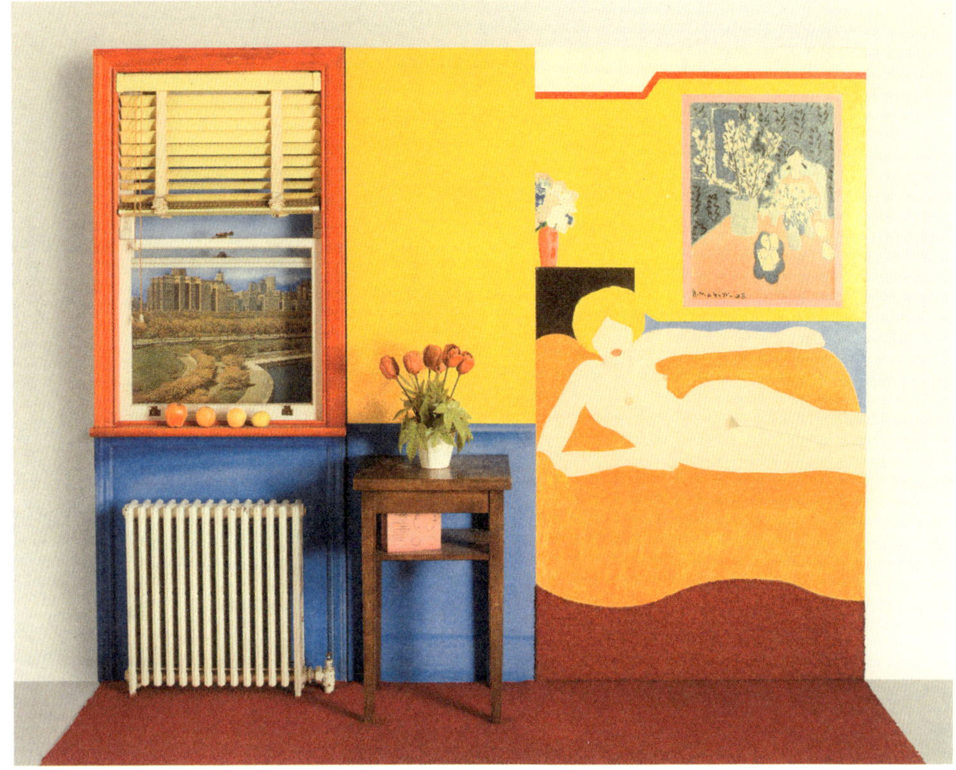

Tom Wesselmann, *Great American Nude No. 48*, 1963, oil and collage on canvas, acrylic
and collage on board, enamelled radiator and assemblage. With his *Great American Nudes*,
Wesselmann brought something new to the tradition of the ideal nude. Sensitive to the past,
in particular Matisse, whose works he often referenced in his paintings, he placed his nudes
firmly in the 20th century via his interest in pin-ups and consumer goods. *No. 48*, with its
Matisse print on the wall and radiator attached, is modern, American and sexy.

than I ever have before or since. I was painting the paisley patterns on the bed and
I remember worrying that my sadness would get into the paisleys and I suppose
perhaps it did. I am just giving you an index of my megalomania.'[9]

While the pitiless painter's eye of Freud and Pearlstein unyoked their nudes
from the flaw-free ideal, the American Tom Wesselmann was driven by a different
desire. He wanted to update the ideal nude. Interested in popular culture and a
competent cartoonist before he trained as an artist at Cooper Union in late 1950s
New York, it was not until Wesselmann escaped the stifling presence of Abstract

Expressionism that he found his way, as he recounts in the autobiography he wrote in the third person: 'Now he decided the only salvation was to tackle what he's always scorned as a student – figurative subject matter – in order to give himself definite elements to manipulate in a very specific and literal framework. The traditional situations of painting would be the subjects – the reclining nude, a still life on a table, a portrait, an interior, etc.'[10]

Wesselmann's achievement was to mate the pin-up with the art of the past. The result is a contemporary challenge to the ideal nude. He was fortunate that the 1960s reincarnation of realism known as Pop art allowed him to make the pin-up a legitimate subject, and it remained his obsession all his life. In 1961, Wesselmann, having given a respectful nod to his predecessors, proceeded to recycle their work in a series of Pop-influenced *Great American Nudes* that went on until he died in 2004.

Wesselmann's combination of tradition with novelty means that the pin-up, the two-dimensional style, and the everyday objects that are as fresh as the latest pop song, live alongside the references to old masters and traditional subject matter in his art. His revelation that the first *Great American Nudes* were inspired by the woman who reactivated his interest in sex after the end of his marriage is a 20th-century retelling of the myth of the painter and muse that Picasso would have recognized. The old-new combination coalesces into an artistic challenge of some boldness with Matisse's lounging nudes in the same image as the American flag and American soft drinks and, in one case, a real American radiator fixed to the canvas.

Deeper than the Pop version of pin-ups which they seem on the surface, Wesselmann's *Great American Nudes* speak clearly of their times. The works made after the mid-1960s offer evidence of an era when the contraceptive pill had faced down the fear of pregnancy and magazines were becoming more open about sex. The women's sexuality as they sprawl with their legs apart is newly outspoken and has nothing to do with the modest presentation of the ideal nude. In fact, they challenge it with the evidence of their sexual selves. In his autobiography Wesselmann is forthright about this: 'Many of the earliest *Great American Nudes* had shaved pubic areas specifically because he found them to be blatantly erotic and consequently visually aggressive. To him a shaved vagina had the same vividness and immediacy as a strong red. … It was this underlying interest in the erotic that caused the conflict between abstraction and realism to be resolved in favor of more realism.'[11] The comparison of colour with sexuality is a neat expression of the meshing of style and content.

Over the decades Wesselmann's *Great American Nude* changed. Pubic hair reappeared; sometimes a breast stood in for the whole; occasionally some facial features were included. But in no sense were these ever portraits. Personality, he felt, would interfere with the bluntness of the fact of the nude. As he struggled to find the balance between abstraction and image, between surface pattern and the three-dimensionality of the TV screens and refrigerator doors incorporated into the paintings, between the high art of Matisse and the eye-popping glamour and pneumatic perfection bordering on sexuality of the demotic pin-up, he succeeded in remaking the ideal nude into something quintessentially modern and American.

For these three major painters, the link between the nude, the model, paint and the past was unproblematic. All were happy to see themselves in a tradition while at the same time transforming that tradition into a contemporary ideal nude (Wesselmann), a kind of dispassionate still life (Pearlstein) and a ruthless look at the human body (Freud). With their formative years overshadowed by such giants of painting as the American Abstract Expressionists and the Europeans Picasso and Matisse, these painters had no reason to question their choice of medium. The nude's link with old-fashioned realism was more of a problem – though de Kooning, Picasso, Matisse and others had already given it their own interpretation. They got round this by making clear their awareness of contemporary stylistic developments. Ours is a 20th-century nude, they said, male as well as female in the case of two of the three, with a 20th-century approach to its making. In its honest modernity, it is nothing like the nudes of the past.

But for painters trained in the 1960s and after, matters were more complicated. For these artists, painting itself had lost self-confidence. By 1960, Andy Warhol, the man now regarded as a modern old master and the source of much of today's art, was delegating the work of making his prints and paintings to his assistants, leaving him responsible for the idea alone. The time-honoured notion of holding a brush in order to create had lost its power, weakening the belief in the importance of the artist's hand as a guarantee of authenticity. When Marxist ideas gained ground in the 1960s and questioned the concept of the individual genius, it seemed that the artist's moment had passed forever. Realism was a style for the old fashioned and painting was seen as a timid choice of medium in a world of video, installations, photography and performance. It seemed that the death of painting constantly predicted since the announcement of the discovery of photography in 1839 had really come about this time.

The fall of painting coincided with the removal of life classes from the art-school curriculum in the 1960s. Students who wanted to paint the nude met with little sympathy. If they wanted to paint, it was frowned on, and if they wanted to paint figuratively, the frown got even deeper. Inevitably they felt self-conscious about their need to paint, their need to paint the nude, or both. Because of the strong belief in the late 1960s and early 1970s that painting was dead or dying, Eric Fischl recalls that he felt outcast as a student. Painting was dead, he has said, and figure painting was really dead. 'When painting became so dominated by abstraction, photography became the dominant language for realism and for the figure itself.'[12]

Marlene Dumas recalls starting out in the South Africa of the 1970s: 'At art school, I remember, my professor told me, "You're a born painter." I replied that I considered painting old fashioned. All the smart artists were doing other kinds of work, so I wanted to do something else, but he said, "My poor girl, what else could you do?"'[13]

All of this lack of interest (at best) and hostility (at worst) meant that artists who wanted to use paint to explore their interest in the nude had to justify their fondness for brushes, oil paint, canvas and the model. For ambitious would-be painters trained after 1960 with their eyes on catalogues, exhibitions and critical acknowledgment, the decision to take the nude as their subject was like running a race with a limp. If you listen hard you can hear the painters' voices above the babble of the dominant abstraction, minimalism, conceptualism, performance, installations and videos as they explain their modern manner of working in an unfashionable medium and choice of subject. Although their justifications strike us as unnecessary, the need they felt to make them reveals a lot about the assumptions of avant-garde art when they were starting out.

Dumas argues for the existence of the painting as an object in its own right, not as a facsimile whose value lies in being 'just like' its subject. 'Once, in North America, someone was interested in these smaller paintings of a naked young girl, and asked, "What is the age of the child?" I said, "It's not a child, it's a painting."'[14] Despite the tinge of ingenuousness hanging over this reply, her demand for her work to be judged as art not life is a classic avant-garde position.

Instead of using models as the basis for her paintings, which take in the whole life cycle from birth to death, Dumas uses photographs, as do several contemporary figurative artists: 'My people were all shot by a camera, framed, before I painted them. They didn't know I'd do this to them.' But in no way is she reproducing photographs. She values the expressive qualities of paint too much for that. The artist's hand is as important to her as it was to earlier painters: 'With photographic activities it is possible that they who take the pictures

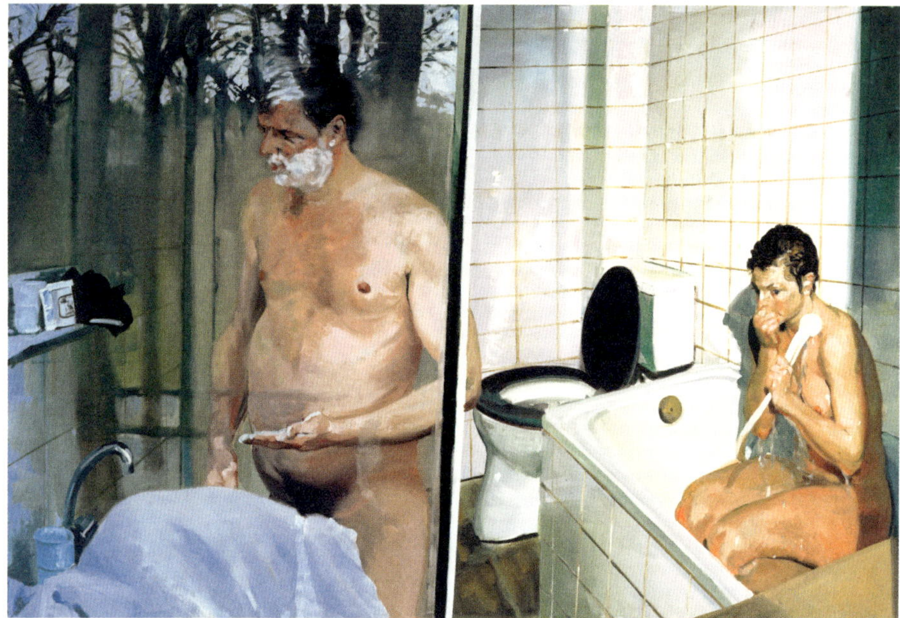

Eric Fischl, *Krefeld Project: Bathroom Scene 2*, 2003, oil on linen. Over the years, Fischl has added middle-aged nudity to his repertoire. For the Krefeld Project paintings, he sent actors to live in a Mies van der Rohe house, photographing them as a couple over several days. The resulting paintings reveal the intimate nakedness of everyday activities.

leave no traces of their presence, and are absent from the pictures. Paintings exist as the traces of their makers and by the grace of these traces. You can't TAKE a painting – you MAKE a painting.'[15]

Eric Fischl, a product of his time, had started out as an abstract artist. When he finally accepted his desire to make figurative art at the end of the 1970s, he brought content back through vast imagined scenes of naked and partially clad figures in disturbing situations reminiscent of the Victorian problem picture whose narrative was always fascinating but never as simple as it seemed at first glance. Superficially transparent, the situations he depicts are filled with ambiguity and a vaguely troubling atmosphere of unspoken tension and desires. They present the complexities of intimacy and relationships in ways we would probably prefer to ignore. It is no surprise to learn that his childhood in a white Protestant suburban family determined to hide the fact of an alcoholic wife and mother stays vividly with him. He is a painter of the secrets of the everyday.

The bodies Fischl paints have begun to reflect his own ageing. In the early 2000s, Middle-aged couples began to enter his art, the men with pot bellies, the women losing that obvious femininity of youth so that you have to look closely to be sure of their gender. As the basis for his Krefeld Project paintings, a group of site-specific works made in a Mies van der Rohe house owned by the German city of Krefeld, he photographed two middle-aged actors left free to develop his suggestions as they inhabited the house as an imagined couple over several days. The interacting painted bodies going about their intimate rituals that resulted are a world away from either the ideal nudes or the grotesque old bodies of earlier art.

Fischl is one of those artists who believes painters can somehow intuit a truth through their practice. Noting the slightly troubled atmosphere in the Krefeld paintings, he said that he later learned that both actors had been having trouble in their respective real-life relationships. It is a variation on Picasso's response to those who thought his portrait of Gertrude Stein, 1905–6, did not resemble her: 'It will,' he said.

Fischl makes huge claims for the power of figurative art, arguing that an art that ignores the body reduces our capacity to understand and feel. He worries that art has lost touch with the big issues of the day. In 2006, in a lecture at the University of Pennsylvania, he argued that removing the body from experience means that we lose the ability to empathize. His example was Iraq: 'And then we get to a point when something really big happens, 9/11 and Abu Ghraib – and now we're a country that tortures people – and we're mute.'[16]

The British painter Jenny Saville wants those who see her paintings to both admire the art and see beyond it. 'Bodies fascinate me,' she says. 'I find having the framework of a body essential. Having flesh as a central subject, I can channel a lot of ideas. I collect images of landscapes, news pictures of war zones, bombed-out carcasses of buildings, disused factories, not just bodies. So far I haven't wanted to paint them directly but these images hold something, they give off a sensation that I'm after, one that I try to transmit through the paintings of a body.'[17]

This desire to endow her bodies with more than is on the surface has been a preoccupation since Saville's first show in London in 1994, when a group of paintings of oversized naked women perched on stools looked out at the spectators. Contemporary attitudes towards what is evocatively called the disorderly body are expressed through markings she adds to her hugely fleshy nudes. By covering the naked body of *Plan* (see page 8) with the concentric circles used in topographic maps to show elevation, she offers the spectator a metaphor from landscape to explain the convex flesh. Poets have used such metaphors for centuries; their verse

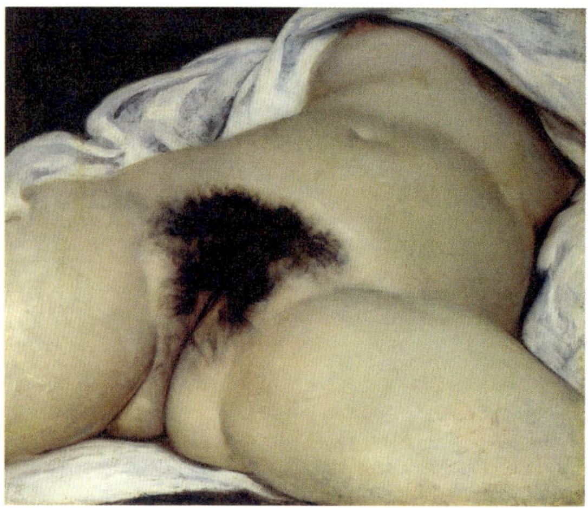

Gustave Courbet, *The Origin of the World*, 1866, oil on canvas.

abounds with comparisons of female bodies to the land – what else is the mons Veneris? Edward Weston took photographs of sections of flaw-free female nudes that can double as hills or sand dunes. Jenny Saville's landscape comparison is grittier, in tune with contemporary female concerns about diet and body image. And landscape is not the only comparison that comes to mind. Those inky circles suggest the marks made by plastic surgeons before their fat-reduction operations. Her picturing of the pressure to own a perfect body shows how the facts forbidden in the presentation of the ideal nude are now the subject of the naked nude.

Saville tracks her fascination with the body's orifices back to early childhood when she saw a small girl fall off a merry-go-round: 'I remember the cut legs, the bloody wound, really bloody, between her legs, and that mix of excitement and worry. I kept going round, seeing snippets, and I couldn't wait till I got round again.'[18] The way she expresses this interest results in some hitherto unseen depictions of the naked body in art. Her curiosity and lack of sentimentality mean that some of her body imagery can be hard to look at. *Reflective Flesh*, 2002–3, shows a naked woman who looks very much like the artist, sitting with splayed legs on a mirror. It brings to mind Courbet's *Origin of the World*, painted in 1866, except that instead of male sexual curiosity it suggests a kind of female insistence on the biology of the body that has nothing to do with erotic allure. *Host*, of 2000, is a pig torso: she has said that when she was painting it, she was struck every time

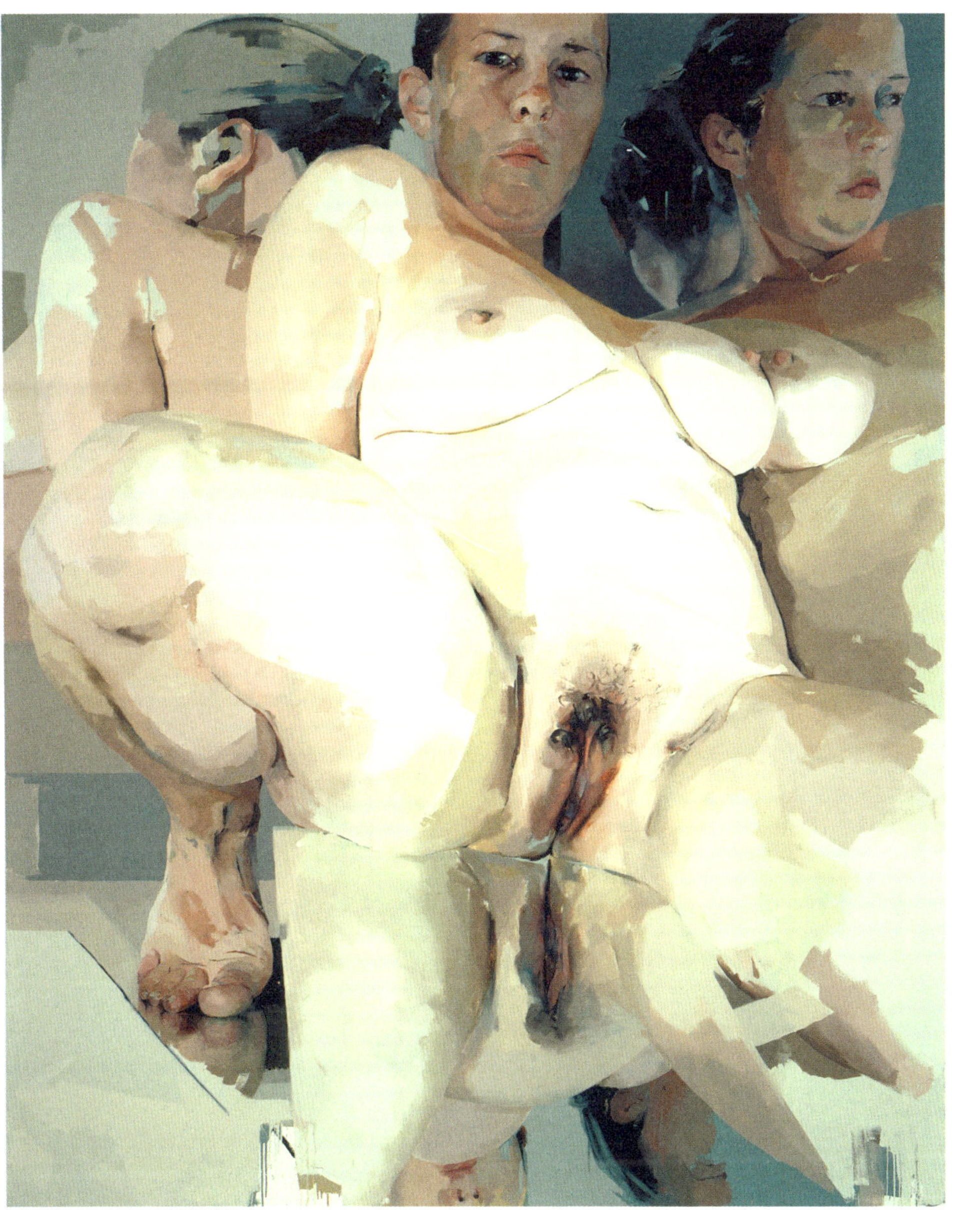

Jenny Saville, *Reflective Flesh*, 2002–3, oil on canvas. These two paintings of similar subject matter are yet totally dissimilar in their approach. Courbet's *Origin of the World* is a sexual invitation to the viewer to do as he wishes. In contrast, Saville in *Reflective Flesh* inhibits spectators' freedom by forcing them to confront the face that watches them.

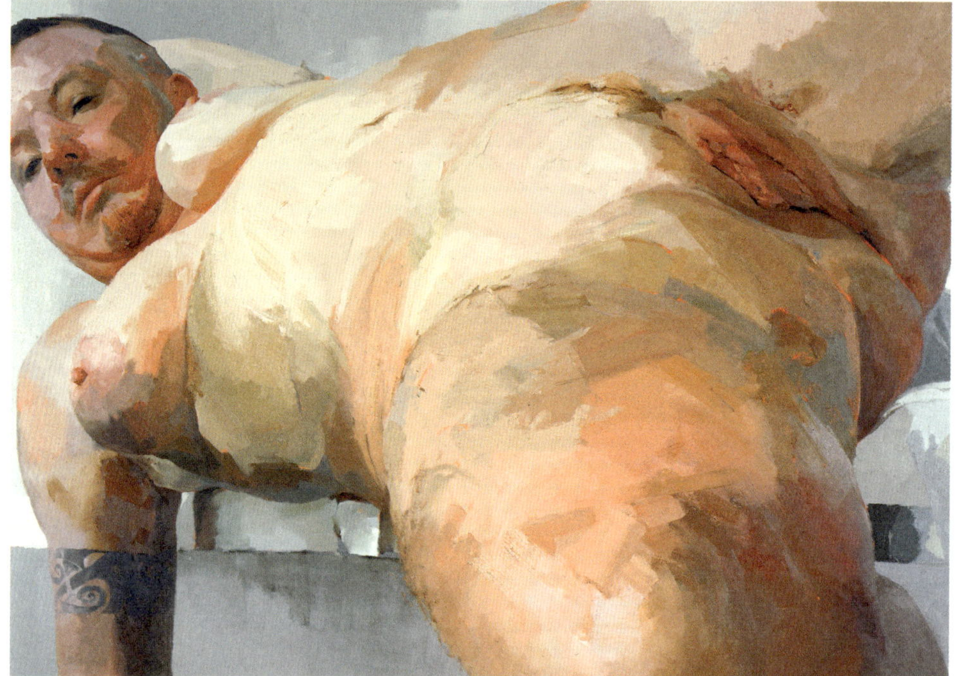

Jenny Saville, *Matrix*, 1999, oil on canvas. 'A gender landscape' was Saville's aim in painting *Matrix*. The pose and blotchy paint suggesting discomfort are very different from Marc Quinn's elegant depiction of two trans subjects in *Buck and Allanah* (see p. 158).

she entered her studio with its resemblance to a female body.[19] *Matrix*, 1999, is a portrait of the artist Del LaGrace Volcano, an intersex, transgender photographer who had been taking testosterone for three years at the time. This depiction, of a person with breasts and a red and angry vulva, shows Saville's interest in the between-gender body. The pose she has chosen is awkward. Their breasts flop to one side and their crotch is up against the picture plane. The obvious brush marks and bruising colours suggest distress and discomfort, powerfully presenting the reality behind gender reassignment.

These new subjects demand new ways of being represented. Speaking in an interview with Simon Schama about *Passage*, another painting of a transgender subject, Saville said: 'Thirty or forty years ago this body couldn't have existed and I was looking for a kind of contemporary architecture of the body. I wanted to paint a visual passage through gender – a sort of gender landscape.'[20]

Saville shares with other artists the desire to establish that she knows she is working in what the art-world gatekeepers perceive as an old-fashioned medium. Fascinated at how a painting can speak in a way that a photograph cannot, she has said that she is 'unapologetic' – a revealing word – for her choice to paint, and produces an impeccable pedigree for her decision. Her interviews are loaded with respectful nods to the great artists of the past: 'The art I like concentrates on the body. I don't have a feel for Poussin, but for Courbet, Velázquez – artists who get to the flesh. Visceral artists – Bacon, Freud. And de Kooning, of course. He's really my man. He doesn't depict anything, yet it's more than representation, it's about the meaning of existence and pushing the medium of paint.'[21] The great abstractionists are her heroes. 'New York represents the last great moment in painting for me – de Kooning, Pollock, Twombly, Johns, and so on. There seems to be a greater receptivity to painting as a medium in New York. A robustness and physicality in painting as a legitimate language of our time…I wanted to see how my paintings stood in that arena – to test them out.'[22]

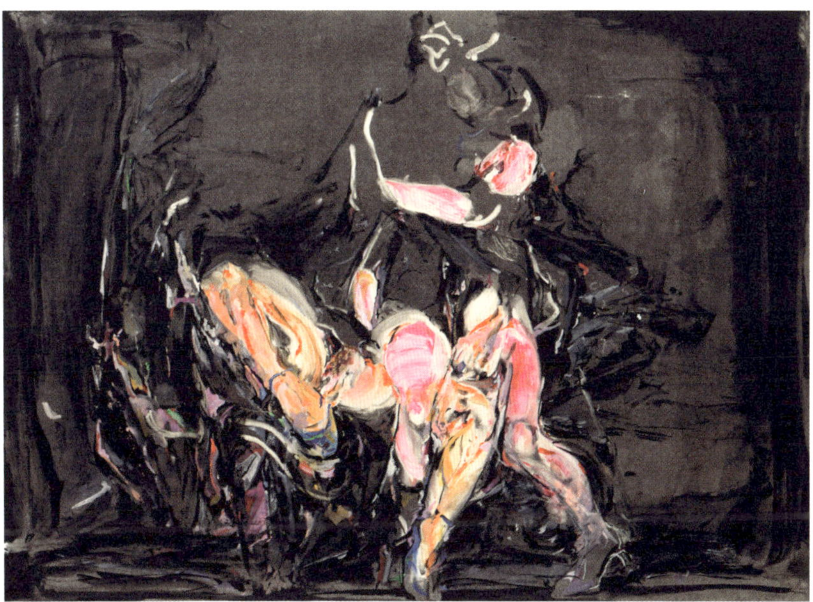

Cecily Brown, *The Skin Game*, 1999, two monoprints with gouache on paper.
Brown wants to paint the body, not the nude. She uses the richness and freedom
offered by abstraction to suggest the intense passion of sexuality. Like many
contemporary painters, she names de Kooning as one of her heroes.

'You just felt such a leper,' says New York-based Cecily Brown about being a painter in the London of the 1990s. [23] It was hard to justify, she recalls. She chose her erotic – some say pornographic – subject matter as a way to draw attention to the painting. Attracted to Picasso, Pierre Bonnard, Bacon and Schiele from adolescence (they taught her that 'art can be rude, outrageous, sexy, nasty'), she says that she 'wanted to use the body but I didn't just want to paint the nude'. An early and important show, *The Skin Game*, depicts sexual acts on gorgeously coloured canvases that look like a cross between Abstract Expressionism and the debris left by the ceiling falling in. 'I used certain erotic images to get attention – especially with my guilt about being a painter. If you want to be a painter, you have to have something that makes people stop in their tracks.'[24] She wonders now if the strategy backfired: 'I think when I was doing a lot of sexual paintings, what I wanted – in a way that I think now is too literal – was for the paint to embody the same sensations that bodies would. Oil paint very easily suggests bodily fluids and flesh.' Her ideal now, she says, 'is to have the tension and intensity of an aggressively sexual image, without actually having to describe that'.[25] Brown has always appreciated de Kooning's observation that flesh is the reason that oil paint was invented.

The painted nude is so deeply identified with traditional art that one canny artist exploited it as a strategy to catch the art world's eye when he was starting out. The American John Currin says that he chose to paint figures in the early 1990s as a way to be noticed in a sea of abstract art: 'It was surprisingly easy to get attention and be different. This is a sort of a glib way to put it, but was sort of like doing conservative paintings with a straight face.'[26]

It says a lot about the American art world of the time that Currin chose painted figuration as a career move. He was well aware that both paint and the nude made his work stand out from the crowd. Asked in 2003 if his work started out as reactionary, he replied: 'Yes, that was on purpose. I was playing into the context of the early 90s, when it was very easy to exploit people's inhibitions about painting, people who felt a responsibility to respond positively to different forms of installation and performance. And it was easy to parody the will to be progressive.'[27] The irony is that his paintings, particularly the surrealistic and grotesquely sexualized makeovers of the great nudes of art history, are not at all conservative. Their cartoonish quality disconcerts many viewers who respect that same art of the past which Currin treats in so cavalier a fashion.

The over-sexualized perfection of women in comics and cartoons inspires many of today's artists. Takashi Murakami is influenced by Japanese sexual culture of the past as well as the present. Recently he has chosen a variety of materials for outspoken

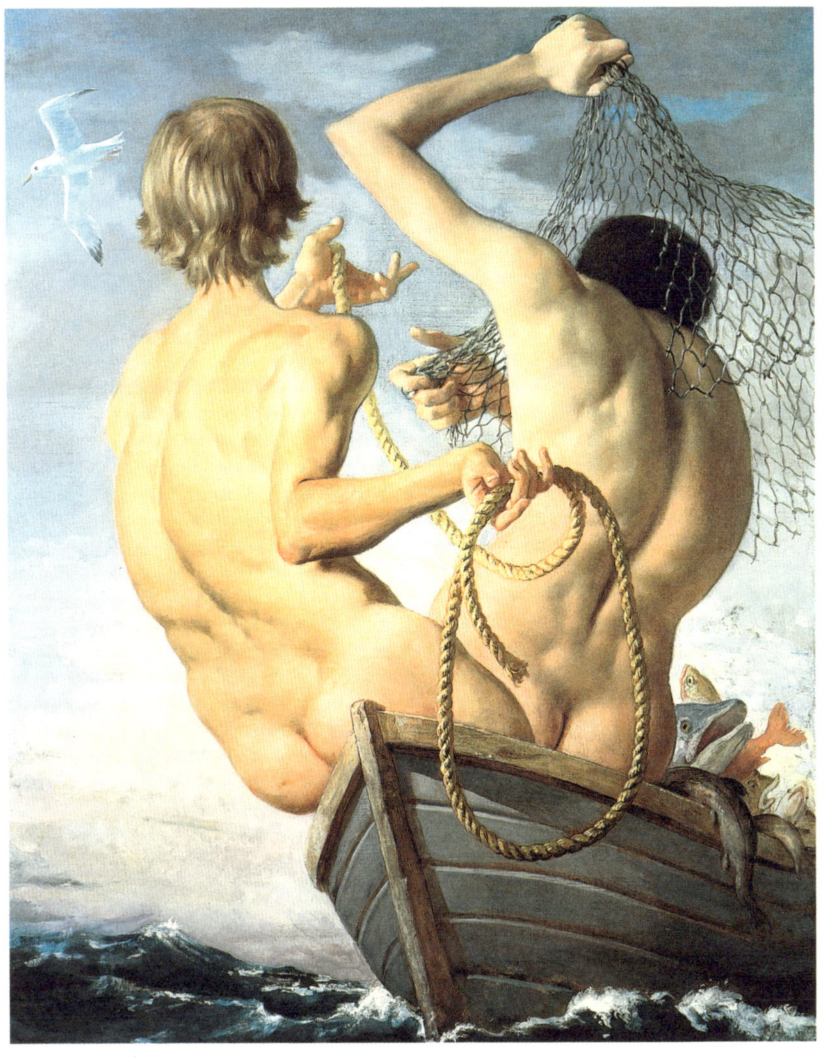

John Currin, *Fishermen*, 2002, oil on canvas. Currin exploits the nude's links to traditional art by modernizing and overtly sexualizing iconic images and styles. Here the handsome male backs, one perhaps older than the other, evoke the magnificent bodies of Michelangelo. The vaguely biblical imagery of the boat, bird and fishes harks back to religious art of the Renaissance.

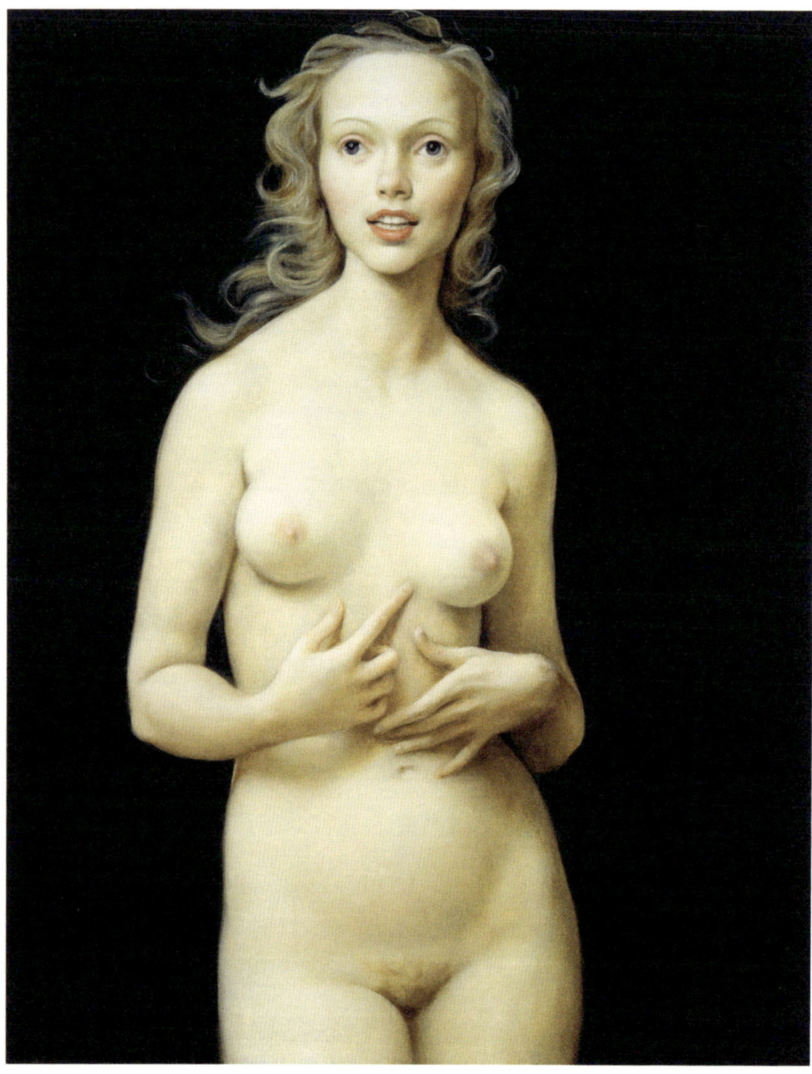

John Currin, *Honeymoon Nude*, 1998, oil on canvas. Set against a timeless black background, the young woman's body recalls Renaissance nudes, especially Botticelli's iconic *Birth of Venus*, while her modern face with open mouth brings to mind film-star poses. In this work Currin knowingly updates the idealized nude as embodiment of male desires, with an added twist – her face is based on his own self-portrait.

sexual imagery based on what he calls the male sexual complex, from sculptures of a penis covered in gold leaf and a vagina covered in platinum set down in front of paintings of traditional erotic sayings to a huge model of a nurse in a tiny uniform that has lost the fight to cover her flesh. A trio of blandly Westernized life-size nudes by the 19th-century artist Seiki Kuroda has been updated at Murakami's request by anime and manga artists into a version of contemporary sexuality familiar from cartoons, complete with pneumatic bodies and childlike faces. Murakami is a type of modern artist par excellence, interested in blurring the lines between high and low art, casting a satirical eye on society, devoted to promoting the works of others, shrewd enough to realize that making his name in the West would open the artistic eyes of Japan to his work.

These post-war painters of the nude brought content back to art. The devaluing of content based on narrative had been a foundation stone of the avant-garde belief in formal values. In this system, abstraction and conceptualism existed alongside life, making sense in terms of the history of art, but not actually referencing the society around it. The link of art to society since the early 20th century has been expressed through art for the masses: the Constructivist designs for tea sets in Russia, the furniture designed on the principles of De Stijl in Holland and the posters commissioned from British artists by Shell in the 1930s. Fine art allowed emotion achieved by abstract means, akin to that aroused by music, as in Rothko's intimations of infinity suggested by the intense colour, huge size and spatial vibration of his painting, but reading meaning through the figure was forbidden.

By the mid-20th century, some brave inhabitants of the art world had begun to voice their unfashionable unease about the defeat of content by the formal qualities of line, design and colour. A suspicion grew that despite the theories, abstraction in the hands of minor artists tended to turn into mere decoration. De Kooning's women were just one example of the new guests at art's table. It was the good fortune of the painters who followed him that they were carried along on this current of change. By taking the hand of the nude and pulling it into painting, these artists not only brought back content, but proved that painting as a medium was not dead.

Once you are alerted to its existence, the painted nude pops up everywhere. Artists keep on challenging the prevailing attitudes to paint and figuration to produce nudes with a contemporary quality. The nude today creates reactions like sparks from a firework. Recycled into the naked body, it continues to surprise us with its relevance to 21st-century concerns.

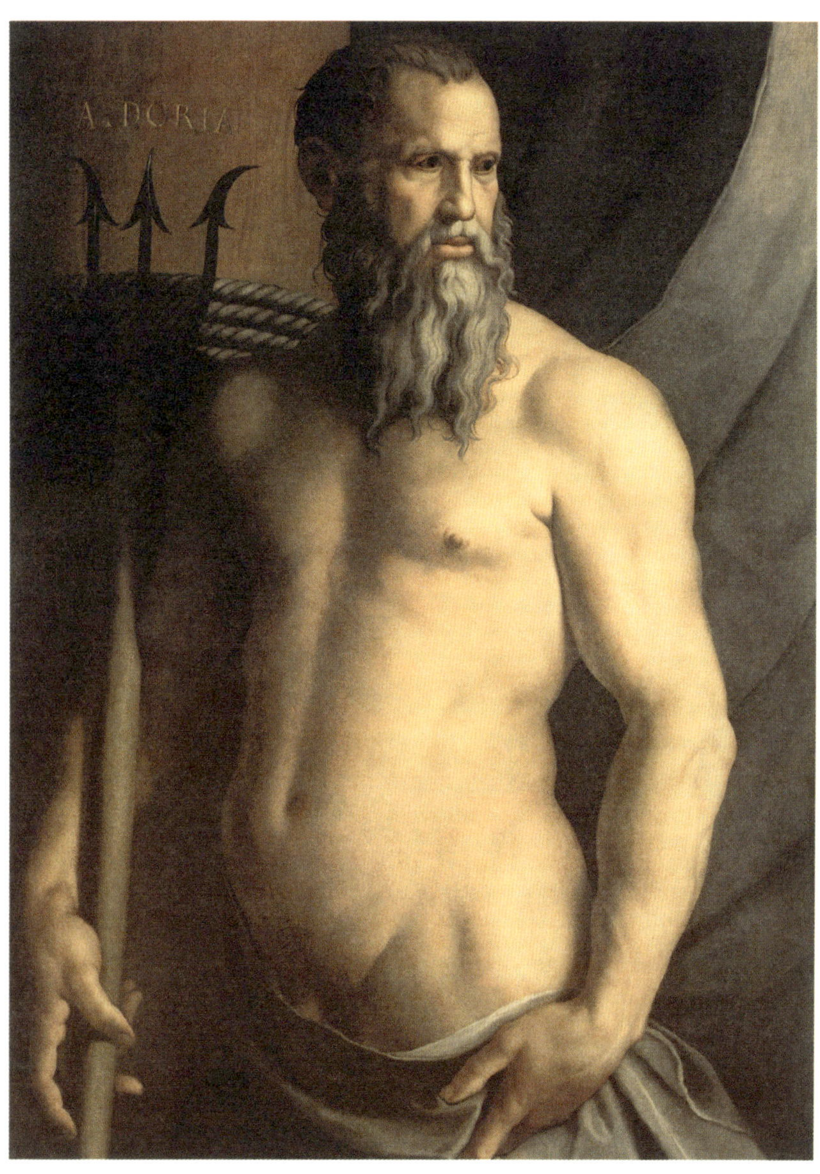

Agnolo Bronzino, *Andrea Doria as Neptune, c.* 1530, oil on canvas. Bronzino's
magnificent 16th-century depiction of the admiral Andrea Doria as the sea god Neptune
sums up the problem of allying the portrait with the nude. The ideal nude presented
generalized perfection, while the portrait, even when 'improved' for art, could never
skimp on the individuality of the sitter's appearance. A naked portrait, given the
conventions of traditional art, stops viewers in their tracks.

5.

THE NAKED PORTRAIT

DESPITE ONE OR TWO EXCEPTIONS – Bronzino's portrait of the powerful Genoese Admiral Andrea Doria and François Clouet's portrait of a woman in her bath once thought to be Henry II's mistress Diane de Poitiers – the nude portrait is a 20th-century invention. The reason is obvious: the nude portrait is a contradiction in terms.

For centuries, the whole point of a portrait was to present a likeness of a particular person polished to its Sunday best. It was all a question of balance. Idealization was part of the portrait painter's arsenal, but not at the expense of the likeness for which the painter was paid. The artist's skill lay in avoiding the brutality of too much realism by enveloping a likeness with a coating of the accepted standards of the day. Beauty was the all-important goal when painting women, a task that sometimes involved a gentle softening of the features: 'I tried as far as I was able to give the women I painted the exact expression and attitude of their physiognomy; those whose features were less than imposing, I painted dreaming, or in a languid, nonchalant pose,' wrote the 18th-century portrait painter Elisabeth Vigée-Le Brun.[1]

There were ways to paint women and different ways to paint men and the public held strong views on who was the best choice for the respective sexes. In the 18th century Thomas Gainsborough was seen as a particularly sympathetic painter of women whereas Joshua Reynolds was more suited to reproducing the *gravitas* of men. When conventions were ignored, the whole of society would take notice. In 1760, when Gainsborough, newly arrived in Bath, painted a dashing portrait of the celebrated musician Anne Ford with her legs crossed, it attracted attention for its daring pose – which was perhaps its aim. The aristocratic Mrs Delany considered it 'a most extraordinary figure, handsome and bold; but I should be very sorry to have any one I loved set forth in such a manner'.[2]

These conventions of portrait painting throw a revealing sidelight on the social scene. The successful Vigée-Le Brun included advice on painting portraits in her *Memoirs*: 'When painting a man's portrait, especially that of a young man, he should stand up for a moment before you begin so that you can sketch the general outline of the body. If you were to sketch him sitting down, the body would not appear as elegant, and the head would appear too close to the shoulders. This is particularly necessary for men since we are more used to seeing them standing than seated.'[3] Her statement magically conjures up an image of tall men hovering over seated women in a genteel setting.

There were theories on the best way of dressing for a portrait: at one stage in his painting career, Reynolds recommended a sort of vague classical dress as less specific, less datable and therefore in his view more acceptable than the modern dress of the 18th century. Facial expressions did not escape the rules. You rarely see a portrait with a smile before the 20th century, and not so often afterwards. Frida Kahlo painted eighty self-portraits over three decades from the late 1920s, and was the subject of many photographs, but she saw to it that her imperfect teeth were kept a secret from the public. Poor dentistry was not the only reason for such sober expressions. Like Reynolds's flirtation with classical dress, painters struggled to produce an image that carried the kind of seriousness that would survive the changing standards and critical eyes of subsequent generations.

The restraint that the need for a convincing likeness placed on the artists' desire to improve the faces before them made portraiture the opposite of the ideal nude. The Venuses and the Adonises of the past are idealized and airbrushed. Freed from the need for resemblance, they are an idea and an ideal, a generalized presentation of perfection. It is for this reason that their faces often seem so bland. The face of Velázquez's 'Rokeby Venus' is only visible in the mirror and is a reflected, slightly blurred impression of pretty, round-faced youth. The artist is following the rule that in order to sustain the illusion of reality, the face must match the body. Too individual or too specific and the door is open for comments and opinions: 'it is too ugly', 'too dark', 'too fair', 'too northern', 'too southern'. In other words, too specific, too individual, both characteristics reserved for portraiture.

Some of the greatest visual shocks in art have come from the uniting of a highly individual face with an unclothed body, as in Francisco Goya's *Naked Maja*. It was for a long time thought to be a portrait of the Duchess of Alba, though scholarship now scorns this interpretation. But it is easy to understand how the wish to claim an identity for it arose, for the striking features are the opposite of the bland and often hazy features of the ideal nude.

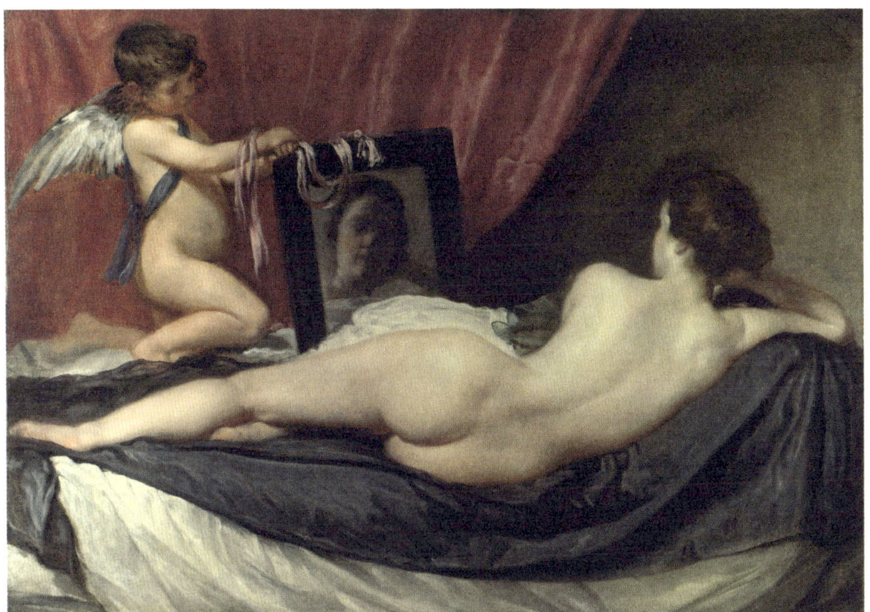

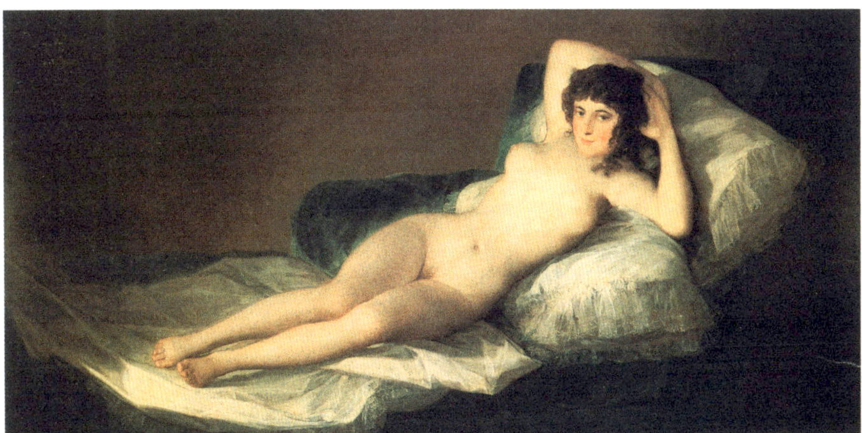

TOP **Diego Velázquez**, *The Toilet of Venus* (Rokeby Venus), 1647–51, oil on canvas. The face of this undulating beauty is blurred in the mirror held by Cupid, leaving the viewer free to explore the body unimpeded by embarrassment or thoughts about the woman's feelings.

ABOVE **Francisco Goya**, *Naked Maja*, c. 1797, oil on canvas. The way the sitter locks eyes with the viewer has convinced many that Goya's extraordinary *Naked Maja* is a portrait and not merely a generalized reclining nude. If so, it was for the owner's eyes only.

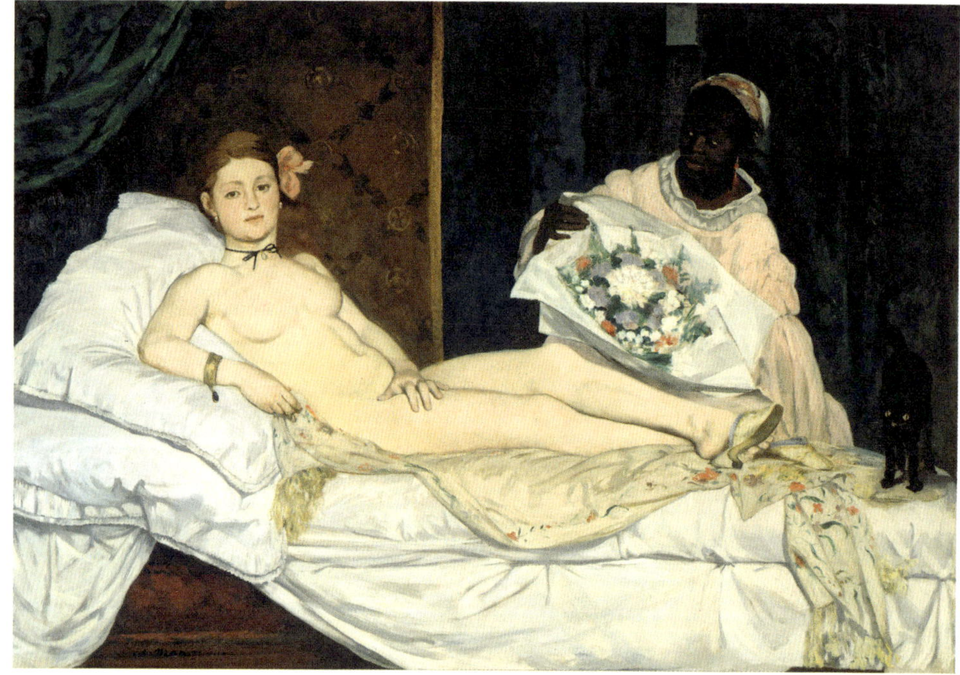

Édouard Manet, *Olympia*, 1863, oil on canvas. Manet's decision to individualize the features of his model for *Olympia* bewildered some and shocked others. He broke the viewing code of the day by making it clear that not only did this body belong to the face above it, its owner was totally comfortable with it.

When Manet painted a well-known model as *Olympia* in 1863, he turned the traditional ideal nude into an image of a sex worker. The clue was not simply in the title – Olympia was contemporary slang for prostitute. It was that the painter had refused to generalize her facial and bodily features: the contemporary hair, the neat modern face, the bold stare back at the spectator, that small, precise and upright body, not to mention the presence of the maid presenting her with flowers announcing a sexual transaction of some kind – all combine to alert viewers that something naughty is going on. She is recognizably modern, the opposite of the lusciously endowed yet coyly modest conventional nudes that came from the easels of the academic painters of the day. There was no chance that bewildered spectators could confuse this alert and pertly seated nude with the undulating ideal nudes they were familiar with, and the way the eyes of this contemporary little face met theirs denied them their customary visual stroking of the image. Since there was no page in their 'Guide to Art Appreciation' on how to cope when the conventions of portraiture were applied to the ideal nude – particularly not when the nude was so oddly alert – confused viewers responded with shock, with jeers and with dismissal.

A similar earlier smashing of conventions marks the portrait of Andrea Doria and that once thought to be Diane de Poitiers. Doria's body is bulked out, as the body builders say, to equate him with Neptune, the sea god this great commander inhabits in this image. It would occur to no one to consider it a portrait if topped by the familiar type of neutrally handsome god-like head. But this grizzled head is so clearly individualized that its combination with the body makes it an image

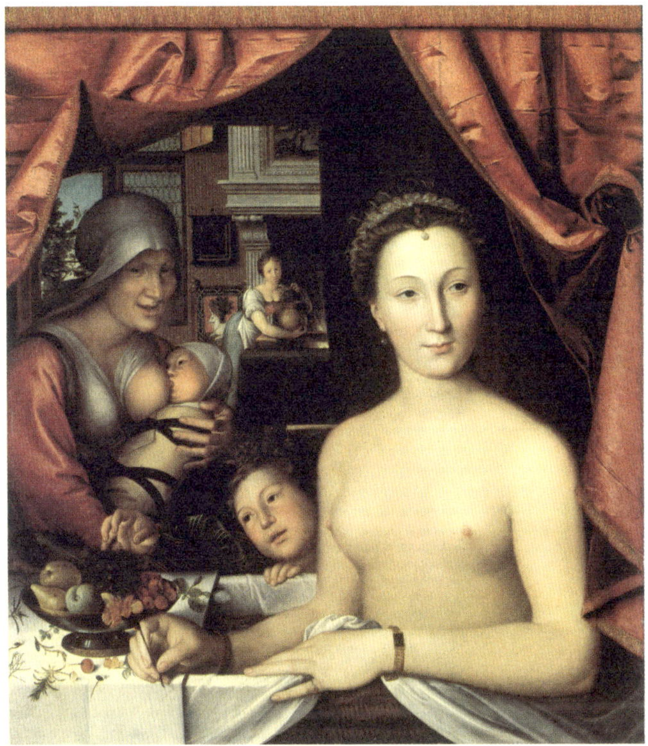

François Clouet, *A Lady in Her Bath*, c. 1571, oil on panel. Though this painting was long considered to be a portrait, scholars now think this is not the case. But despite the complex symbolism and the link to other 16th-century French paintings of this type, the extraordinary individuality of the facial features encourages the illusion that it is a portrait of an important member of the French court.

that contains much strangeness. The female figure's nudity is explained by the fact that she is in the bath and legitimized by the allegorical programme of the image, but the self-control of those sharply arresting features which are the opposite of the dreamily lowered eyes of the traditional nude begs one to read it as a portrait. Scholars now think that rather than a portrait, this may be no more than an example of a type of painting fashionable at the French court in the 16th century. It may not even be by Clouet. But the truth is no one knows, and the interest lies in why so many think this work must be a portrait.

Towards the end of the 19th century, at a time of intellectual tumult, some painters began to experiment with the idea of painting themselves naked. The most uncompromising paintings emerged from Germany and could be seen as remaking an earlier tradition of their own. For as Kenneth Clark had pointed out, the ideal nude was not the only type of nudity in art. A more expressive nude was used by Northern painters to underline attitudes and elicit emotions. Instead of visualizing Christ as the personification of god-like qualities in the Italian manner, the German and Netherlandish painters of the Renaissance showed him as a tortured unidealized man to help viewers relate his suffering to theirs. And in Southern as well as Northern art, evil was often expressed through ugly bodies. When command of the cooking pot and the rituals of birth and death was enough to frighten those in power, society's retaliation was to label as witches these unconfinable old women whose skills had survived their social sell-by date. In cruel visualizations of a negative nudity, artists depicted them with withered naked breasts and hideous bodies as a metaphor for their wickedness. Clark's name for this was the alternative convention.[4]

In intellectually exciting Vienna, the interest in understanding the workings of the mind, symbolized by the theories of Sigmund Freud, found visual expression in the works of several artists. Richard Gerstl painted a self-portrait in 1904–5, when he was twenty-two years old and in thrall to the avant-garde painters' belief in their bohemian freedom to paint how and what they wanted. Calm and hieratic, with a long white cloth around his hips, he resembles Christ and, at the same time, is a young man studying himself with curiosity in the mirror. Four years later, in the year he killed himself, he painted a rawer image in which he faces us as a man of sexual maturity before a swirling background that projects a turbulent state of mind. It was in the same intellectual climate that Egon Schiele painted his notorious *Self-Portrait Nude Facing Front* of 1910 and the tormented *Self-Portrait Masturbating* of 1911. The Norwegian Edvard Munch made his naked *Self-Portrait in Hell* in 1903 when he was working in Munich.

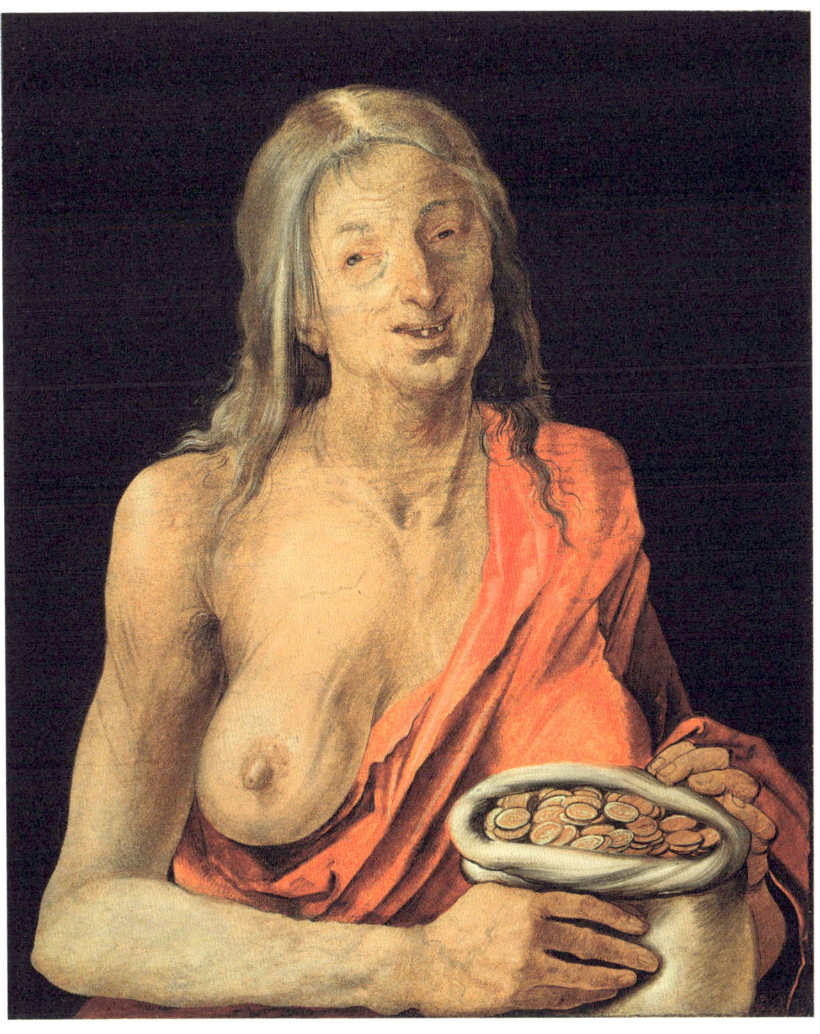

Albrecht Dürer, *Old Woman with a Bag of Money*, 1507, oil on panel. Dürer's allegory
could never be mistaken for a portrait. The cruelly painted body and the gap teeth and red-
rimmed eyes are designed to warn of the transitory nature of wealth and youthful beauty.

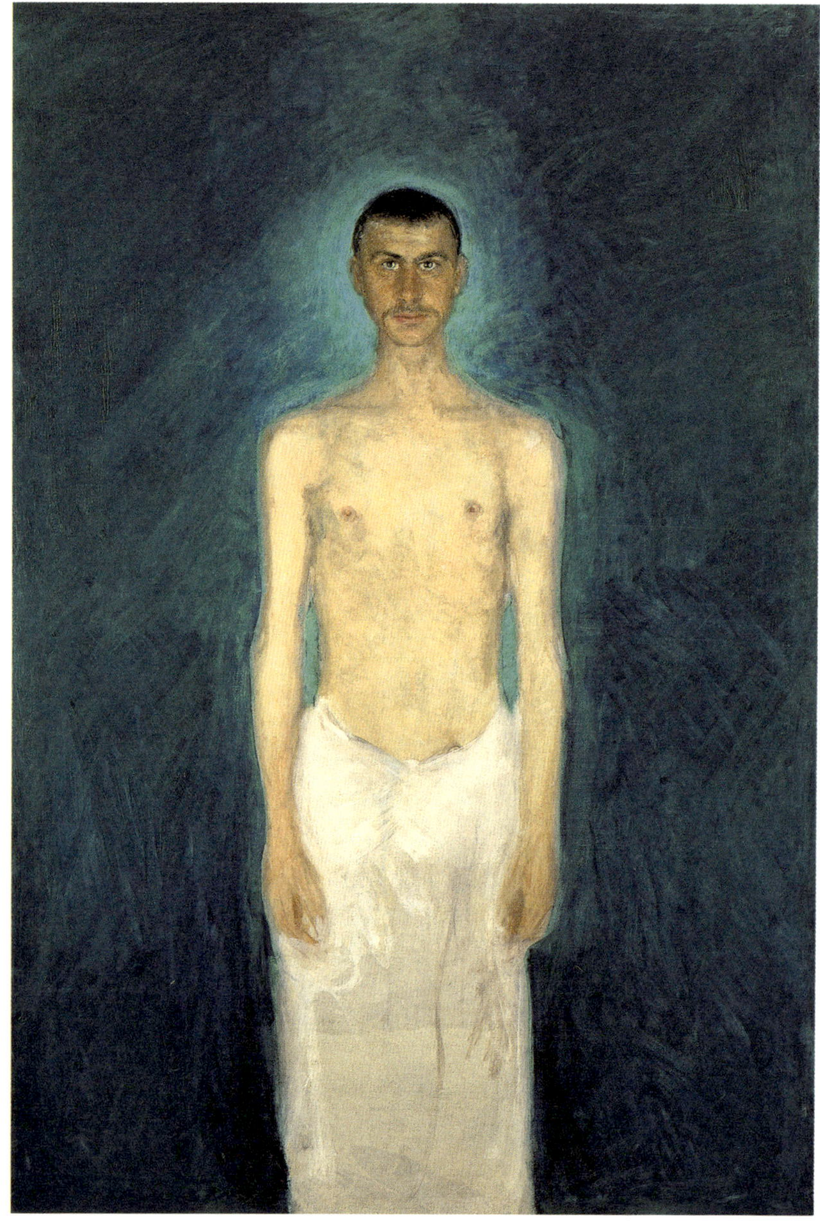

Richard Gerstl, *Semi-Nude Self-Portrait*, oil on canvas, 1904–5. Naked self-portraits were produced by a number of Viennese artists at the start of the 20th century. The young Richard Gerstl gazes at himself with intensity, clad in a white cloth that adds religious overtones and backed by a sumptuous blue, with lighter shades surrounding him with an aura.

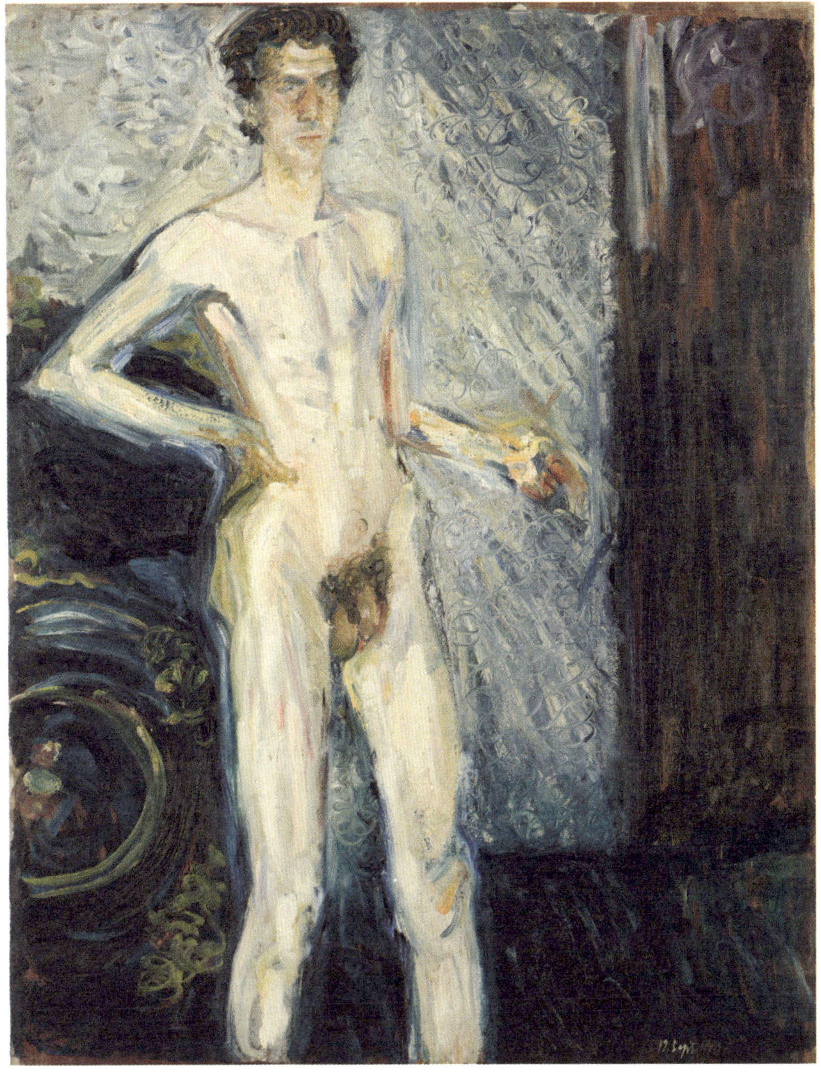

Richard Gerstl, *Nude Self-Portrait with Palette*, 1908, oil on canvas.
Three years later, the background is more turbulent than the earlier luminous blue
and the presentation of his face and body more uncompromising as he asks himself
who he is. The work was painted in the year he killed himself.

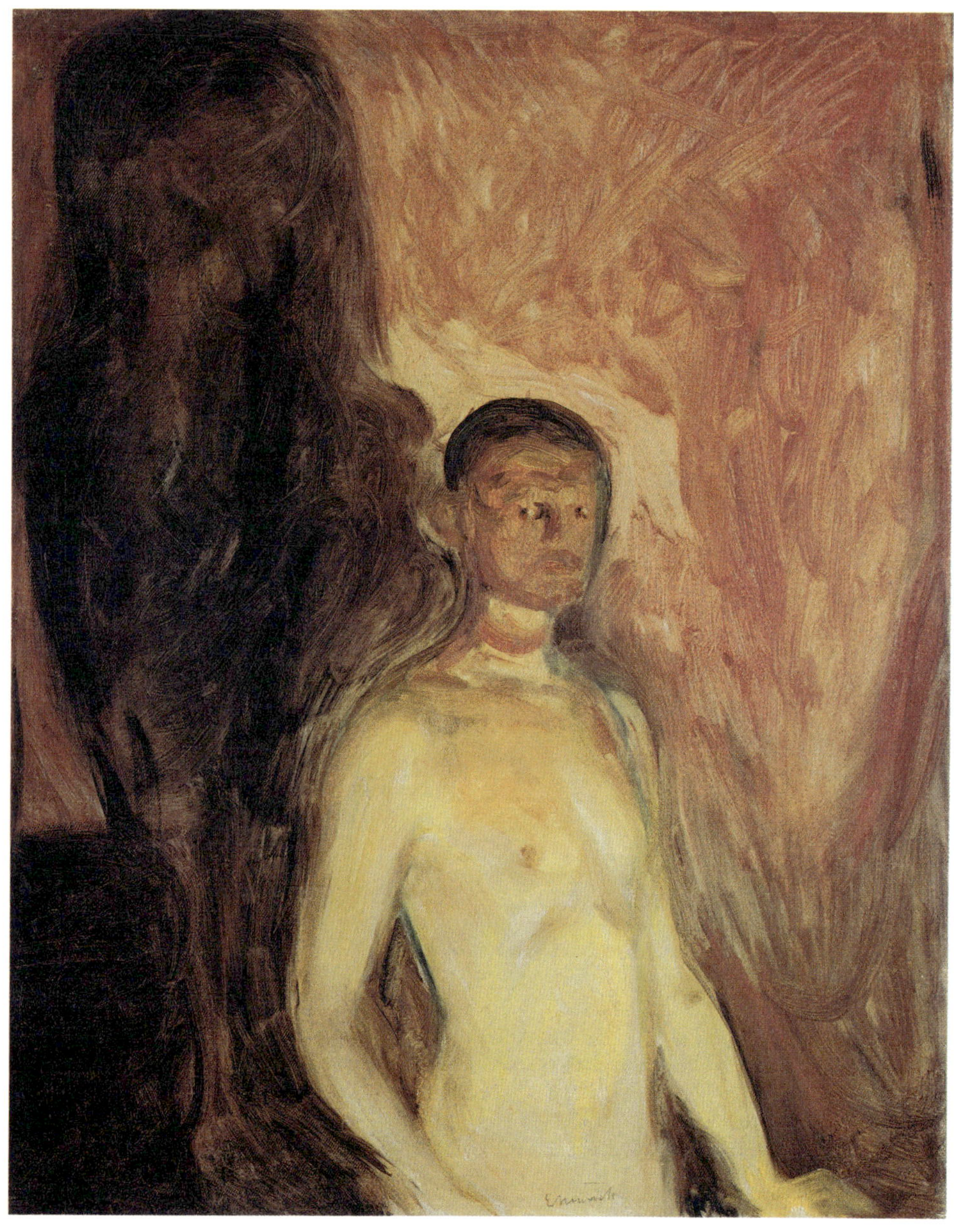

Edvard Munch, *Self-Portrait in Hell*, 1903, oil on canvas. The wilful brushstrokes and Expressionist colour make this an unforgettable image of torment. Munch's haunted eyes stare out of his heated face against the flame-like oranges and reds of the background.

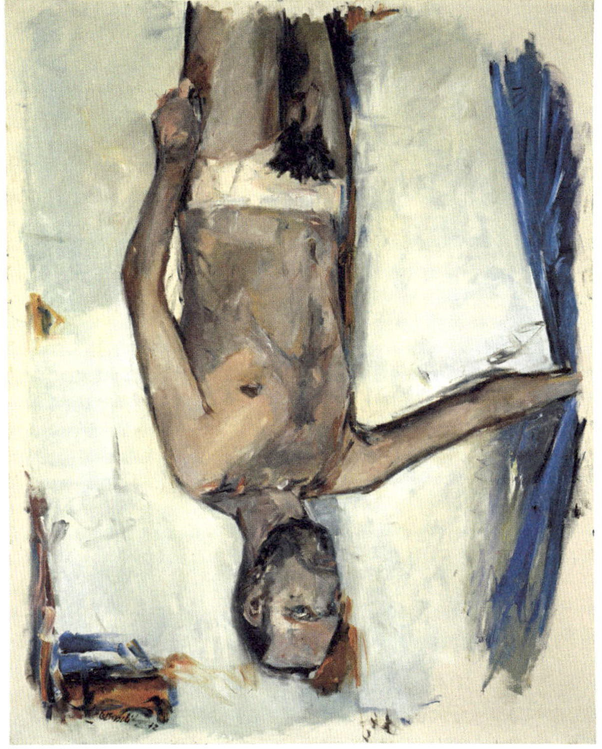

Georg Baselitz, *Fingerpainting – Nude*, 1972.
By painting portraits from photographs positioned upside down, Baselitz
draws the viewer to the colour as much as to the content. During this
period, he was shaping and sculpting the paint with his fingers.

These artists' daring treatment of the body as a portrait as well as the face was
only possible because they had no one to answer to but themselves. The emaciated
Christs and ugly witches of their heritage may have given them a helpful push
but no more than that. These naked portraits follow no tradition. They are new.
They make the private public. And they left a legacy. In 1923, Anton Kolig, who
frequently painted men without their clothes, painted a self-portrait in which, in
a most unusual reversal, he wears a top but no trousers. In 1972, Georg Baselitz
painted himself upside down, as had been his manner since 1969, and naked, a
more acceptable successor to the notorious depiction of masturbation he painted
a decade earlier, *The Big Night Down the Drain* of 1962–3. Here, he used the private to create a public confrontation with what he considered post-war German

blandness. Its sexual outspokenness led to its confiscation by the authorities and a fine for himself and the gallery that showed it.

Many naked portraits these days are – just as they were at the start of the century – self-portraits. It is just so much simpler for artists when they are their own models. In 1993, aged seventy, Lucian Freud joined his interests in nakedness, painting and portraiture in a self-portrait: 'The very least I can do is paint myself naked.'⁵ *Painter Working: Reflection* is a portrait of the vulnerable artist, a vulnerability underlined by the unlaced boots, which add an air of the tramp to the image. If ever a painting confirmed the existence of Clark's 'nude' as a subject category with its own rules of beauty and the heroic, it is this small rectangle of the nakedness of an old man. The power that is exuded by the huge paintings of his naked sitters shrinks here to the pathos of unheroic truth. It seems fitting that this grandson of Sigmund Freud was born in Germany, the home of the ruthlessly revealing naked self-portrait.

When they are not their own models, artists tend to use their friends and relatives as sitters for naked portraits. In 1966, the young Gerhard Richter painted his wife in *Ema (Nude on a Staircase)*, which is an early example of his technique of abstracting a realist subject. Traditionally trained as a painter in what was then East Germany, but amazed at the end of the 1950s by the work of the Italian Lucio Fontana and the American Jackson Pollock, he has spent subsequent decades testing the line between realism and abstraction. In this work, the gold-red hair, white breasts and dark pubic hair of the elegant Ema emerge from the soft horizontal lines signalling the stairs.

One of the biggest changes in the nude over the last half century is the way that the tabooed relationship of portrait face and portrait naked body has wormed its way into conventional portraiture. At the end of the 1960s, a new portrait alliance of body and face confounded theorists who argued that the two should not and could not come together. The agent of this change was the painter Sylvia Sleigh and the subjects she chose to paint were male. Sleigh was influenced by feminist investigations into the roles of women as artists and models, and her rethinking of how to present the male nude in art was a response to the recognition that nude had come to mean passive female with its own specific visual vocabulary of representation.

There must be thousands of art-school students who stuck male heads on the female ideal nudes of art history, inspired by John Berger's challenge in *Ways of Seeing* to test the fact that the assumed viewer of the ideal nude is male and the image of the woman designed to flatter him. 'If you have any doubt that this

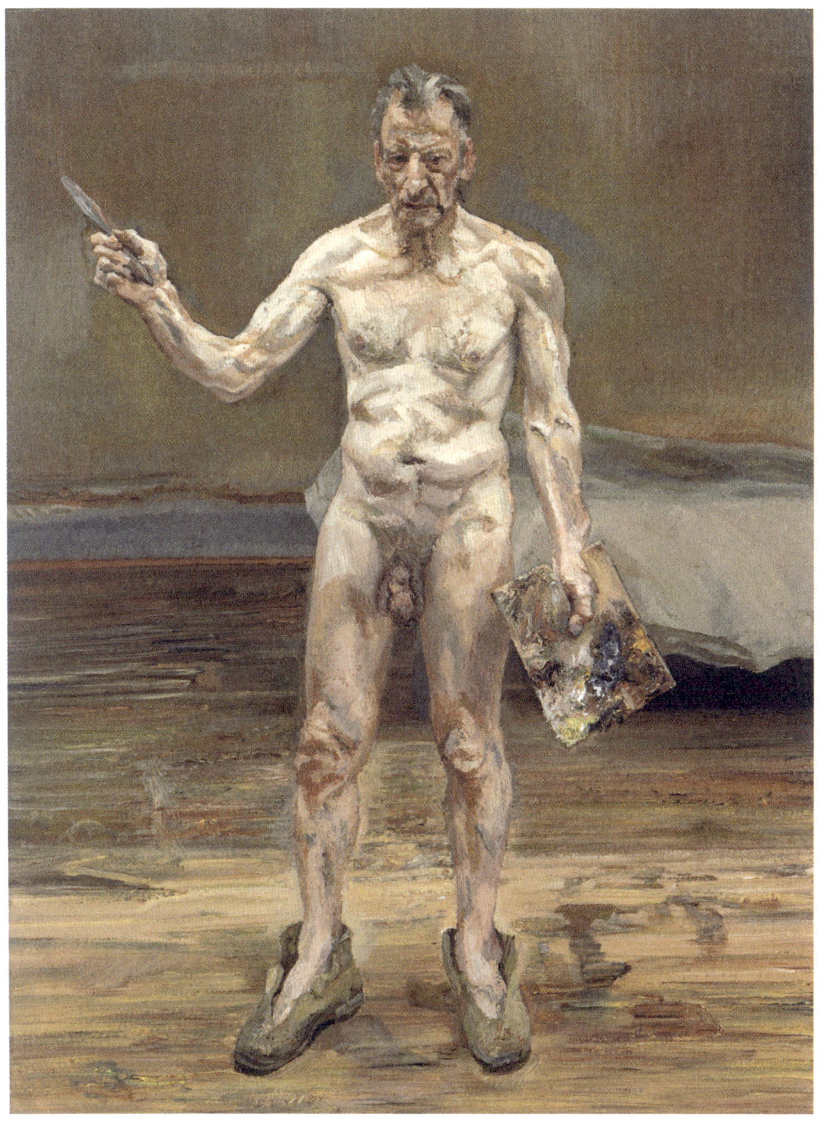

Lucian Freud, *Painter Working: Reflection*, 1993, oil on canvas.
A great contemporary painter of the naked body, Freud turned his gaze on himself
when he had just turned seventy. There is nothing heroic about his self-portrait as
an old man with stooped posture and the unlaced boots that protected him
from the paint and splinters of the studio floor.

is so,' Berger suggests, 'make the following experiment. Transform the woman into a man. Either in your mind's eye or by drawing on the reproduction. Then notice the violence which that transformation does. Not to the image, but to the assumptions of a likely viewer.'[6] (A home-made collage with a male head ridiculously placed atop the body of Giorgione's languid reclining Venus has sat with tatty curling edges on my pinboard since the early 1980s, made in response to Berger's challenge.) It was clearly impossible to paint a male as an object of desire, at least not in the conventional reclining pose with lowered lids and coyly covered genitals.

It was this kind of thinking that lay behind Sleigh's decision to paint her naked male portraits. She wanted to change Berger's 'ideal' spectator from man to woman through the vehicle of the naked male portrait. And she also wanted to see if a woman artist could paint a new kind of portrait of a naked man. Her goal was to produce a sympathetic portrait of a man in the nude that did not objectify him according to some general rules of beauty as had been the lot of women, but treated him as an individual with his own attractive quirks.

The project of presenting the identified male nude in a way that revealed his own particular beauty involved Sleigh for several years from the late 1960s. In 1968 she painted a portrait of Allan Robinson stretched out on a sheepskin rug, his young face turned trustingly towards the painter, evidence of her habit of chatting with her subjects as she worked. The result is touching and dignified as well as visually interesting, with Robinson's chest hair creating a pattern in its own right. This fascination with male body hair is Sleigh's particular contribution to the vocabulary of male beauty, a visual equivalent to the woman's perfect breasts or tiny waist.

In 1973, Sleigh made *The Turkish Bath*, an ambitious painting measuring nearly 2 x 2.5 m (6 x 8 ft), which epitomizes her method of remaking the great nude paintings of the past with men instead of women. For this group portrait, she reworked Jean-Auguste-Dominique Ingres's *The Turkish Bath* of 1863 to produce her startling line-up of relaxed masculinity. But unlike the female nudes of Ingres, who were not portraits and who all conformed to an oddly sinuous and vacant type, Sleigh's work stresses the individuality of the sitters through their poses, body shapes and assorted 1970s hairstyles. The artist's delight in the patterns that distinguish the men's bodies, from the white shapes left by swimming trunks to various whorls and distributions of body hair, is as evident as her pleasure in showing the facial differences between the men, an aim that clearly had no interest for Ingres in his harem fantasy.

Because her practice was to base her portraits of men on famous paintings of female nudity, there were criticisms that all Sleigh had done was replace art's objectified female nudes with their male counterparts. But because she made each man a portrait, taking great care to distinguish his bodily as well as facial particularities, the criticism misses the point. The variety of types draws our eyes as much as their nudity. It is not just that she finds a way to make a naked portrait of a man acceptable; she does it without smoothing away irregularities, proving that it was not necessary to divorce the painted nude body from the specific characteristics of the everyday body we all inhabit. The naked portraits that result are as redolent of their era as flared trousers and tank tops.

Since her death in 1984, the portraits by the American Alice Neel have become increasingly visible in books, catalogues and exhibitions as her originality and contemporary sensibility become ever clearer. She painted naked portraits of men and women from the start of her career, and this, combined with her lack of interest in the ideal, her eye for emotion and psychological disposition and the overall boldness of her approach, has ensured her continuing relevance.

Neel had always been a painter's painter, admired by an inner circle of those in the know, but after her talent was brought into the spotlight by a retrospective at the Whitney Museum in New York in 1974 and her inclusion in the Los Angeles exhibition 'Women Artists 1550 to 1950' in 1976, which recognized her as an exciting and unappreciated feminist foremother, she began to explore the nude portrait with new enthusiasm. Her interest in nakedness as a way to touch the truth, which was evident from the start, exploded in the 1970s into portraits of children without clothes, couples without clothes, friends and family without clothes and expectant mothers without clothes.

In 1930 Neel had painted *Couple on a Train*, an image of a young man and his pregnant partner. In the late 1960s, she began to paint pregnant women again, but this time with no clothes on. Her portrait of the naked pregnant Margaret Evans made in 1974 is typical of her clear-eyed but somehow sympathetic stare and her belief that nakedness revealed an individual's essence. The culmination came when in 1980, aged eighty, she turned that stare on herself in a naked self-portrait that is done in an abandon of light, bright colours that one would expect in a painting of spring. She did it, she said, in order to undergo the same experience as her sitters. It reveals that she kept her enthusiasm for life and art right up to the end.

In the 1970s, the decade of her rising profile, Neel painted several portraits of naked men from the New York art world, taking up a theme she had begun much earlier with her notorious portrait of the balding, scrawny Joe Gould in 1933.

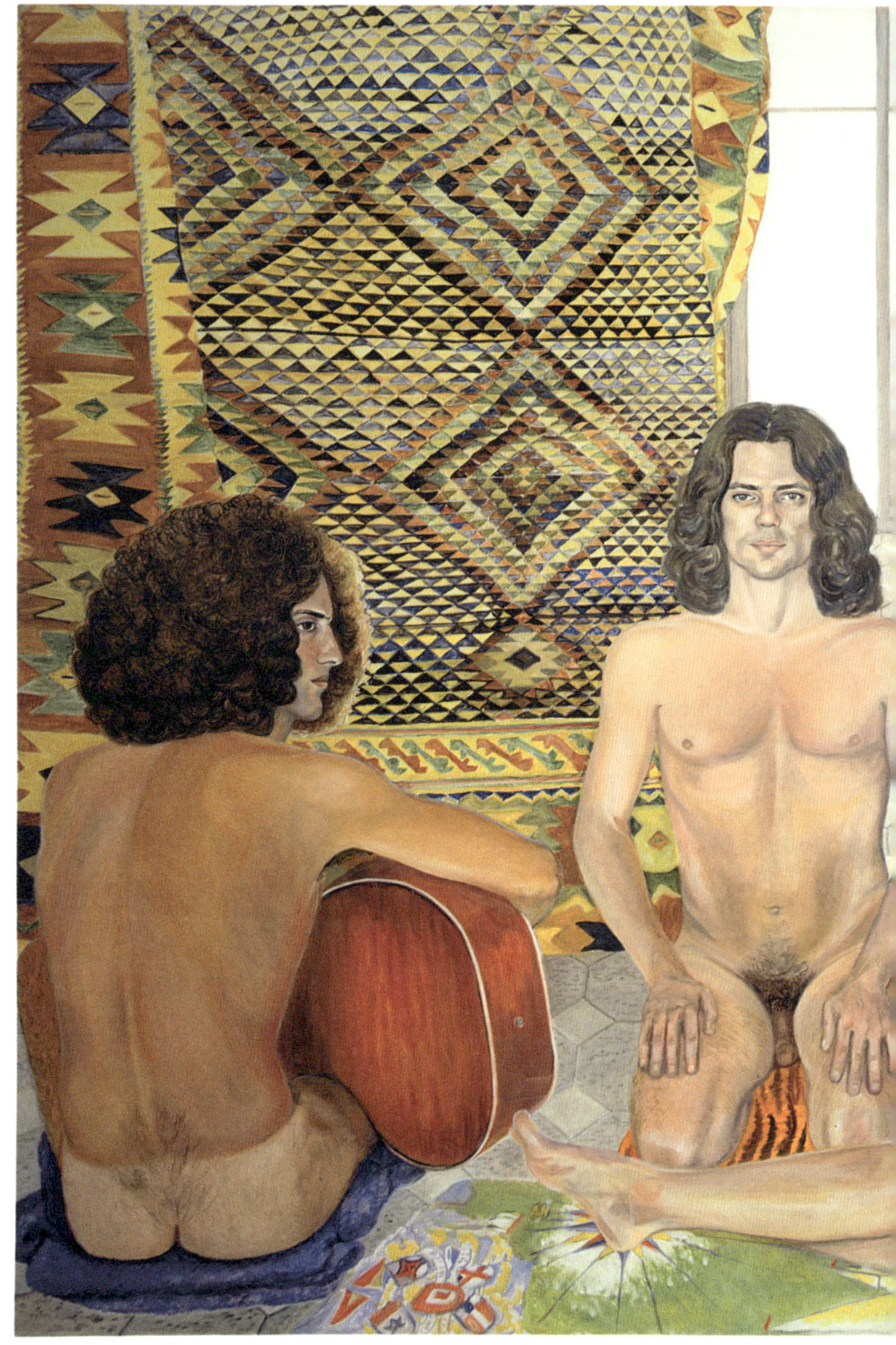

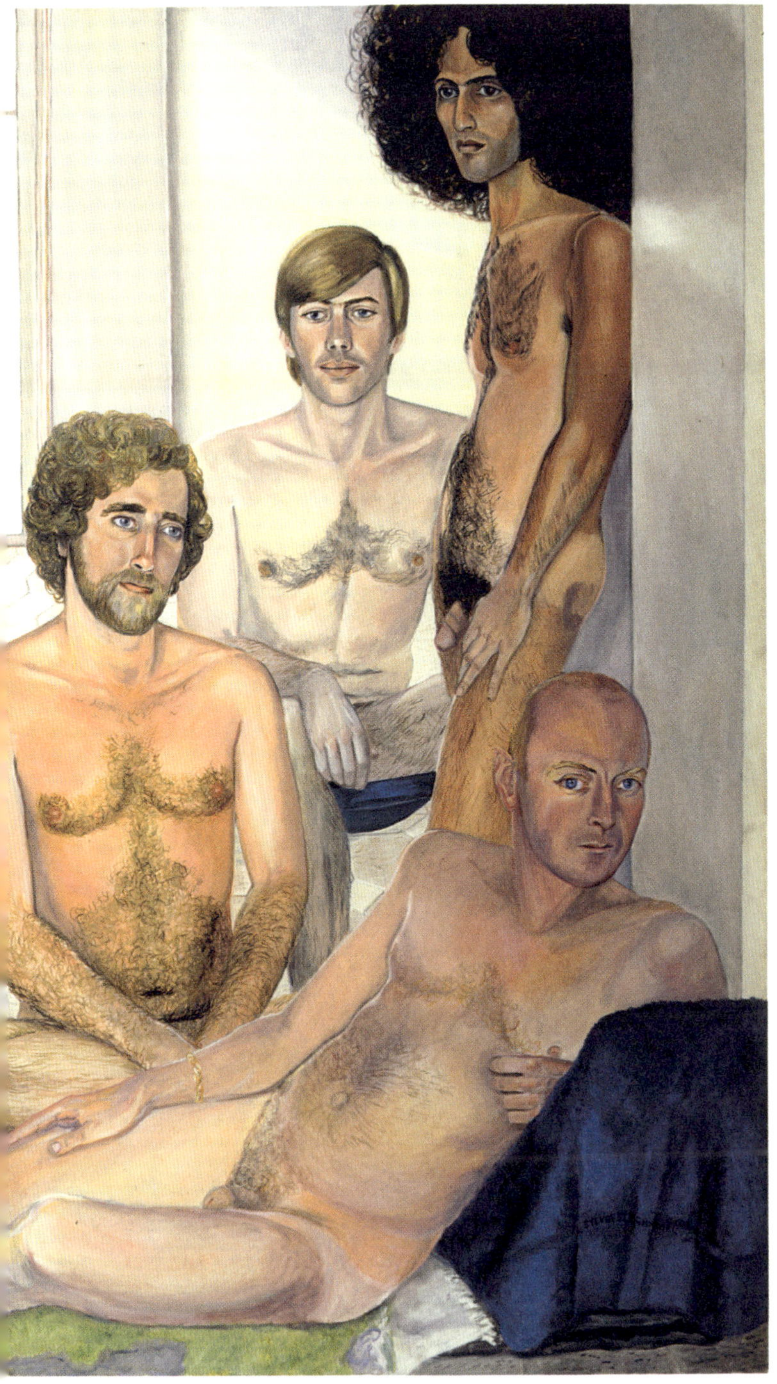

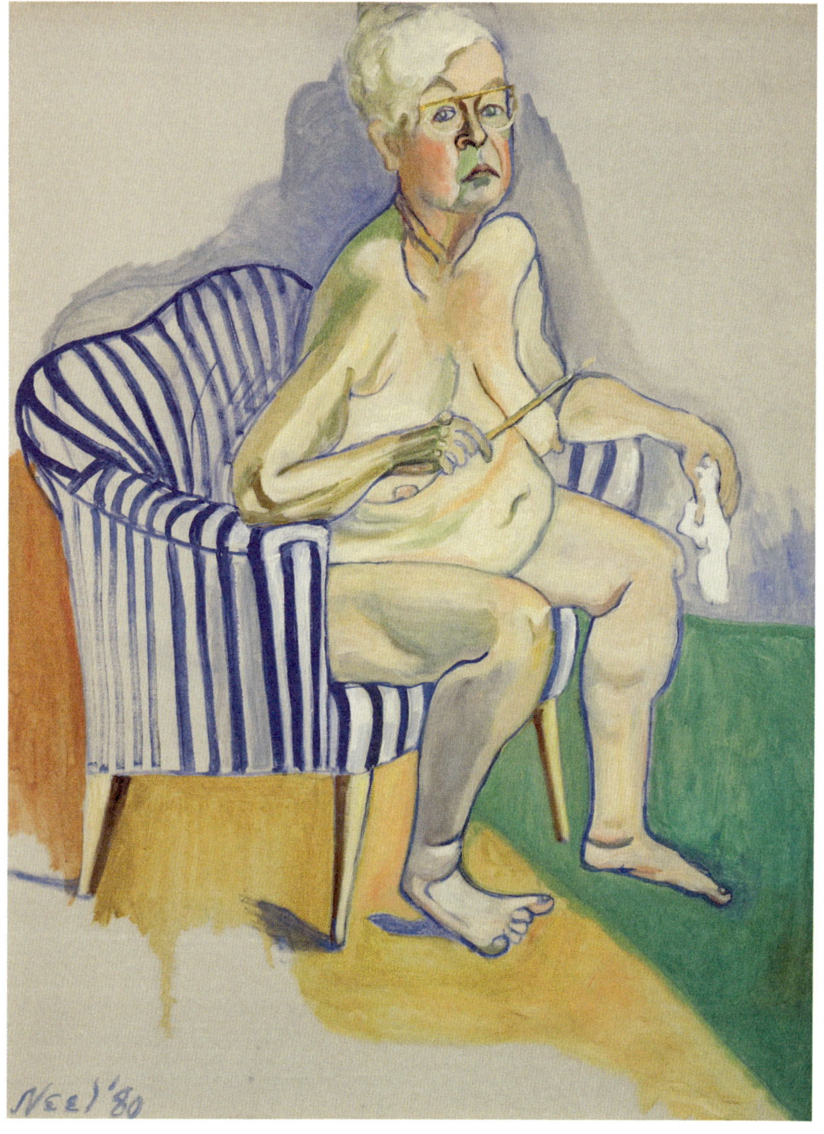

PREVIOUS PAGE **Sylvia Sleigh**, *The Turkish Bath*, 1973, oil on canvas.
A presentation of the varieties of male beauty was Sleigh's goal in this huge work.
Unlike Ingres, whose *Turkish Bath* inspired it, she painted portraits of the men she
knew (she was married to the man, bottom right) and not a generic type.

ABOVE **Alice Neel**, *Self-Portrait*, 1980, oil on canvas. Neel turned her
gaze on to herself in this image of an unconventional woman artist aged 80.
She is grandmotherly but alert, and her right foot is flexed with energy.

Her view of this slightly crazed offspring of an intellectual Boston family has him seated facing us with three sets of genitals extruding from his body and framed with torsos complete with yet more genitals: 'Joe wanted this painted, and I was still imaginative enough to give him a whole tier of penises. I thought that was so clever, hanging that one set from a stool. He was uncircumcised. This could be a propaganda picture against circumcision. Malcolm Cowley saw it one time, and he said: "The trouble with you, Alice, is you're not romantic."'[7]

The painting Neel made in 1970 of a shirtless Andy Warhol two years after he had been shot by Valerie Solanas is a fine example of her skill in using the body to say something new about the sitter. In contrast to most photographs of Warhol, in which he appears opaque and stylized, with his unsmiling face, huge glasses and deep blond fringe, Neel's portrait is shocking in the almost feminine vulnerability of its soft flesh, which looks as if its protective shell has been removed. A rare example of the reclining nude as male is her 1972 portrait of the critic John Perreault. Somehow she has made him look masculine: perhaps it is the confidence with which he meets our gaze, the strongly bent leg, the vehement body hair. Where Warhol looks as if he has been unwrapped and his tender parts revealed, Perreault tells us that he is the same relaxed and confident man undressed as dressed. Given that the naked portrait in which the sitter's body is as much a portrait as the sitter's face is such a collision of artistic codes – the portrait face being public while the naked body is private – it seems amazing that these portraits were painted at all. Self-portraits one can understand, but it says much about the regard in which Neel was held that the sitters consented. It also says much about how attitudes to nudity were changing.

Neel has had a huge effect on several painters in ways that show how influence is rarely a straightforward transference but something more subtle and sideways. The American Elizabeth Peyton, who has made many portraits of her friends and of celebrities, respects Neel for her ability 'to connect with all kinds of people'.[8] It is a mark of Neel's hold on her imagination that in 2007–8 Peyton painted a small imagined nude portrait called *Alice Neel in 1931*, the year in which Neel was released from hospital after the series of unbearable personal events caused her to break down and attempt suicide. The portrait has none of Peyton's familiar clear colour, but is instead a small and painful work in greys and blacks, which shows the utterly unluscious naked torso of her heroine below a face whose eyes look down. It is as if by eschewing both her own and Neel's strong colour and direct face-forward style, she is suggesting Neel's discomfort with the distressing world she inhabited at that time.

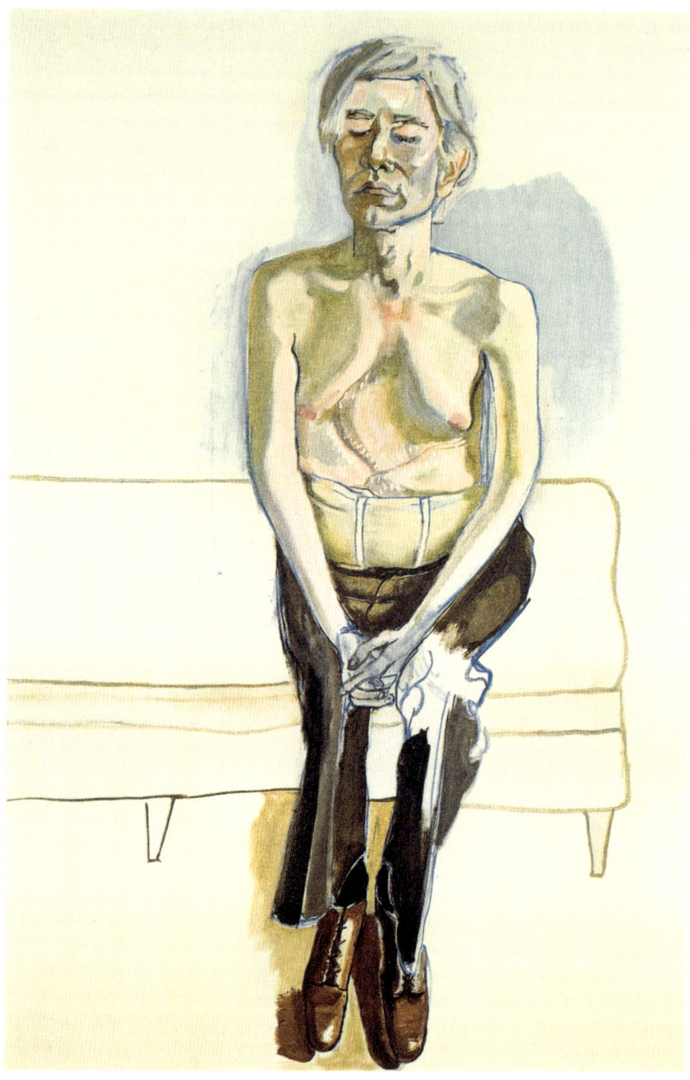

ABOVE **Alice Neel**, *Andy Warhol*, 1970, oil on canvas. Neel's portrait of Warhol is one of several works she made of men without their clothes. Here, what is striking is the vulnerability and oddly modest femininity of the artist who is now seen as the wellspring of contemporary art.

OPPOSITE **Elizabeth Peyton**, *Alice Neel in 1931*, 2007–8, oil on linen over board. Alice Neel's work haunts subsequent figurative artists. Here, Peyton imagines her heroine at a time when she suffered great personal stress. The artist abandons her taste for strong colour to produce a painting of symbolically subdued tones.

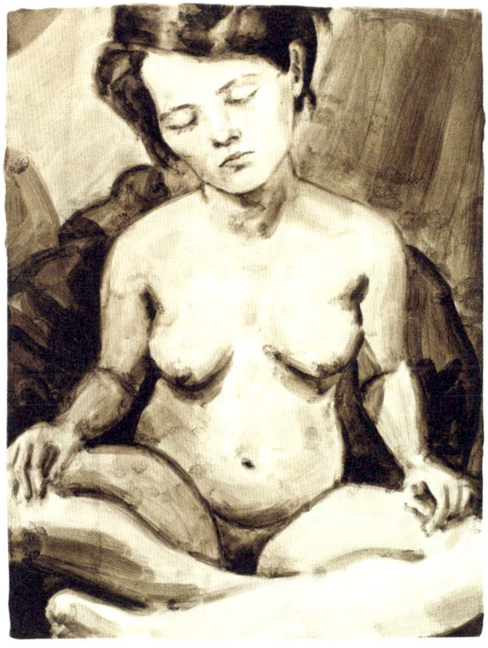

Eric Fischl is another admirer. 'I look at Alice Neel's paintings and wonder how she talked people into sitting for her. But then you're so happy they did because they're such fabulous, interesting paintings. And the world isn't just about being vain. I think it's that people perceive the artist as capable of truth. I think we all want to participate in truth, and we want to be seen as an example of truth. Maybe it's just that they want to be seen. I think that's the other thing: people really want to be seen.'[9] In 2003 he was having a problem with the portrait of auctioneer and art-world grandee Simon de Pury and his partner Anh Duong, a portrait painter Fischl describes as a kind of primitive Alice Neel. De Pury suggested that he paint Duong naked, which still did not work 'because they were so stiff together … I went up on this ladder to get a different perspective and she comes and sits on his lap and then she lays on him and I'm clicking away. Suddenly, I know what it's like to be Helmut Newton … She's a big girl and she literally didn't fit and also they didn't fit, and by the time I'd finished the portrait they had broken up.'[10] No wonder he believed paintings could reach a truth beneath the surface.

Marlene Dumas thinks highly of Neel's economy of means: 'It's very difficult to do a complicated subject in a single image.' To Dumas, Neel's Warhol 'looks a

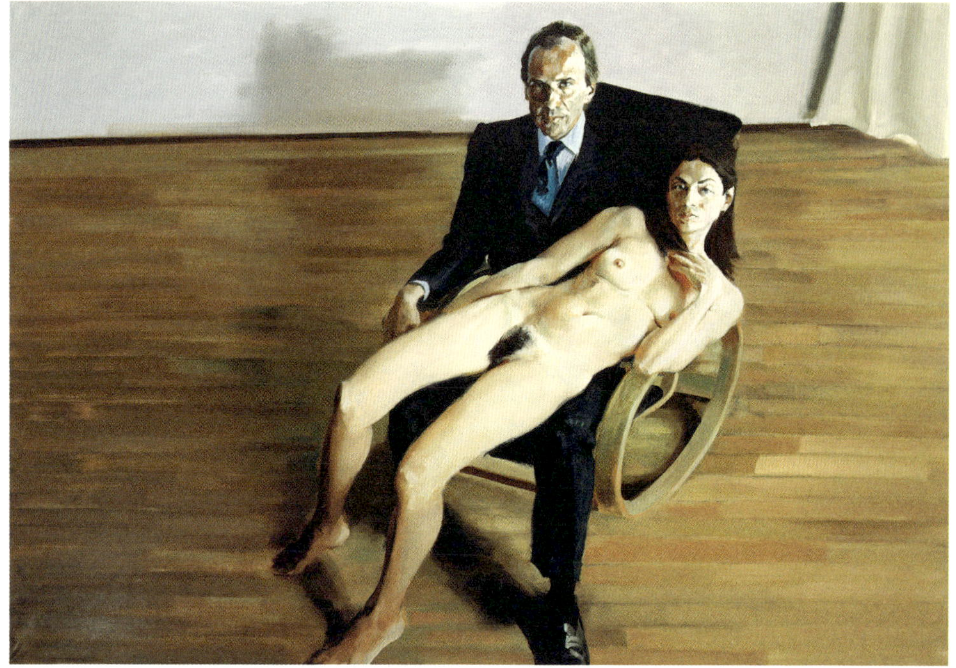

Eric Fischl, *Simon and Anh*, 2003, oil on linen. For this double portrait,
Fischl painted Simon de Pury wearing a suit and his then partner, the artist Anh Duong,
nude. Fischl said later that the discomfort of the image foretold the couple's break-up.

bit like a woman, male and female in one. Warhol was also enigmatic; there is a
total fake, artificial aspect, then there is the lonely aspect of an alienated character.'
Dumas thinks that Neel's portrait of Andy Warhol may have unconsciously played
a part in her complex portrait of her own naked daughter, called *The Painter*. Or
is it her daughter? Based on a photo of a young girl, it also bears a suggestion of
psychological self-portraiture with its adult and oddly malign expression and its
blue and red paint-stained hands, which suggest guilt as well as art: 'I use the body,
and Neel uses the body, to get to the spirit, because the spirit has some form. It's
not about flesh or about materiality, it's about trying to capture the spirit.'[11]

Despite these examples, the naked portrait remains a rarity. The division of
Lucian Freud's paintings into commissioned portraits whose subjects wear clothes
and the naked portraits, which are not commissioned and which occupy a sort of
Freudland between the portrait and the traditional nude, suggests a reason. Even

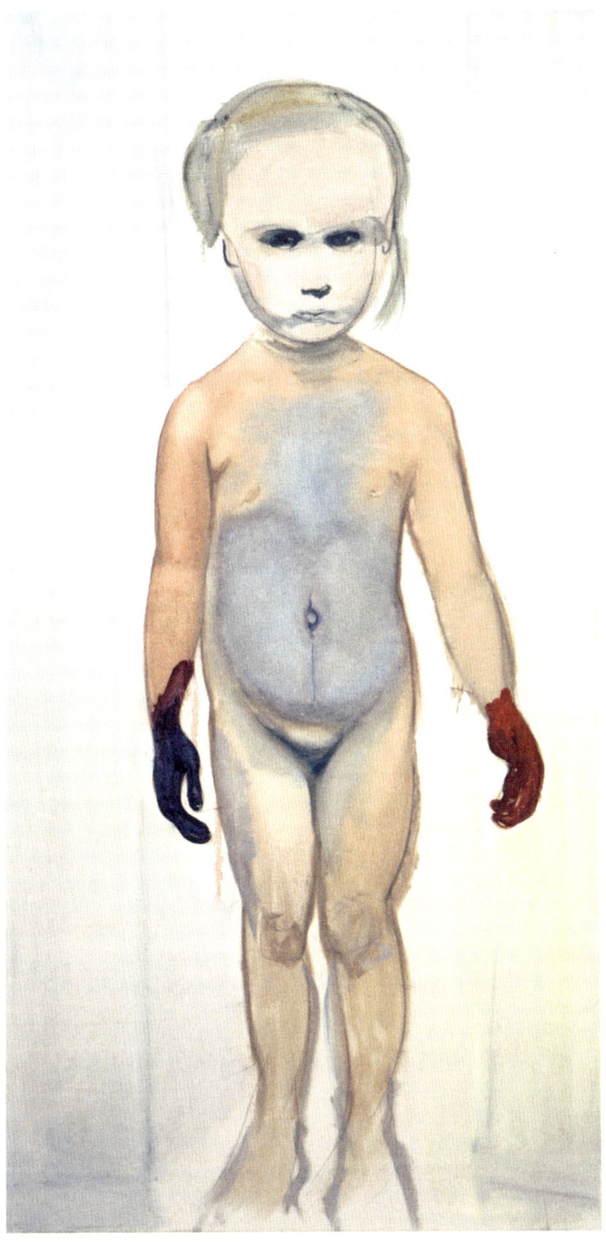

Marlene Dumas, *The Painter*, 1994, oil on canvas. This work is many things:
a portrait of Dumas's daughter, one of herself as a child, and an intimation
of the malignity of the child and the adult artist.

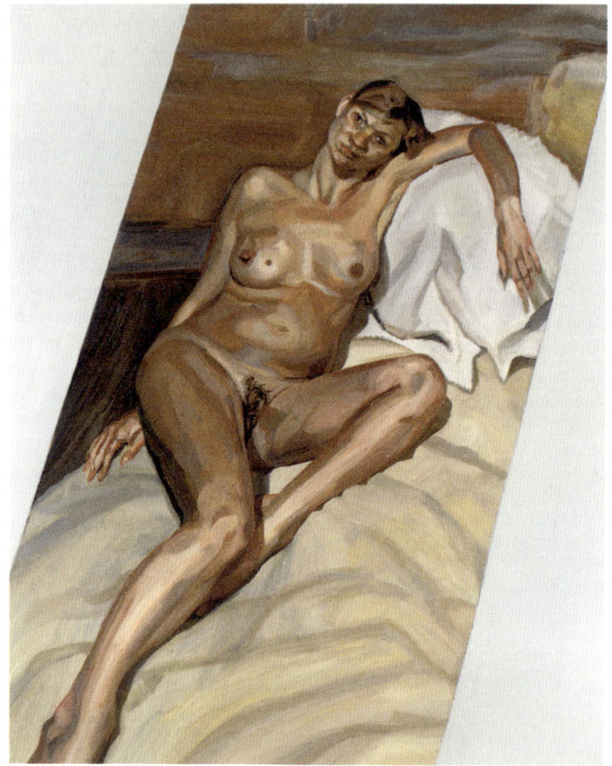

Lucian Freud, *Naked Portrait 2002*, oil on canvas.
Fashion model Kate Moss sat for Freud when she was pregnant.
The result is far removed from her airbrushed presentation in the media.

today, portrait painters follow the artists of the past and help their sitters to put their best face forward. Their task is still to present their subjects in an acceptable manner (one thinks of wedding photographers helping brides and grooms to look their best) in order to satisfy the sitters who pay and the public that looks, be it the sitter's social circle or society at large. Since a portrait carries within it the weight of centuries of subjects who could afford to commission a work of art, who were important enough to commission a work of art, whose families loved them enough or whose professional colleagues respected them enough to pay an artist to make them look as good as possible, it is hardly surprising that when it came to the sitters who paid huge sums to commission their portraits, Freud restrained his analytic gaze to their faces and hands. There is status involved in commissioning a portrait and an artist will do nothing to undermine the acceptability or seriousness of the finished product. The portrait painter has to please the sitter; the painter of the body can please themself.

Freedom to paint with the brutal eye which is Freud's trademark came with subjects who had no problems with their nakedness in front of an artist – friends, family or paid models. The subjects of his naked portraits are not named in his titles (though, interestingly, the portraits of his daughters are often excepted from this rule) even though in this media-soaked age several of them are either known to the public, like performance artist Leigh Bowery, or become so, like Sue Tilley, the subject of *Benefits Supervisor Resting* (see page 101) and *Benefits Supervisor Sleeping* of 1995, a huge painting about 1.5 m (5 ft) square, which set a new record for post-war art when it sold for $33 million at auction in 2008.

One person who has no problem with being painted or sculpted naked and is happy to be identified is the British fashion model Kate Moss. Like Bowery, whose life was built on self-display and for whom modelling for Freud was just one more performance, she was a willing subject. Used to being on display and regarding her body as a career tool in the way opera singers do their voice, she had no reservations about being depicted as he wished. The resulting almost life-size portrait Freud made of her naked and pregnant has more in common with his resolutely unglamorized unnamed nudes than it does with the airbrushed photographic model familiar to us from fashion magazines. But even though this naked sitter would willingly have been identified, the work is titled *Naked Portrait 2002.*

The truth is that neither the ideal, handsome, youthful, beautiful and anonymous nudes of past centuries nor the brutal nakedness of so much art involving today's bodies offers scope to be borrowed for an official portrait, destined to be hung in a public place. When artists try it, yelps of offended sensibilities arise. In 2007, the Irish American Daniel Mark Duffy began to work on a series of naked portraits of the over-forties. One of these, a frontal naked portrayal of the lived-in body and face of sixtyish Irish writer Nell McCafferty, provoked a strong reaction in 2008 when it appeared on the wall of the Royal Hibernian Academy. Because it was 2008 and not 1908, the shrieks of outrage faded as fast as yesterday's sunset, but nonetheless the fact that these very strong shrieks were uttered at all showed that many continue to feel that some things are better kept for private not public consumption and are certainly not suitable to be displayed as art. There is a squeamishness about too much realism in portraiture even in today's been-there, done-that society.

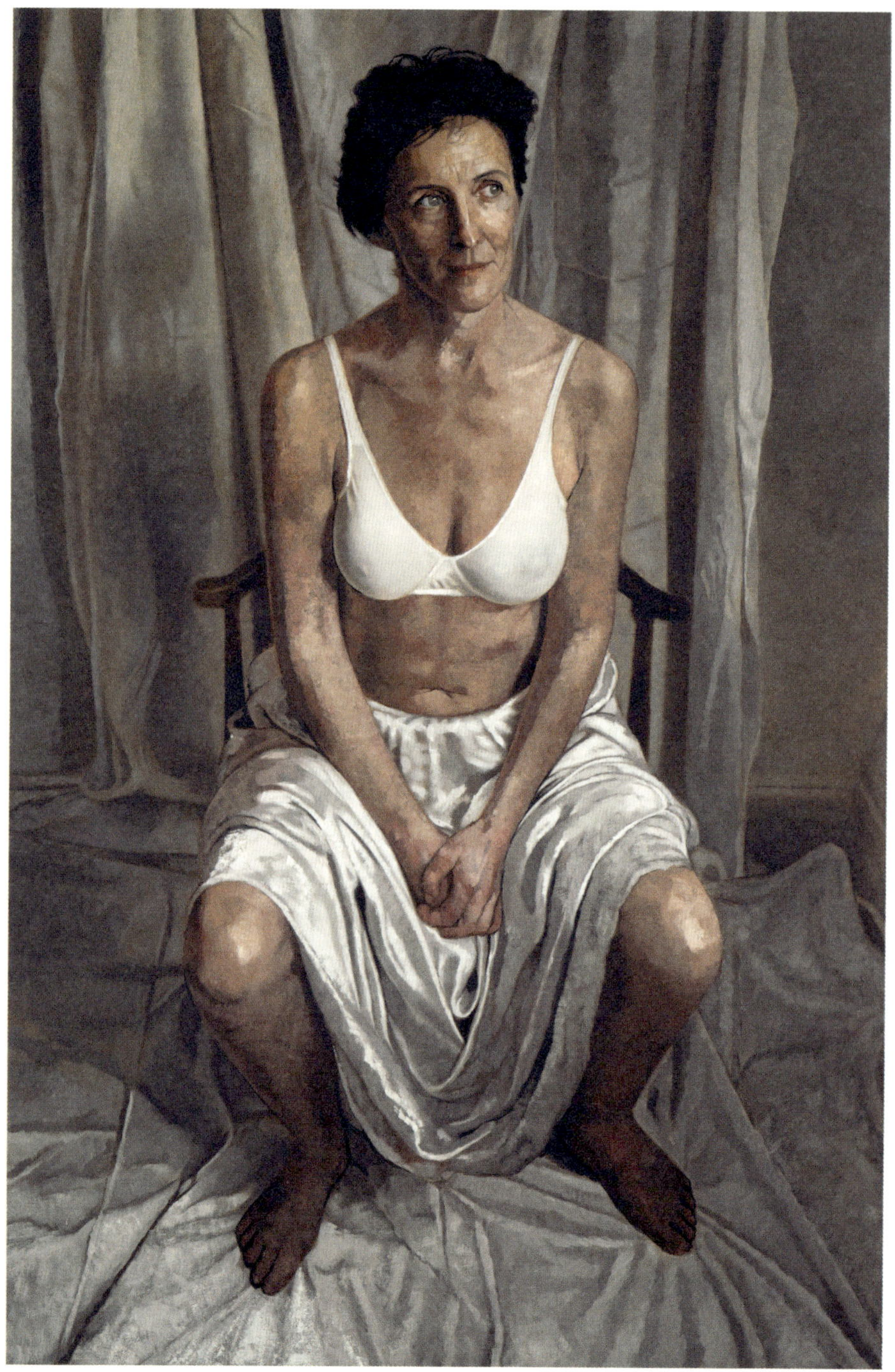

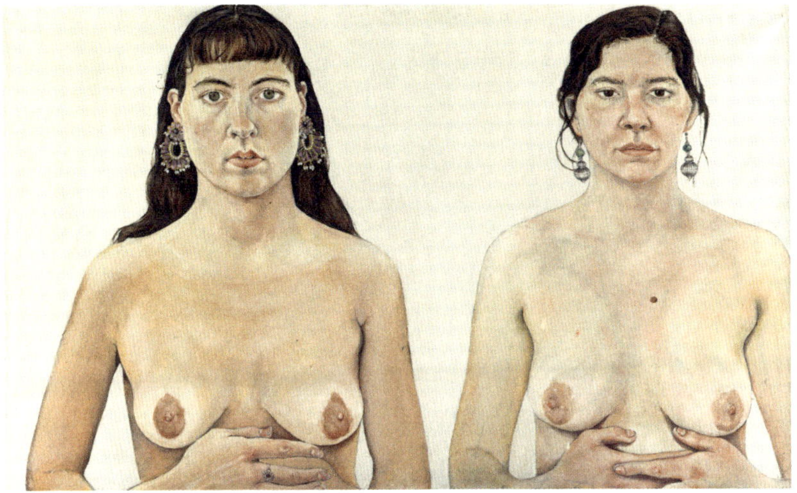

OPPOSITE **Victoria Kate Russell**, *Fiona Mary Shaw*, 2002, oil on canvas. The intimacy
of this life-size image of the actor Fiona Shaw derives in part from her semi-clothed state. Head
turned up and slightly to the side, she appears to be contemplating her next role – and costume.

ABOVE **Ishbel Myerscough**, *Two Girls*, 1991, oil on canvas. Friendship portraits are
a small but distinct strand of portraiture. The intimacy and trust between these two artists
who studied together at the Glasgow School of Art are expressed by their nakedness.

All this ensures that where nudity is concerned in portraiture, a compromise
works best. For most of us, the reality of our bodies makes us loath to put them on
display in a portrait destined for a public space, be it hallowed hall or living-room
wall. There is a sense in which the body represents our private animal self, which
is the opposite of the social self that the painter is being paid to celebrate.

Proof of this comes from an imposing life-sized painting of the actor Fiona Shaw
in London's National Portrait Gallery, which shows her facing the viewer with her
thighs covered with a hitched-up skirt, her feet planted firmly apart and her torso
bare except for a bra. With her bumpy and variegated coloured flesh and her fine
bosom supported in the kind of sensible white bra unknown to seductive lingerie
boutiques, she comes across as handsome rather than pretty, womanly rather than
waif-like. Above all she seems confident, ready for whatever costume the next role
demands she wear. Victoria Kate Russell, who painted it in 2002, says: 'She is a
very strong, lively woman, and the painting shows this. It's an honest portrait.
The things artists find interesting about sitters are often the things that sitters are
most ambivalent about, but it wasn't true on this occasion.'[12] The portrait always

attracts a crowd, not just because it is an arresting image, which it is, but because it is so unusual to find a portrait of someone in their underwear. The reasons for this tell you all you need to know about the taboo of pairing portraiture and the unclothed body. In 2013 the gallery was presented with Ishbel Myerscough's *Two Girls*, a double portrait of herself and her fellow student Chantal Joffe naked from the waist up painted for the artist's degree show at the Glasgow School of Art in 1991. An intimate portrait of friendship, painted within the permissive art-school atmosphere and modest in size, it has ironically ended up in a national gallery of art.

These days, portraits of unclothed sitters are more likely to be made by photographers than painters, underlining the way in which the ideal nude has migrated from painting to photography. A line of naked photographic portraits has earned a place in galleries, from Alfred Stieglitz's portraits of the painter Georgia O'Keeffe's nude body in the 1920s to Robert Mapplethorpe's gleaming Amazon-like definition of the bodybuilder Lisa Lyon in the 1980s. An alternative and more recent trend, epitomized by Nan Goldin's intimately honest photographs of her friends and family, which she calls a visual diary, is the elevation of the snapshot of one's circle into art. Although he began as a compulsive snapper of his friends, often unclothed and enjoying private moments on summer trips across America, Ryan McGinley has begun to compose his naked subjects in a studio while still trying to encapsulate a golden, youthful atmosphere. Wolfgang Tillmans wants his viewers to question the standards and assumptions surrounding photography and its exhibiting conventions, sometimes displaying his work on tables, sometimes without frames, sometimes stuck on to walls, often combined in a variety of sizes and formats. His presentation of the world as he sees it frequently involves his friends in moments of intimacy. But far from documentary, these images are artfully posed and presented. In 1992, he created *Lutz and Alex Sitting in the Trees*, in which a man and woman wear open raincoats – and nothing else. Not glamorous and not overtly sexual, they are like adults reverting to a childhood innocence and sense of fun – or would be if their expressions did not carry a warning. The woman is confident and curious as she looks into the camera; the man is more withdrawn. The reference to 16th-century German paintings of the knowing Eve and the too-suggestible Adam is inescapable.

It does seem as if photography, with its digital improvements and its airbrushing, has, in some cases, inherited the idealizing habit of fine art. In 2008, Anderson & Low produced a group of photographs of nude athletes. The words of the press release show them inhabiting the traditional high ground of the ideal nude: 'Transcending cultural and socio-economic boundaries, the universal appeal of these athletes made them the ideal subjects of this project. Their nudity in the

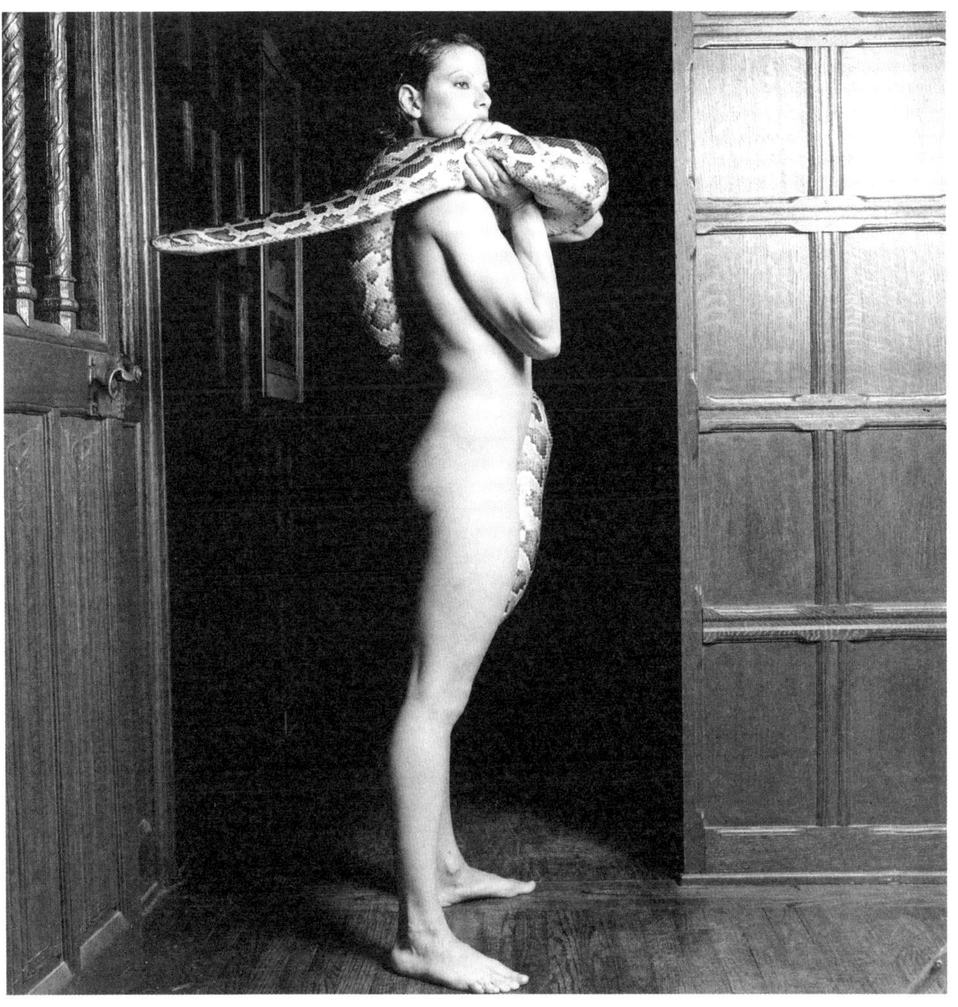

Robert Mapplethorpe, *Lisa Lyon*, 1982, gelatin silver print. Naked portraiture
seems more at home in photography than it does in painting. Mapplethorpe's images
of the bodybuilder Lisa Lyon offer an intriguing update on traditional art's conception
of the ideal body, as well as questioning contemporary notions of perfection.

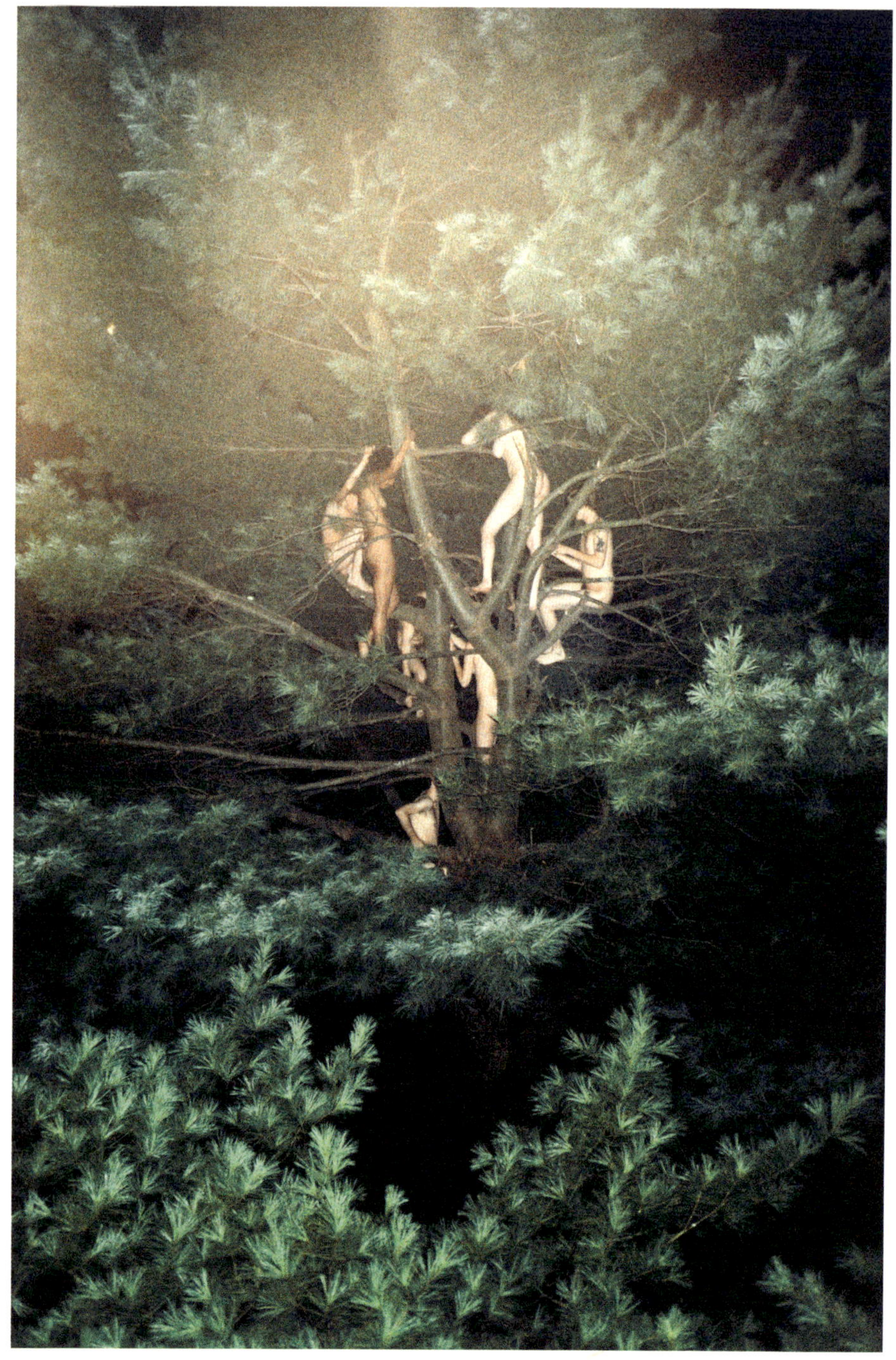

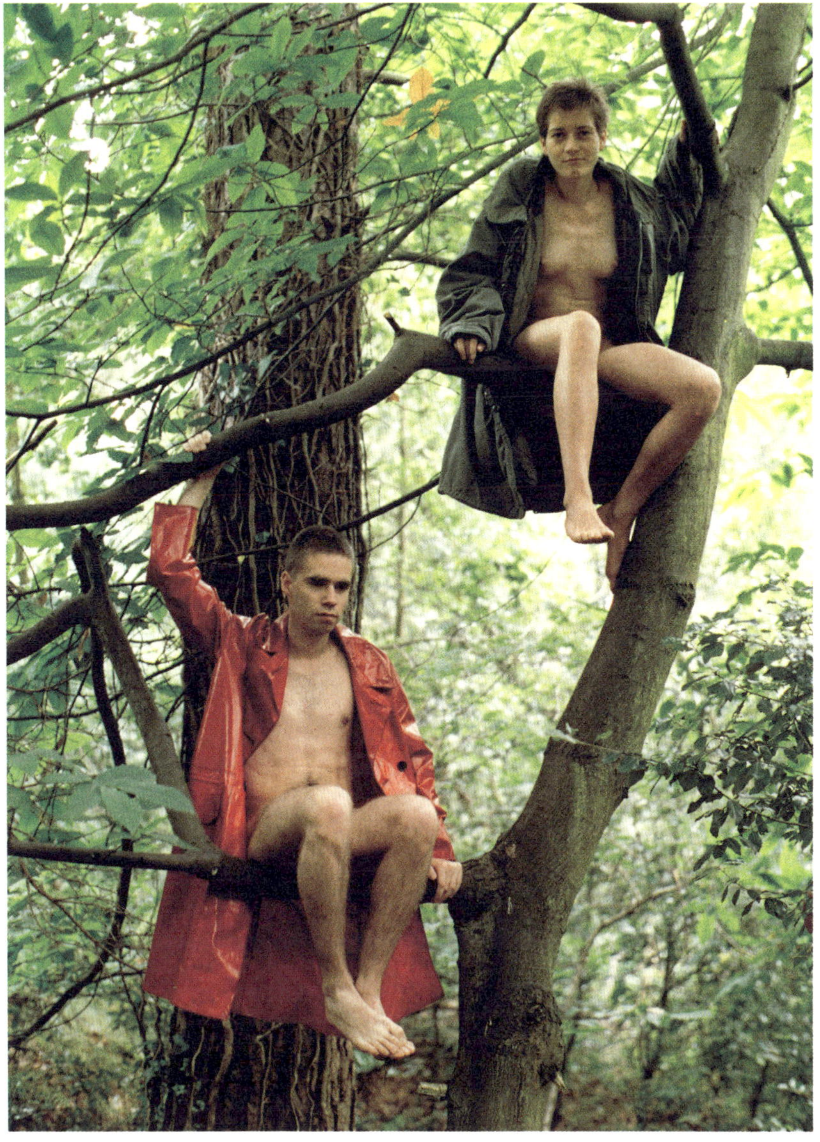

OPPOSITE **Ryan McGinley**, *Tree No. 3*, 2005, C-print.

ABOVE **Wolfgang Tillmans**, *Lutz and Alex Sitting in the Trees*, 1992, inkjet print. McGinley's orchestrated vision of spotlit youths in a tree suggests the idea of a golden age. Tillmans's print is more complex. What started as a fashion shoot for raincoats evolved into a meditation on the relationship between the sexes.

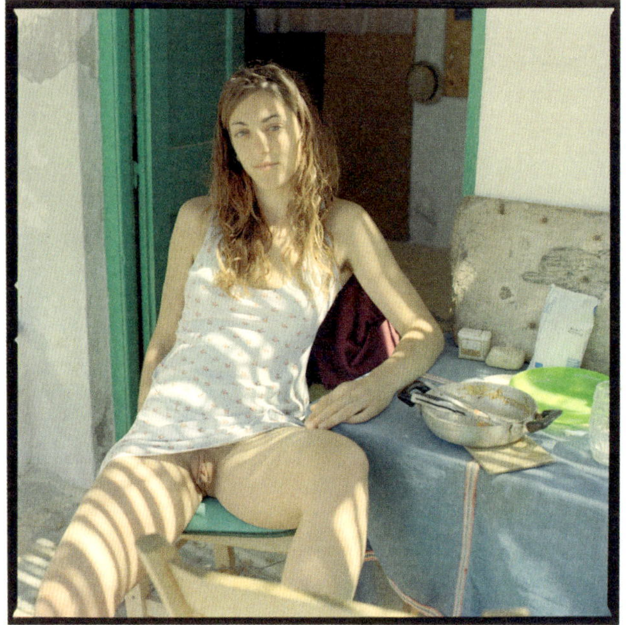

Panayiotis Lamprou, *Portrait of My British Wife*, 2010, digital
chromogenic Fujicolor Crystal Archive print. It is beautiful. It is honest.
It is ugly. It is obscene. The confused response to this work shows that when
the private and the public collide, we have no formula to deal with it.

portraits is symbolic, illustrating both their physical beauty and prowess alongside
their vulnerability and humanity.' The downplaying of cultural, social and eco-
nomic differences and the stress on universal appeal and values are exactly what
the defenders of fine art's ideal nude did in their attempts to elevate it above the
sometimes squalid facts of the everyday body.

Even the terms of photography have descended from art history. An internet trawl
of 'nude portrait' overwhelms the seeker with photographers who want to photograph
you in the nude, promising to make you look more beautiful than you ever have
before. While serious contemporary painters are unwilling to tell a lie about their
sitters' bodies, commercial portrait photographers have no such problems. In their
hands, the camera is a glamorizing agent, a tool to render the sitter jaw-droppingly
perfect in a portrait that is anything but naked in an honest sense.

This takeover of the ideal nude by commercial portrait photographers is now
inspiring a response from photographic artists. *Portrait of My British Wife* by

Panayiotis Lamprou was exhibited in 2011 at the National Portrait Gallery in London. Lamprou shows his wife, dressed in a long tee shirt, sitting with her legs apart and her genitals displayed in explicit detail unknown in traditional Western art. In fact, after the first shock of such an unusual image, its particular individuality and beauty take over. The Japanese erotic illustrations of the Edo period, which include images showing the genitals of famous courtesans, would be a possible ancestor; the closest artist photographer would perhaps be Robert Mapplethorpe, whose images of male genitals are as magnificently gorgeous as the photographs of food in expensive cookery books; as for a woman artist, the butterfly vagina plates of Judy Chicago's *Dinner Party* installation of the 1970s come to mind. But even though vaginal imagery is not unknown in art and has in fact inspired some interesting semi-abstract work in the last few decades, this naked portrait is new and daring. The public's responses to Lamprou's image represent a collision of contrasting attitudes. It is beautiful. It is ugly. It is erotic. It is pornographic. It is realistic. It pushes the boundaries of the portrait photograph. It is a strategy to attract attention. The opposing opinions highlight the problems caused for the viewer when, in artistic terms, the barriers between categories break down or when, in everyday terms, a photograph that would normally be private goes public.

The confusion the photograph causes proves that we have no formula to deal with the truthful naked portrait. It has escaped from all our comfortable classifying attempts to control it. Our comfort with it as a portrait of a beautiful woman is disturbed by the shock of what she displays. Kenneth Clark's nude/naked line is powerless today because the art world has moved on – the work was considered sufficiently acceptable to be shortlisted for the Taylor Wessing photographic prize in 2010. The photograph of Lamprou's wife expands the category of artistic acceptability and widens our idea of the kind of beauty that is allowed to enter art, just as Manet's *Olympia* did in 1863 with her pert and individualized face and figure. Embarrassing. Shocking. Disconcerting. A terrific photograph. The ideal nude recycled for our times into the naked portrait.

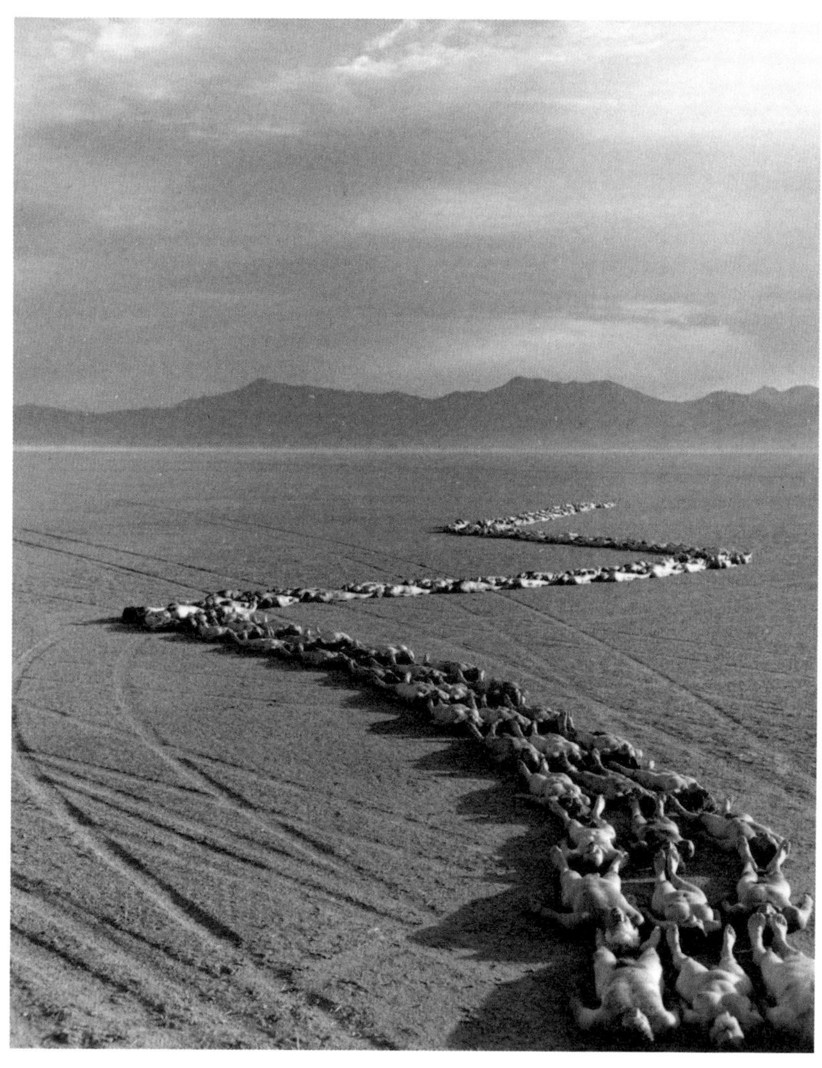

Spencer Tunick, *Nevada*, 1977, gelatin silver print. Tunick uses the body instead of traditional sculptural materials. In *Nevada*, naked bodies lie three in a row on their backs, snaking across the desert and into the distance to create a piece of Land art that alludes to the American westward trek.

AFTER RODIN, IS THERE ANYTHING LEFT TO SAY?

ONE OF THE EARLIEST SURVIVING SCULPTURES is of the unclothed human body: the Palaeolithic *Venus of Willendorf*. However, in the classifying system of art history, the enormously exaggerated breasts, stumpy legs and skinny arms ensure that the Willendorf Venus and her little group of sister sculptures are described as fertility goddesses, a label that moves them outside the box of 'proper' art and into the one marked archaeology.

The sculptured human body's story is one of a long journey towards the classical perfection of works made in Greece in the 5th century BC. Art history's conventional line of development starts with the *kouroi*, stylized naked male figures of 7th century BC Greece, formal, frontal, slightly schematic young men, who in their turn lead to the refined and more naturalistic statuary of the golden age of classical Greece. The first nude female sculptures came later: the goddess Aphrodite was said to be so jealous of the *Aphrodite of Knidos* made by Praxiteles in the 4th century BC, and allegedly based on the courtesan Phryne, that she came down from Olympus to inspect it. These fusions of perfection and realism are not men and women in their everyday state of nakedness; the accounts of the Greeks using gymnasts as their models suggest that they are designed to be examples of the human body at its peak, a perfection demanding to be gazed on and admired – ideal nudes, in other words, as traditionally understood. Unlike the *Venus of Willendorf*, they exhibit no tell-tale signs to remind us of the ruder, cruder side of nakedness. The women are well proportioned, their modesty protected by a hand or drapery about their hips. The men are broad shouldered and small bottomed, with untroublingly tiny genitals.

This classical standard remained the pinnacle of sculptural achievement for centuries, only temporarily displaced in the medieval era with the spread of Christianity

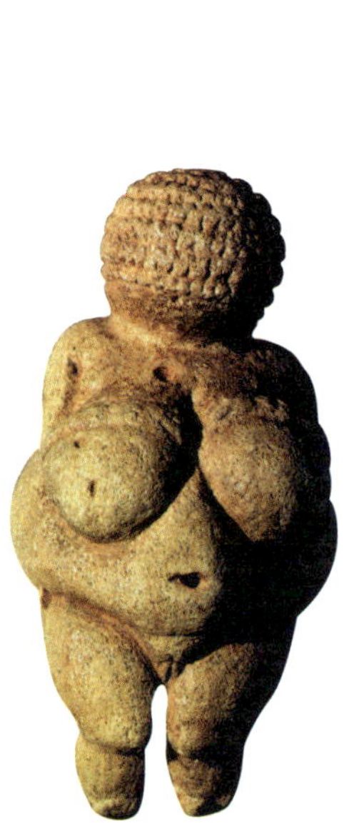

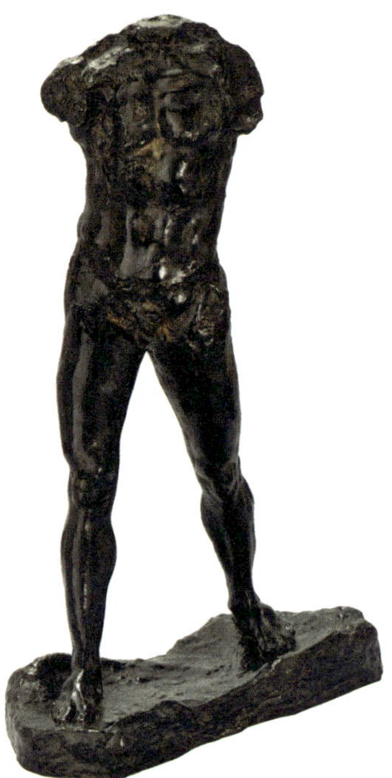

LEFT *Venus of Willendorf, c.* 20,000 BC, sandstone with red chalk decoration.
Archaeology, not art, is the category the *Venus of Willendorf* is placed in today.
Her heavy proportions have nothing to do with the idealization of the human
body that had its source in the sculpture of classical Greece.

RIGHT **Auguste Rodin**, *The Walking Man, c.* 1890–5, bronze. Rodin's work
marks the turning point between the idealized and the contemporary nude.
The body of his headless *Walking Man* incorporates the handsome proportions
of the ideal male body with a new Expressionist treatment of the surface.

and its dismissal of the body. It emerged again in the Renaissance with Donatello and
reached a peak with Michelangelo. Gian Lorenzo Bernini carried on the tradition
in the 17th century and Antonio Canova in the 18th and early 19th. At the end of
the 19th century, Rodin was both the last of the old, with *The Age of Bronze*, 1877,
a nude male so realistic it was accused of being a cast not a sculpture, and the first
of the new, with the expressionistic carving of the headless *Walking Man* (above).

Until about 1960, sculpture and painting walked happily hand in hand, in one
mind about the changes art flung at them as they negotiated the 20th century. But

whereas painting faltered around 1960, sculpture began to gallop ahead of its former partner. No one ever said sculpture was dead as they did continuously of painting. Its potential excited artists, who realized it could do anything they wanted.

For many, the bricks and stones and strings and gloriously crazed assemblages of objects met with in galleries today symbolize contemporary art much more than painting does. Cornelia Parker comments on the eroding chalk cliffs of the southern English coast by threading fallen chalk clumps on to a dense square of hanging threads. The Brazilian Cildo Meireles creates a maze of hanging tape measures bordered with little clicking, ticking letters and numbers, overwhelming us with the realization of the way our lives are measured out by clocks and calendars. The themes sculptors deal with are immense and the means they choose to deal with them unimaginable before the mid-20th century. And yet despite this, some sculptors go against this trend and choose to work with the unclothed human body.

Today, like a singer unwilling to retire, the sculptured nude has made another of its comebacks. Several sculptors are looking at it with fresh eyes, less interested in it as a container for heroic characteristics in the case of the male, or ideal beauty in the case of the female, than as an expression of modern ideas about the body. Taking as their starting point the revered ideal nude sculptures of art history, which now strike us as so bland they have ceased to rouse our interest, these sculptors play a clever game by using them to examine controversial issues of our day.

Classical sculpture is the basis for the eye-catching and seductive male and female nudes of the Portuguese artist Joana Vasconcelos, familiar figures from the past startlingly encased in webs of patterned black crochet. The artist buys her nudes online from garden centres specializing in reproductions of the Greek and Roman gods to be used as garden accessories, or wired to carry electric lights. First, she paints them, then she covers them with scraps of antique crochet, which she has collected painstakingly for years. The effect is everything art should be: not only beautiful, the sculptures excite the mind, sending it off in all sorts of directions.

Vasconcelos is fascinated by the contrast between the ideal body of the past and the bodies of today, which are not just different from the classical ideal but are often displayed and decorated in ways that past generations would never have accepted. Her arrangement of the crochet pieces, an artwork in itself that takes months to piece together, makes several statements besides the inevitable comparison with the contemporary beauty of tattoos. One of the most surprising effects of the lace-like crochet is to introduce a sexual element to the ideal nudes, which art history has tried so hard to deny them. Not only does the lace covering make the female bodies more alluring, it also feminizes the male bodies and, when it covers

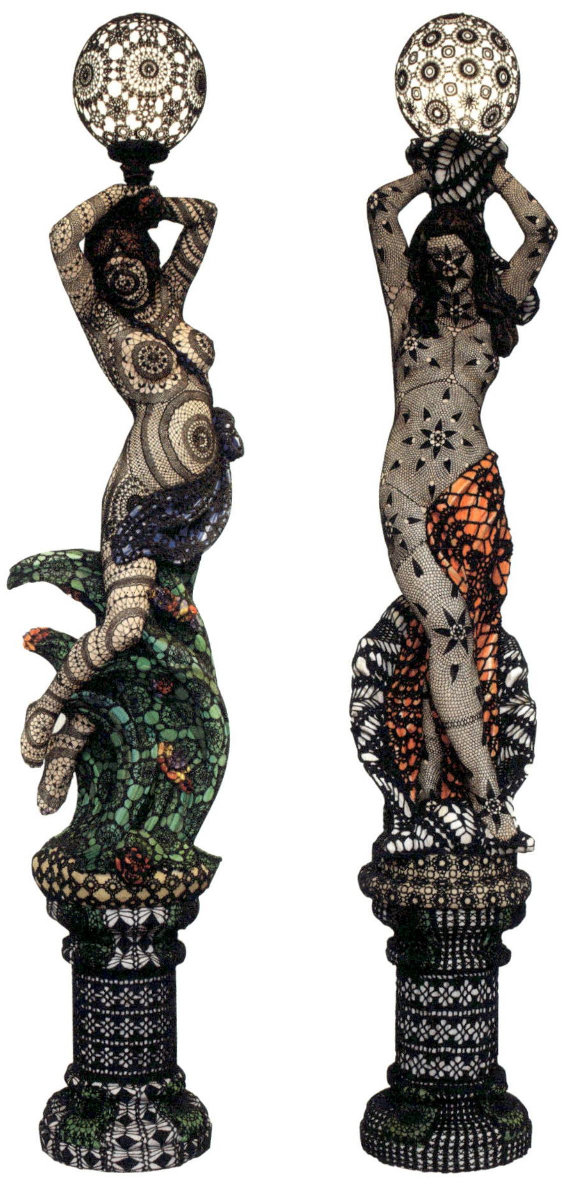

Joana Vasconcelos, *Juliet* (left) and *Guinevere* (right), both 2010, concrete statue, acrylic paint, handmade cotton crochet, plastic globe, light bulb, electric system. Vasconcelos turns casts bought from garden centres into surreal images of modernity. The black crochet in which she covers them emphasizes the sexuality that was only politely suggested in idealized sculpted bodies.

the heads and faces of either sex, adds a disconcerting hint of sexual aberration. The crochet-covered statues also raise issues about the way that the admired ideal nudes of history have become part of today's currency of commerce. Nothing is sacred any longer, the lace says, not even the ideal nudes of high art. Everything is open to questioning, to selling, to debasing, to borrowing.

For over a decade, the British artist Marc Quinn has made subversive use of the traditional sculptured body in order to comment on the present. His target is our contemporary attitude to perfection. For *The Complete Marbles* of 1999–2001, he sculpted men and women who through birth or accident had lost a limb, and exhibited this group of works in the cast court of London's Victoria and Albert Museum. The collecting of plaster casts of the most celebrated classical and Renaissance sculptures reached its height in the 19th century, when institutions saw their role as educating and informing their visitors about the best of the past. Museums and art academies made sure they owned a selection of casts of the greatest sculptures like the *Venus de Milo* and the *Apollo Belvedere* in order to spread a visual knowledge of landmark examples of fine art. The cast court's reproductions are in white plaster, but Quinn expressed his respect for his sitters by having them represented in Italian marble, the material used for the originals of the cast court's copies.

Quinn's placing of the flawless sculptures of his limbless sitters in the cast court next to the classical statues, whose absent arms or legs seem normal when seen through the spectacles of art appreciation, was an inspired way to point out the instability of our ways of judging beauty. His choice of finest white marble aestheticizes his sitters, turning their missing limbs into something we can regard without embarrassment or sympathy. The lack of sympathy is important because sympathy can diminish the reality of others' lives. In other words, they are as handsome and beautiful as the casts, whose missing limbs do not diminish their artistic quality or the respect they elicit from us.

Ten years later, a new group of gorgeous life-size bronzes and marbles was shown at London's White Cube Gallery. At first glance they looked exactly like the nudes appreciated by connoisseurs of past centuries. A second glance revealed that those beautiful surfaces showcased some extraordinary bodies, unlikely to have been depicted by a classical sculptor. A male body had a pregnancy bump, while a woman had breasts so large she supported one balloon-like in her palm.

As an artist interested in contemporary social developments related to the body, Quinn is presenting a modern phenomenon, the urge to tailor the reality one is born with to one's deepest dreams and desires, in the manner of the most admired traditional sculptures. The bodies of this group, based on portraits of real people, illustrate the spectrum of change achievable these days from surgery and chemicals. On the one hand, there are the breast implants of actor Pamela Anderson and the nose of Michael Jackson. On the less well-documented end of the body spectrum are the trans porn actors Buck Angel and Allanah Starr, whom Quinn presents facing us hand in hand (see page 158).

Again, it is celebration and not shock or patronizing sympathy that drives Quinn: 'I'm just presenting reality – well, re-presenting reality. I'm not taking a moral view on it but on the other hand, of course, there's a celebration of humanity. I think what I'm looking for is humanity in areas in which people might immediately write off its presence; when, in fact, there is something there, a spiritual or a human interest.'[1] Spiritual might seem an odd word to use, but Quinn is convinced that the contemporary desire to change the body one is born with is a kind of quest to align one's outer with one's inner needs.

The strategy forces us to consider the whole question of the way the ideal is becoming ever more attainable. Not just the ideal found in the surgically enhanced bodies of the glamour models or in the impossibly long and slender digitally adjusted bodies on which the clothes in fashion photographs are displayed, but more personal ideals tied up with people's sense of self. With a range of interventions becoming ever more available, from lunch-hour Botox sessions to banish lines and wrinkles through breast enlargements to the drastic desire for gender reassignment, the possibility of matching outer and inner has become a reality. Quinn's decision to present his subjects in the shining, smooth bronze associated with the perfect bodies of the past both dignifies the subject in a way the spectator understands from work of previous centuries and reveals to us the truth of what goes on in some people's lives today. It is as if he hopes that the deference due to the art of the past will help us understand the people who have posed for him.

Quinn exploits our comfort with the ideal, a kind of art we rarely bother to look at twice these days, by forcing us to do just that – look at it twice. The deadpan presentation is disconcerting: just what is the viewer to do with this array of humans who pursue their unfamiliar goals inside the clean white spaces of a gallery of contemporary art? His decision to stand them on the gallery floor so that we come face to face with them allows us no escape into the mythology and distancing of traditional sculpture. By representing them in the form of the ideal nude, imbued with the respect of a costly and traditional material, he suggests the way his subjects are in fact striving for an ideal of their own and asks why, if they exist in real life, should they not exist in art?

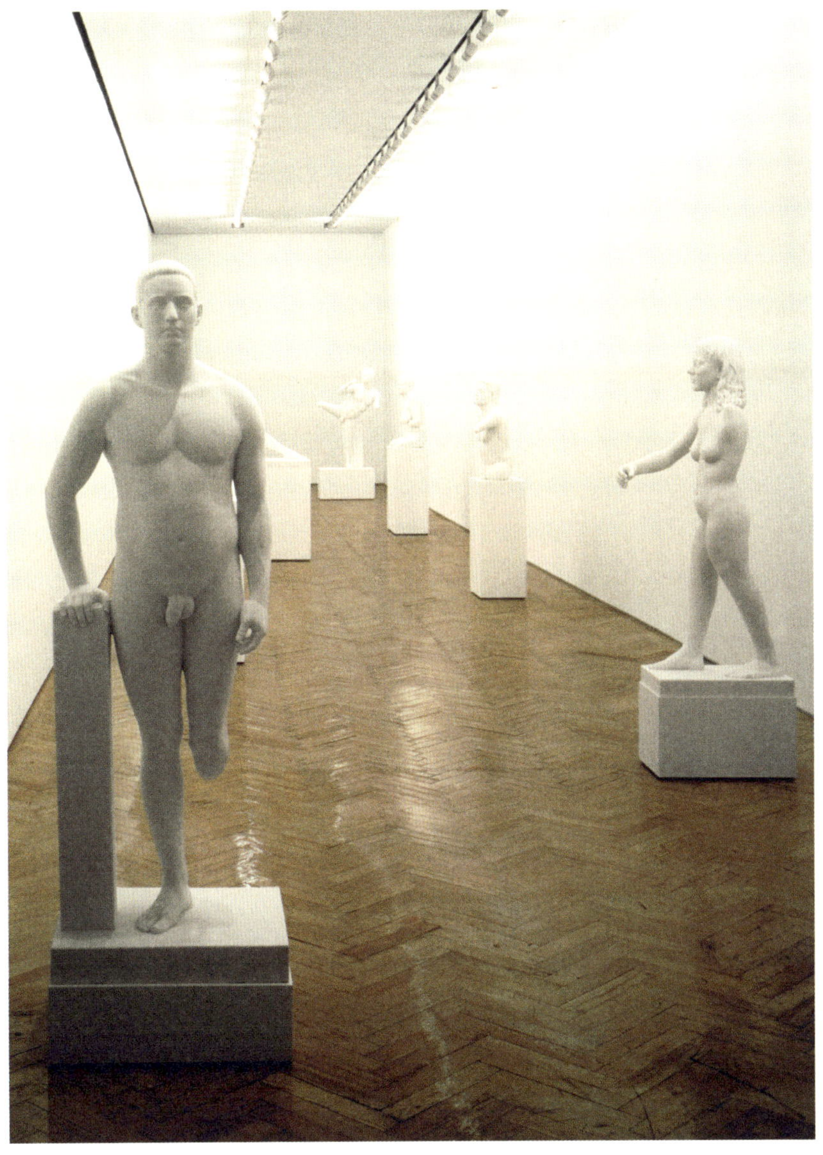

Marc Quinn, l to r, *Jamie Gillespie, Stuart Penn, Alexandra Westmoquette,
Peter Hull, Catherine Long*, 1999–2000, marble, installation at the Prada Foundation,
Milan, 2000. Quinn links contemporary bodies marked by accident or birth
to the admired classical sculptures of the past. By respectfully sculpting his sitters
in the finest marble, he underlines their resemblance to the revered Venuses and
Adonises whose missing limbs are accepted without question.

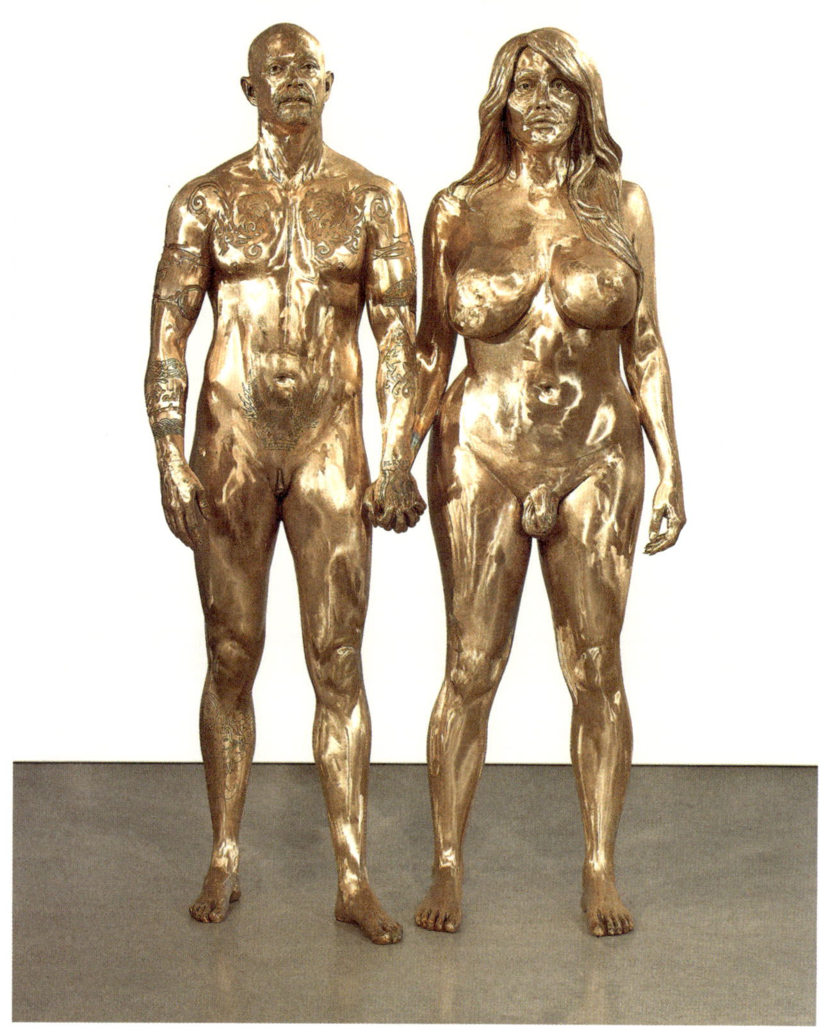

Marc Quinn, *Buck and Allanah*, 2009, lacquered bronze. Quinn believes that his sculptures are illustrative of more than simply the subjects they depict: 'I like the idea that if you left them [Buck and Allanah] in the desert and somebody found them in 5,000 years, it would probably tell them something about the society we live in now.'

Given the human figure's importance in the history of sculpture, it is impossible to look at contemporary sculptures of the nude without thinking about their relationship to the art of the past. Sculptors who work with the nude figure seem to be in constant debate with their predecessors. Far from finding it inhibiting, Quinn is clearly stimulated by his relationship with the past's great sculptures and happy to reference the masters. In case anyone thinks that Michelangelo left artists nothing to free from a block of marble, in 2008 Quinn exhibited a series of larger-than-life-size sculptures of the development of a foetus. He said that the foetus emerging from the stone was both like the practice of Michelangelo and the creativity of making a baby.

But not all sculptors react so positively to tradition. While Quinn's work provocatively references art history, the British sculptor Antony Gormley insists on distancing himself from his predecessors. Despite the fact that his sculptures are casts of his own body, which inevitably brings to mind – and to life! – the Vitruvian concept of the human figure as the measure for architectural proportions visualized in Leonardo's famous drawing, Gormley insists that his work marks a break with the past: 'I did not simply want to continue where Rodin left off; I wanted to reinvent the body from the inside, from the point of view of existence. I had to start with my own existence.'[2]

Gormley made this point in his 1996 discussion with the art historian Ernst Gombrich, in which he attempted to explain what distinguishes his art from that of his predecessors: 'We have somehow to acknowledge the liberty of creativity in our own time, which has to abandon tradition as a principle of validation, to abandon the tradition of mainstream Western art history and open itself up. Any work in the late 20th century has to speak to the whole world.' To which a sceptical Gombrich replied: 'It may have to, but it won't.'[3]

The determinedly contemporary Gormley seems to carry remarkably little weight from the art of the past on his shoulders: 'I think that we all are very visually informed these days. Maybe classical education within the visual arts has been replaced by a multiplicity of visual images that come through computers and advertising and all sorts of sources.' His view of the problem is that sculpture, which he calls 'something still, silent, and therefore rather forbidding because it isn't like a moving image on a screen. It is not telling you to buy something', has to speak to people who are used to a succession of immediately appealing pictures from films and computers and advertising. 'It may have within it a residue of 5,000 years of the body in art, but it must be approachable to somebody whose main experience of visual images is those things.'[4]

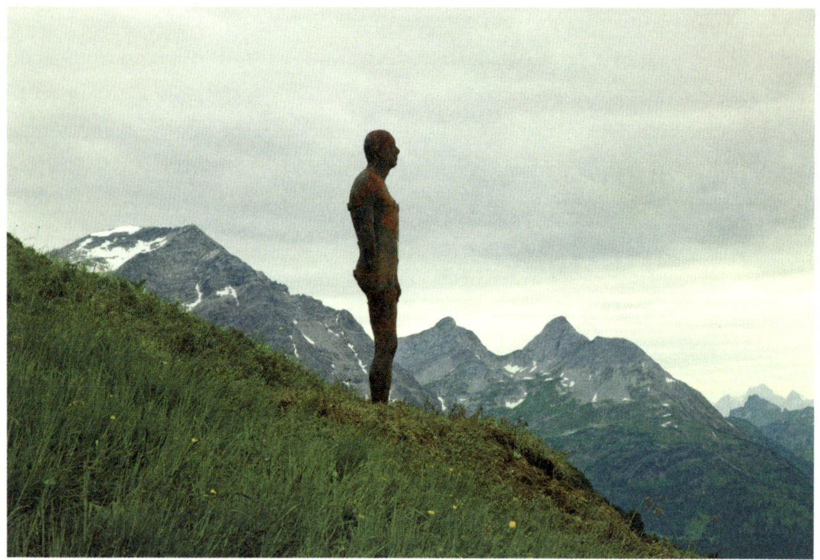

Antony Gormley, *Horizon Field*, 2010–12, landscape installation in the High Alps of Vorarlberg, Austria. The photograph shows a single example of the 100 life-size, solid cast-iron figures spread over an area of 150 km² (*c.* 58 sq miles). Whether facing out to sea or standing on mountains, Gormley's casts of his own body act as a medium to involve spectators in the world around them.

Like many artists who work with the nude, Gormley believes the task of art is to find a new relationship between art and life: 'In trying to deal with what it feels like to be alive, dealing with the body the other way round – from the inside, exploring it as a place rather than an object – I am countering both the contemporary obsession with bodily appearance and the historical one of idealization.' However, his way of doing so is singular for an artist. He has no desire for the casts of his body to carry any aesthetic value or interest in their own right. Instead, their value lies in the uses to which he puts them: 'I think of the work as a catalyst or resonator whose value or significance is not intrinsic but is generated in relation to the viewer and to its context.'[5]

Since 1997 Gormley has been populating a series of landscapes with iron casts of his own body. Among the most ambitious of these sited sculptures is *Horizon Field*, situated high in the Austrian Alps and composed of a hundred iron bodies spread over seven valleys with all the sculptures positioned at a height of 2,039 metres to create an artistic field that makes its own horizon. He says such works represent his attempts to ask a simple question in material terms: Where does the human being fit in the scheme of things? 'Sculpture doesn't need a roof or a label. You don't need to pass over the threshold of an institution in order to experience something that engages your imagination and, with luck, your body. When placed in the outdoors in rain and sunshine, in summer and winter, in daylight and moonlight, sculpture, in my view, begins to live and its silence becomes a potent marker in time and space. People may well ask "What the hell is this thing doing here?" and the work returns that question and it responds reflexively "What the hell are you doing here?"'[6]

Despite Gormley's denial of the usefulness of the art of the past, it is hard to divorce his nudes from it, even if just as a point of comparison. There is something of the Renaissance about his goal of using his body as a kind of surrogate for us to view the world. Is that so very different from the miraculous one-point perspective of the 15th century, which offered an optimum spot from which the viewer could see a painting in its full three-dimensional glory? A journalist once put this link to humanity and to the sculptural tradition in a less elevated manner: 'Some lonely art lovers have probably spent more time scrutinizing his rough-cast bottoms than they have a living human's. In the world of sculpture only Michelangelo's *David* and the *Venus de Milo* are more gawped at.'[7] In 2011 Gormley faced up to his sculptural heritage – literally. Invited to show at the Hermitage in St Petersburg, he 'deplinthed' a group of classical sculptures by sinking them into a false floor, enabling visitors to come face to face with these personified icons of humanity at its best. For the adjoining courtyard, he constructed a group of pixelated, blocky humanoids, crumbling and wavering in the confusions caused by life today. His aim was to present a modern dystopian contrast to the classical confidence of the perfect body.

Hyperrealism and change of scale are the tools of Australian sculptor Ron Mueck, who has taken great pains to leave behind the traditional materials of sculpture and to choose as subjects any body other than the ideal. His sculptures seem closer to the art of making waxworks than to the bronzes and marbles of high art. Mueck is tight-lipped about his art, preferring to let it speak for itself, but he has said that he is fascinated by other people and often wonders how it would feel to be in their place. He seems drawn to all humanity, people of all ages, from babies to elderly women. Sometimes he chooses to reproduce his subjects naked, as if removing their clothes can bring them closer to him.

It is this fascination with how people look that comes across in Mueck's art. His eerily realistic copies of his models are the product of a series of complex stages, starting with clay modelling and incorporating polyester resin or silicone or both in the transformation of malleable mud to lifelike surface. The sculptures are nearly always scaled up or down so that you cannot avoid staring at the sheer wonder of a giant baby or a smaller-than-life man. His facsimiles are as realistic as a reflection – or would be if the artist had not changed the scale. The result is to make the ordinary seem extraordinary, like a hand viewed through a magnifying glass or a portrait miniature.

Visitors to the legendary 1997 'Sensation' exhibition, which showcased the Young British Artists generation, found themselves peering down at a wax reproduction of the artist's father on his deathbed. Everything about *Dead Dad*, from the toenails and eyelashes to the skin's unnerving similarity to flesh, seemed as real as the gallery-goers who clustered around the body, except for one thing: Mueck had slightly reduced his father's size and placed him stretched out on the floor, a brilliant move that made one feel like a scientist inspecting a specimen. By naming the body as his father, he personalized the sculpture, making it impossible for the viewer to escape involvement. The strategy aroused unease and fascination in equal measure.

Mueck has made a giant baby and a giant naked man by the same technique, the results rendered monstrous by the change of scale. In 2001 came *Mother and Child*, which includes, in what must be a sculptural first, the umbilical cord of a baby lying on their mother's stomach. Mueck, like Quinn, has expanded the repertoire of the nude in ways that would never have been permitted or understood when sculpture served to embody the impersonal and the perfect. This is the nude recycled for our time into images of nakedness – defenceless in the case of his father, almost grotesque in the case of the baby. And individualized in a way that has no link at all with the generalized nudes of the past.

Even with the contemporary freedom to use anything one wants as a basis for sculpture, it is nevertheless an extraordinary innovation to use massed living bodies as sculptural material. The American Spencer Tunick makes new kinds of shape

OPPOSITE ABOVE **Ron Mueck**, *Dead Dad*, 1996–7, mixed media. Everything about this work operates in opposition to the notion of the ideal nude. Instead of generalized perfection, Mueck reproduces every wrinkle, hair and vein in his detailed portrait of his father's body.

OPPOSITE BELOW **Ron Mueck**, *Mother and Child*, 2001, mixed media. A first in the history of art is this larger-than-life sculpture of a mother and newborn child with attached umbilical cord. Its replacement of the classical ideal of exterior perfection with the interior functions of the body makes this indisputably a nude for our time.

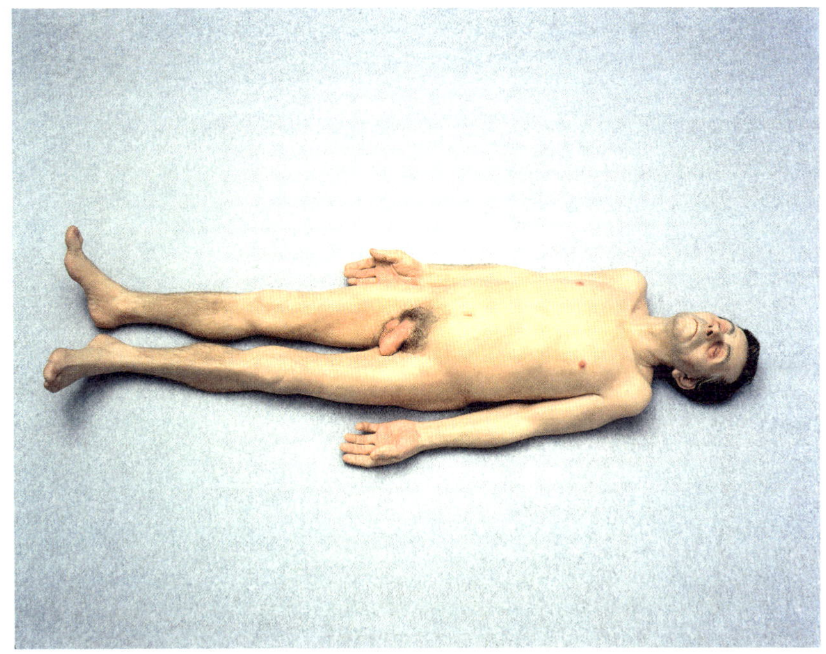

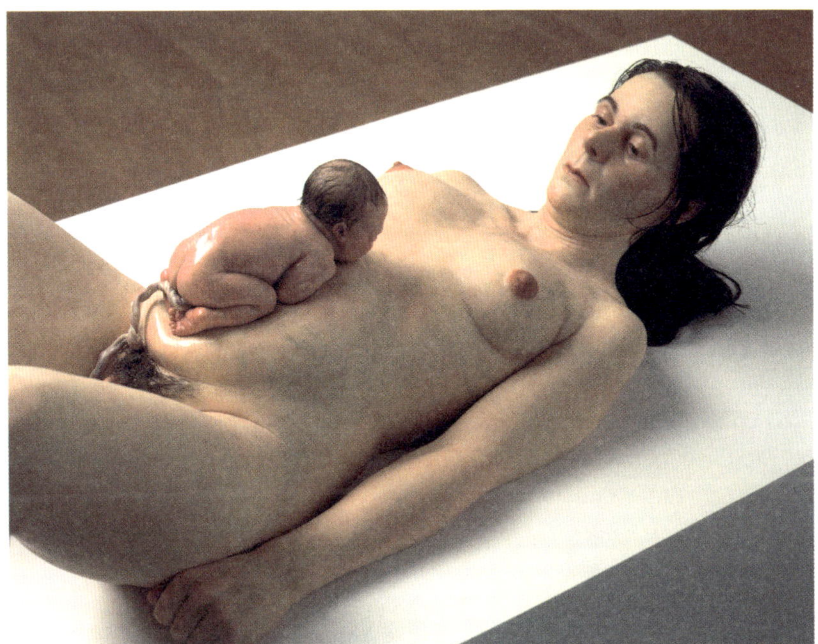

and form by massing hundreds, and often thousands, of naked bodies whether on the steps of Sydney Opera House or an eroding Swiss glacier, and then photographing them, in the process of which the bodies take on a united form with a character of its own. Tunick's work is an original combination of performance, sculpture and abstraction. *Nevada*, 1967, with its path of prone bodies winding off into the distance resembles nothing so much as Land art – Robert Smithson's *Spiral Jetty* comes to mind. The plane of horizontal bodies in *Maine*, 1997, suggests ripples on the sea.

Tunick says that he sees art in every stage of the process: 'From the moment my projects are announced, to the day of the installation, and the feeling the participants take away with them. I like to think my work is a continuum of experiences that asks people to think differently about themselves, and the world they live in; about how they move through each day.'[8] However, for those not involved in the process of making and who are unable, as with conventional sculpture, to visit the original, these multi-bodied sculptures exist only as photographs, which makes the photographs themselves the work of art. Tunick sees them as 'quasi-documentary and quasi-conceptual'. He photographs these human masses as a phenomenon of nature, waiting for the light to hit the bodies in the perfect way to satisfy the aesthetic demands of the final image.

On the one hand, Tunick is aware of the power of the naked body en masse to attract attention even in our sex-saturated culture, and on the other, he is aware of the need to produce work that excites or pleases in artistic terms: 'Maybe my dream would be to take the human form vertical…building structures to place people on and sometimes these structures holding the people would be invisible, blocked from view by the bodies themselves. Working in a more choreographed way for video…to create large abstract moving installations.'[9]

Tunick was once asked how he saw himself in the long artistic tradition of the nude. He replied that his art allowed people to know the human form differently as a sort of colour-field painting of pinks, tans, blacks and browns: 'Sometimes I feel a close association to painters such as Ellsworth Kelly.'[10] Of course, comparing his work with massed nudes to that of an abstract painter who sometimes raises the surface of his paintings to resemble sculpture is a reply that deals only with its artistic side. It ignores Tunick's interest in the underlying social purpose of his work, which he defines as 'letting go of your individuality and connecting more with each other's common humanity. It is not about standing out, but connection to what is mutual between us.'[11] A perfect example of this is the bridge of people he created across a canal in Amsterdam.

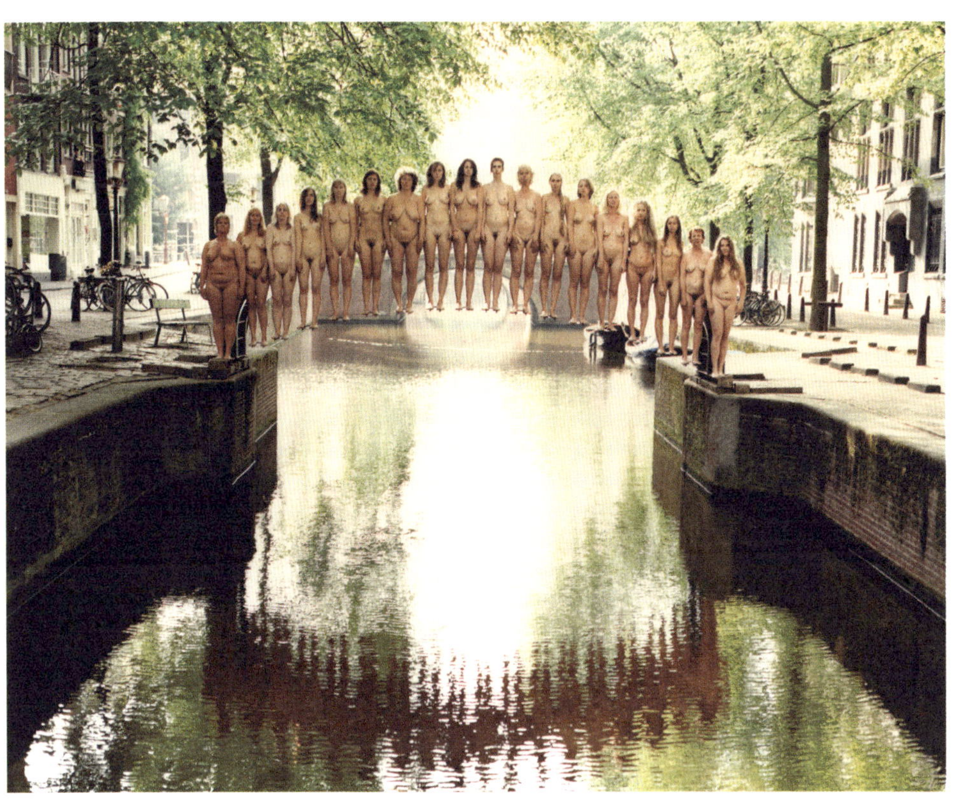

Spencer Tunick, *Netherlands 13* (Dream Amsterdam Foundation), 2007, C-print. A bridge of women across an Amsterdam canal is a literal illustration of Tunick's interest in the power of nudity to create a mutual connection between people that transcends their individuality.

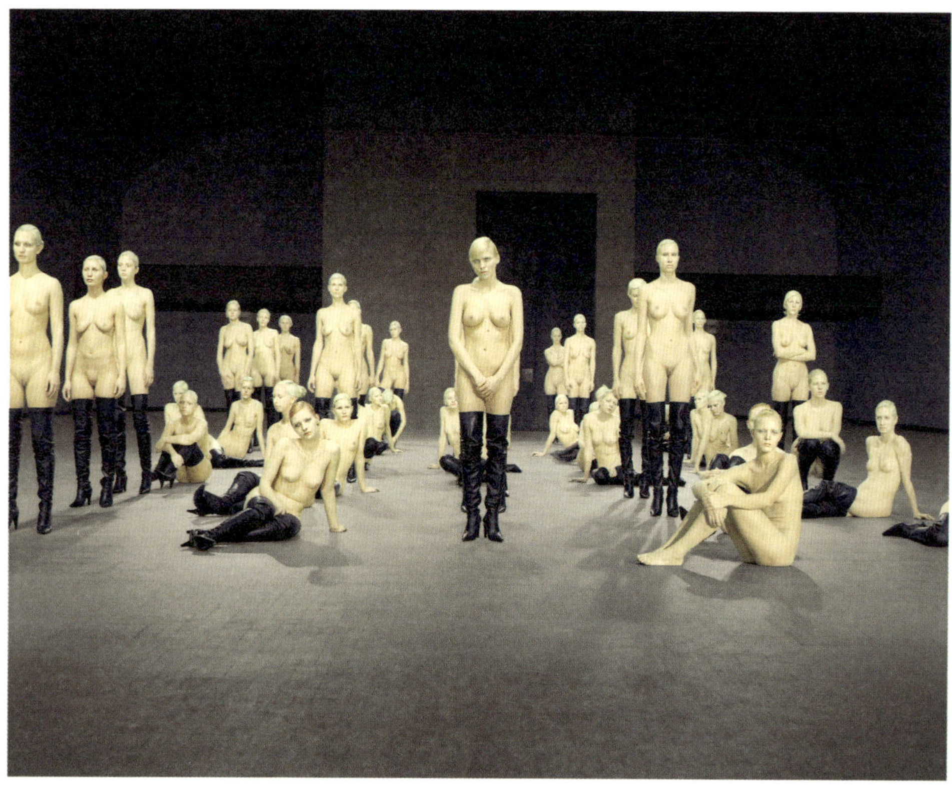

Vanessa Beecroft, *VB.45.107dr*, performance photograph, Kunsthalle, Vienna, 2001. Beecroft's art made with living nudes reveals the truth behind the ideal. She sets up her young, attractive models but then steps back as over the hours of the performance they tire, sit, sag and droop.

A different way of creating art with the living nude is offered by Vanessa Beecroft, an Italian-born artist living and working in the United States, who over the years has produced a succession of time-based works centring on nude or partially nude women standing in formation in a gallery for anything up to three hours at a time. Beecroft is one of those artists who makes art out of her own obsessions. Famously anorexic, she combined paintings and live models for her graduation piece, inspired by the colour-coded food records she used in her teenage diaries and the types of female faces and bodies that she admired. With this, she had found her medium. Before long, the models took over and a series of artworks of female formations ensued, each titled by initials and a number. Sometimes the women wear identical wigs, sometimes high heels, sometimes tights, sometimes nothing at all. Beecroft places them in the desired formation then leaves them and the situation to develop. As the women stand silently in the gallery space, their cohesion breaks down and their frailty and individuality emerge: they shift, stagger and slouch, and this combined with their silent unapproachability and sexuality creates a fascinated confusion in the viewer. Although the point of these performances can seem mysterious, the mutation of the ideal into the naked nude suggests that one source of their power lies in the visual crumbling of perfection. All Beecroft's women are ideal nudes. But as they reveal their individualities, they expose the reality behind the ideal nude. A resonant way of explaining her work comes from Jeffrey Deitch: 'While sitting in her figure drawing class at the Art Academy in Milan in 1993, Vanessa Beecroft had a simple but radical insight. She decided that the live models were more interesting as art than the drawings for which they were posing … A strange tension existed in the classroom as the students looked at the models in front of them and at each other. Conventional reality was suspended.'[12]

Not all today's sculptors work with the complete body. One group, while fascinated by the body, dissects it or amends it, sometimes taking it far from conventional realism. For half a century until her death in 2010, Louise Bourgeois explored the confusing and complex area of gender in works that in their conflation of male and female characteristics have the power to touch our deepest feelings, making the ground beneath our feet a little less firm than is comfortable. Bewilderingly, her art seems to speak for neither one side nor the other. Her subject is the relationship between men and women, masculinity and femininity, and her work seems to delight in wrecking received ideas. *Femme couteau*, for example, a concept she explored through several decades, represents women as both seductive and destructive. The pink marble version of 1969–70 encases soft, cleavage-like folds within its narrow shape, and yet the title, 'Knife Woman', calls to mind unpleasant thoughts of castrating women. In other works, groups of round ball- or breast-like bronzes attributable to various sexual organs rise from a tray-like base in a manner suggestive of gender similarity rather than gender difference. These disturbing shapes derived from the male and female sexual body are part of her strange new landscape of sexual imagery.

Bourgeois always claimed that her art emanated from her childhood knowledge of her father's affair with the governess, and this suggests a way of reading the ambivalence of her sexual shapes. For while her mother was soft and betrayed, her victorious governess was the opposite. It replaces 'woman good, man bad' with an altogether more complex attitude to the potential for softness and hardness in men and women. 'There has always been sexual suggestiveness in my work,' she said. 'Sometimes I am totally concerned with female shapes – clusters of breasts like clouds – but often I merge the imagery – phallic breasts, male and female, active and passive.'[13] There is something very mischievous about Bourgeois's talent for leaving us bewildered while at the same time creating art that takes us into unfamiliar sexual and sensuous depths.

Bourgeois's disconcerting body-based sculptures have encouraged several contemporary artists to surprise us with their powers of innovation. Rebecca Warren makes lumpy, bumpy females out of unfired clay, all protrusions and wobbly bits, which have more to do with an overflowing female energy than with ideal female form. In 2003 she produced a group of almost life-sized sculptures entitled *She*. Their roughness suggests they were never completely finished, and displaying a striding leg here, a giant breast there, they exude a crazy energy and sense of movement. Her final brilliant stroke was to place the *Shes* on low wooden boards on wheels, which made you feel they would skate away the minute you turned your back. This exhilarating image of womanhood has no links with the past, even if the past helped the artist arrive at it.

Warren's relationship to the art of the past ebbs and flows like a tide: 'There are things I really loved when I was young and first studying art history, like de Kooning and Rodin. When I later went to art college, I neglected these things because that wasn't what was going on there at that time. My studio at Goldsmiths was ridiculous: there was nothing in it.' And then, as she puts it, the policemen in her head vanished and 'suddenly everything became possible'.[14]

Rather than turn her back on the sculptors who preceded her with their masculine preferences for the female form divine, Warren seems to roll their works around in her mind, finally producing her response in her sculptured mountains

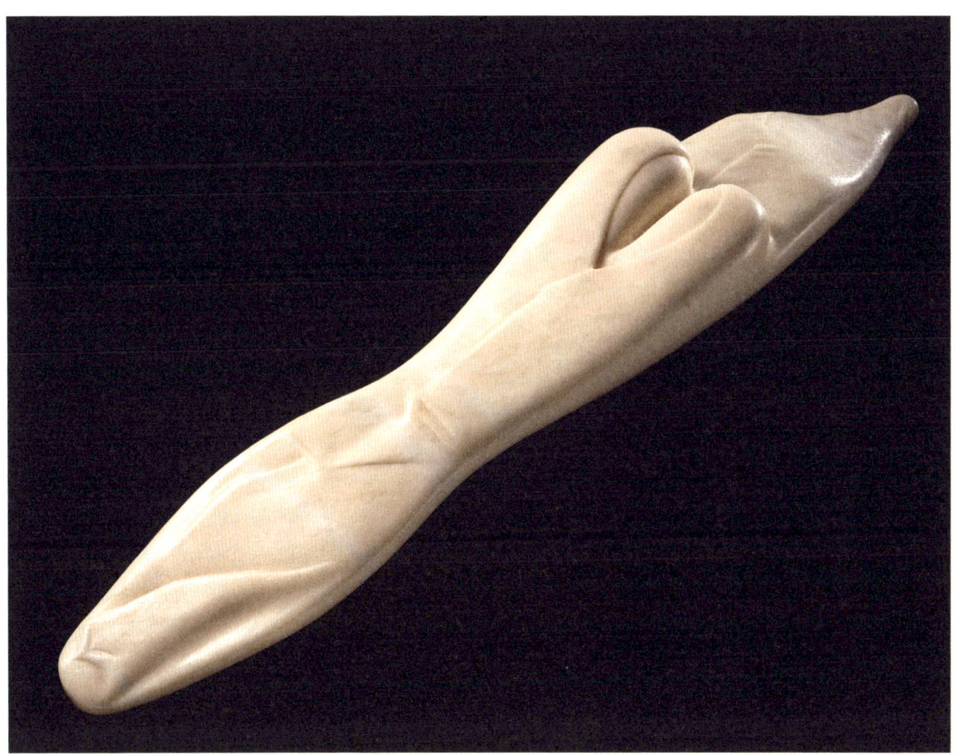

Louise Bourgeois, *Femme couteau* (Knife Woman), 1969–70, polished marble. This subject fascinated Bourgeois over the decades. At first the delicate pink marble makes this example appear all pretty femininity, until the phallic references emerge at second glance.

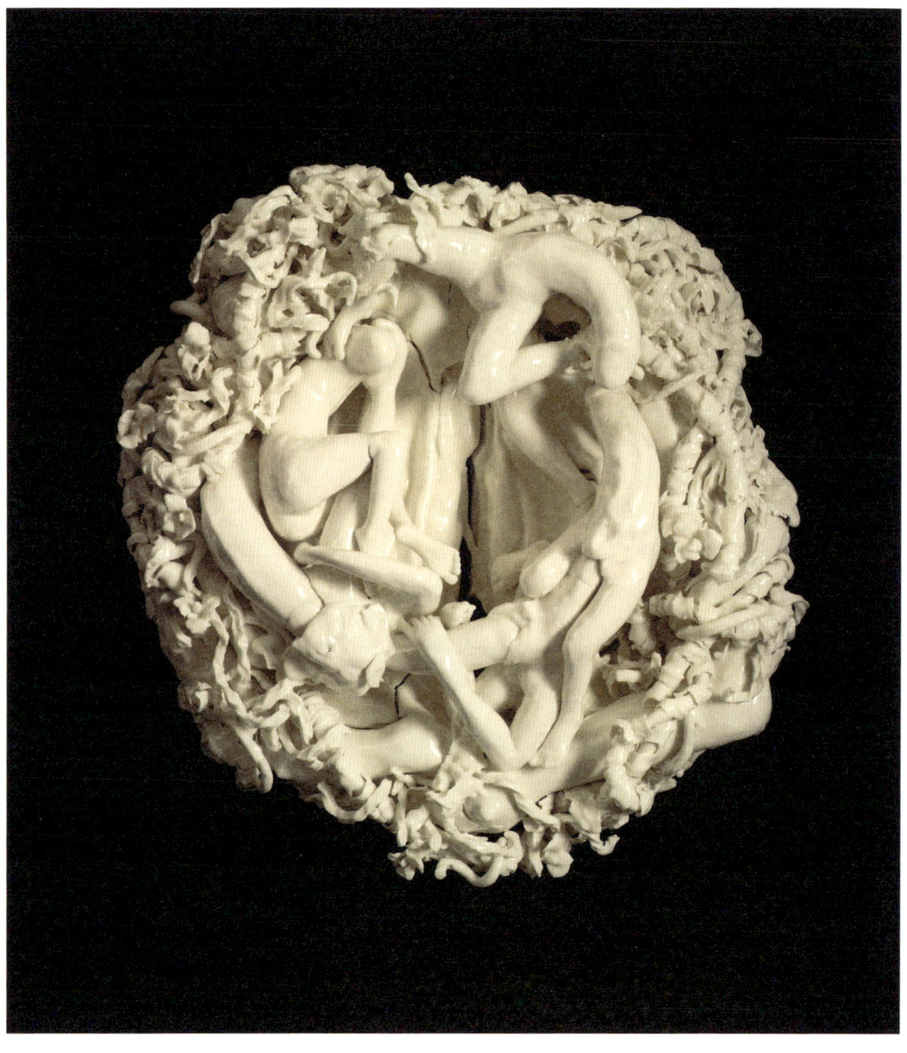

Rachel Kneebone, *Shield II*, 2010, porcelain. Classical myth and 18th-century
porcelain may lie behind the sculptures of Rachel Kneebone, but the imagination
they spring from belongs to the 21st century. Her urns and wreaths are alive
with writhing shapes of sexual body parts entwined with plant forms.

of unruly female shapes, which one feels would fit no imaginable masculine fantasy. She is fascinated by *Little Dancer Aged Fourteen*, which Degas made in 1880–1 and kept beside him in his studio: you can see a trace of her in the oddly unbowed pose of *Pony*, 2003. And Warren looks around as well as behind her. *Helmut Crumb* is an early work of 1998, which combines the immense thighs and balloon-bottomed women beloved of the cartoonist Robert Crumb with the long-legged perfection of the equally obsessed photographer Helmut Newton, in an attempt to construct something of her own out of these men's fixations. The resulting double pair of legs, one divided by a bottom, the other by a vagina, is both shocking and very funny in its presentation of the absurdity of obsession.

The British artist Rachel Kneebone attempts to deal with the huge emotions of loss and grief by replicating bits of bodies in that most refined of materials, porcelain. In *Lamentations* and *Shields*, two series of expressionistic works made in 2010, she ignores religious references suggested by the titles in favour of writhing, entwined masses of body parts and plant forms. Look closely and feet, legs, breasts, clitoral and penile shapes, flowers and vines emerge, sometimes realistically modelled, sometimes in the process of changing into something else. A figure lies stretched on its back atop a tangled pile of vegetation, at one end an exaggerated vaginal shape, at the other a penis shaft. The sexuality is graphic and yet it is carried out in the most delicately detailed manner imaginable and in china of the purest white. The viewer faces something beautiful yet tormented: Hieronymus Bosch without the ugliness. Memories of Michelangelo's *Pietà* or the entwined figures of Rodin's *Gates of Hell* hover round the edges of your brain, but the effect Kneebone creates with her cold white porcelain pile-ups is of something new and very modern, visceral rather than transcendental. There is grief and beauty but no God.

In 2009 the British artist Sarah Lucas unveiled her *Nuds* series. Made from tights filled with kapok, fluff and wire, twisted and moulded into sexually suggestive shapes, they are obviously related to the nude. Lucas shows these soft sculptures on traditional plinths, but they are a novel kind of inhabitant for the arty pedestals that support them. The limb- and torso-like shapes arouse thoughts of limp penises, an anus, arms clutching bodies or shielding eyes, and a confusion as to whether the contortions belong to two people or just one.

Lucas has taken sex as her subject from the start of her career, but it is sex presented with a sense of amusement as well as amazement at the role it plays in contemporary society. The *Bunny* sculptures that emerged at the end of the 1990s were made of tights stuffed with fabric and then placed on chairs in the kind of loose and lewd poses that had bad-girl associations. By calling them 'Bunnies', she

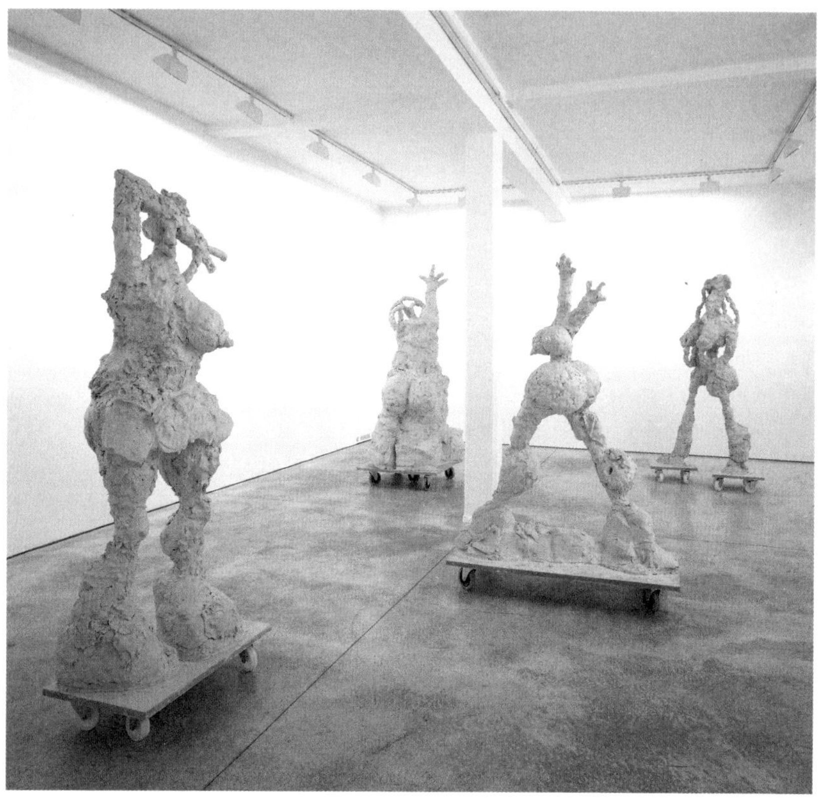

ABOVE **Rebecca Warren**, *SHE* series, 2003, l to r: *Untitled, Homage to R. Crumb, My Father, No. 6* and *South Kent*, reinforced clay on MDF on wheels, installation at the Maureen Paley Gallery, London. The wheeled boards on which Warren stands her unrefined, unidealized representations of crazy female energy are the complete opposite of the plinths that support the perfect female sculptures of the past.

OPPOSITE **Sarah Lucas**, *Nuds Cycladic*, 2010, tights, fluff, wire, installation view, Museum of Cycladic Art, Athens, 2010, in the foreground *Nuds Cycladic 8*. These distorted and contorted body shapes arouse thoughts of the greatest sexual intimacy. They have more in common with the *Venus of Willendorf* than with the *Venus de Milo*. The artist herself calls them primitives.

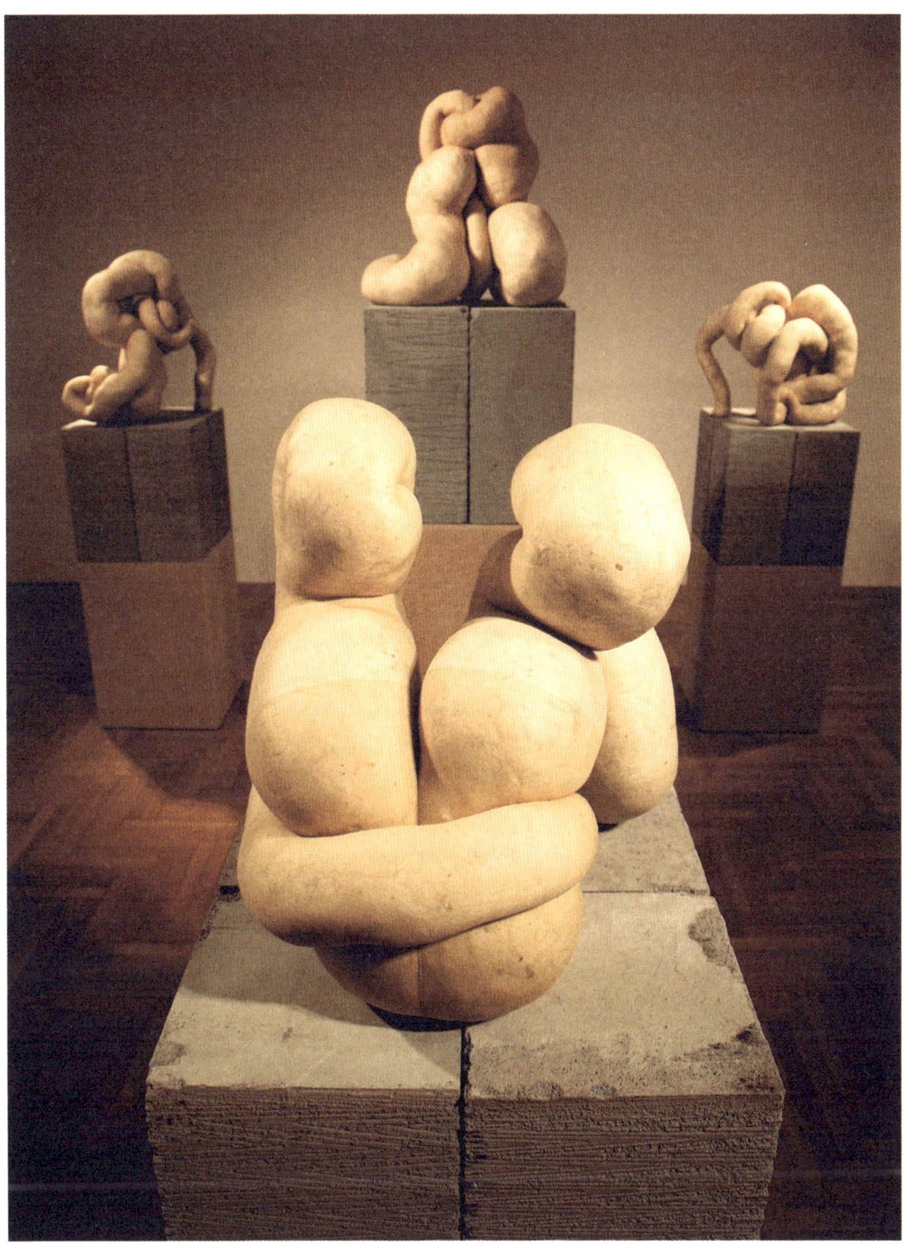

was referencing *Playboy* magazine, that playground for male watchers of compliant female flesh. Two things in particular mark her art: a love of puns, metaphors and jokes and a taste for making work out of everyday materials, not just tights but cigarettes, the pages of popular newspapers, toilets and kitchen chairs. Managing to be both imaginative and sexually obvious at the same time, the *Nuds* are a development of these interests.

To anyone familiar with English wordplay, the name 'Nuds' will be read as a jokey reference to the nude, but Lucas sidesteps interpretation: 'People ask me what the Nuds mean. I don't know what sort of answer they're expecting. What the Nuds mean is what they are. Exactly that. They don't illustrate an idea or refer to other art. They're primitives … I'm thinking God, Mum, Dad, Sex, Art. The Nuds, being primitive, required a three-letter designation, I felt.'[15]

Primitives. She is making primitives. So it seems only fitting that they were made for a show at the Museum of Cycladic Art in Athens. In their economy, these suggestively sexual human shapes share more with the simplified bodies of Cycladic art than with the ideal nudes of the succeeding centuries. Closer, in other words, to the *Venus of Willendorf* in their directness. The *Nuds* series joins the naked Willendorf Venus of prehistory to the naked nude of today.

Whether they make their points through expressive distortion or by subverting the classical nudes of the past, all these sculptors are interested in using the body in ways that are relevant to modern life. Gender confusions, imperfections, emotions, sexuality, all the things that were excised from the record under the rule of the ideal nude, are dealt with in their art, thereby creating a nude for our times – a naked nude. Is there anything left to say after Rodin? Plenty, it seems, and plenty of sculptors to say it.

7.
GOING TO EXTREMES

ARTISTS, AND THIS IS PARTICULARLY TRUE of contemporary artists who work with the nude, like to see how far they can go. When artists go to extremes, they by definition abandon the ideal and general. When those extremes centre on the naked body, they can involve the viewer in a great deal of discomfort. The artists always seem one step ahead of the audience as they find ever new ways to present us with the previously unvisualized. This is where discomfort can arise for today's art audiences. For centuries, art's role and responsibility were to support authority. The church employed the greatest artists of the day to make visual its beliefs. The Bible came alive in pictures. Wicked Eve succumbs to the serpent's words while a bemused Adam looks on. The Virgin Mary and her son portray the perfection of motherhood. The saints are depicted in ghastly detail as they endure pain and horror in the name of faith, an example to us all. Painted miracles give hope to the poor and sick. And everywhere the body of Christ on the cross, dying in agony for us. How could we not believe?

As for secular authority, rulers since antiquity have understood that the power held by their image could substitute for their presence. Roman emperors sent portrait busts to the provinces as stand-ins – just as photographs of royals and presidents decorate government offices today. English aristocrats in the 16th century placed bulk orders for imagined portraits of their antecedents to line the long galleries where they strolled on rainy days. Likeness was not the point – no one knew what they looked like in any case – but proof of ancestral pedigree legitimized the family's standing.

The role of art as an arm of the state changed forever with the development of bohemianism in the 19th century, first described to the French public by Henri Murger in the short stories he wrote in 1848, *Tales of Bohemian Life*. Derived from the region of Bohemia, now in the Czech Republic, which the French associated with 'gypsies' and an unconventional lifestyle, Bohemia came to be seen as a sort of alternative state within the official state, made up of artists of all sorts and defined by its defiance of the standards of the surrounding conventional community. In Paris, among the top hats and the crinolines of the mid-19th-century bourgeoisie, a group of singers, dancers, painters, sculptors and writers lived by their own rules: midnight flits when the rent was due, affairs without marriage, a casual and witty mode of dress and an art in revolt against the approved art of the day, all marked Bohemia's territory.

By the end of the century, the bohemian way of life had spread, and its values were adopted by avant-garde artists in many countries. It also enjoyed a fascinated acceptance by the society that surrounded it, as *La Bohème*, the popular Puccini opera of 1896, makes clear. Instead of making art as a reflection of the official French state, the artists of Bohemia used their art in the service of their own particular set of beliefs. Since Bohemia was a state of mind marked by individuality and defiance of the norm, the art spoke only for the values of the artists and their circle.

Bohemianism gave sex a legitimate place in fine art, which meant artists no longer had to be coy or to restrain themselves when it came to painting nudity. By the start of the 20th century new theories about sexuality offered artists new avenues to explore. The Surrealist interest in psychoanalytic theories inspired such intriguing works as Frida Kahlo's *The Bride Frightened at Seeing Life Opened*, with its use of split and oozing fruits to signify female sexuality, and Dalí's *The Great Masturbator*. Today's artists have gone further. They no longer need an excuse to legitimize their interest in sexuality. They have unyoked sex from its Freudian explanations and treat it as just that – the sexual act in all its variety. And not just sex: bodily functions and gender confusions come under their scrutiny as well in an artistic response to the permissive society. As one would expect, there are as many responses as there are artists. Tracey Emin paints watercolour representations

OPPOSITE ABOVE **Salvador Dalí**, *The Great Masturbator*, 1929, oil on canvas. New ideas about sexuality gave the Surrealist Salvador Dalí the freedom to explore his personal desires and terrors in works of dream-like intensity. *The Great Masturbator* encodes portraits of himself and Gala, his future wife, in an image abounding in sexual symbols. Her lips and nose savour the man's genitals, while his mouth hosts a locust, an insect of phobic horror for the artist since his childhood.

OPPOSITE BELOW **Tracey Emin**, *Masturbating*, 2006, acrylic on canvas. Ideas about what is suitable for public viewing have changed in recent decades. Emin treats the subject of masturbation with great delicacy of line and colour.

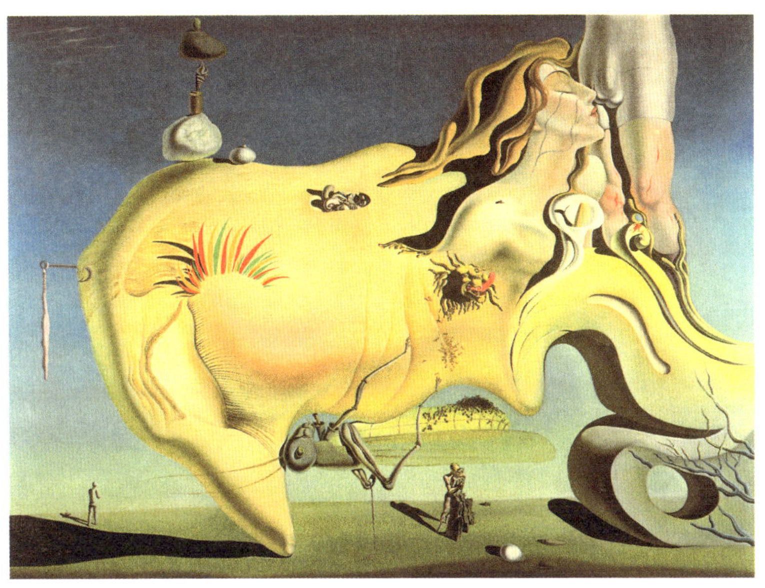

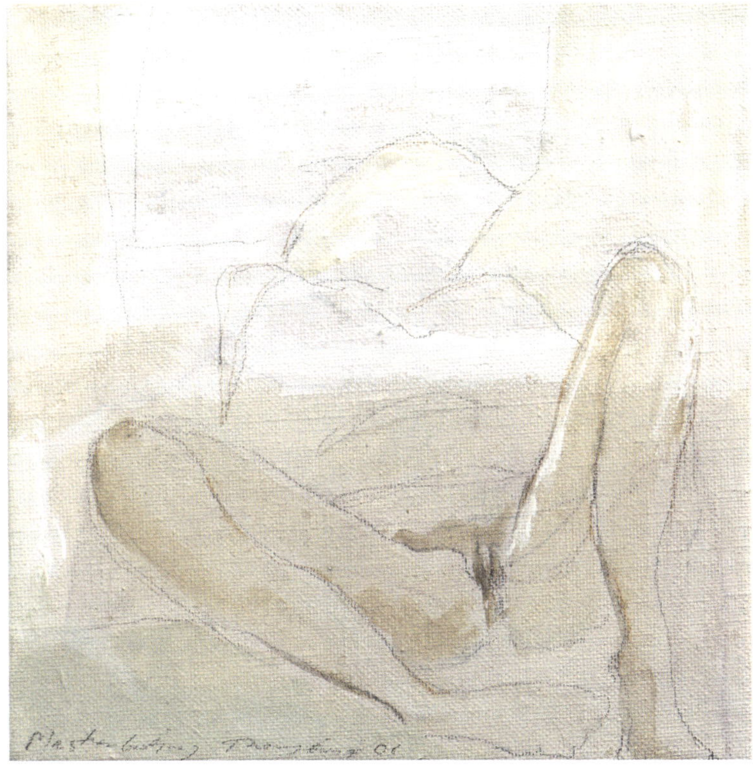

of female masturbation, less violent, more delicate and less disturbed than Egon Schiele's work of almost a century earlier, but masturbation nonetheless. In 2009, she made a flicker-book-style animated film of the subject, which was based on her drawings of her hands and open legs. Robert Mapplethorpe presents the viewer with gleaming photographic images of gay sexual activities. Nancy Spero's delicately coloured works on paper reveal on close inspection the sexual horrors that women suffer at the hands of men in wartime. The less repressive sexual climate of today offers retrospective possibilities as well. In the last two decades, the erotic drawings and paintings of Klimt and Schiele have been exhibited internationally in public institutions.

Few if any ideal nudes of the past express the artist's view of the controversial concerns of the era. Whole dormitories of reclining nudes were painted to show off the artist's skills at painting gorgeousness, to help tell a story, to offer a kind of drawing-room erotica or to attract attention and hopefully a buyer with the development of selling exhibitions in the 19th century. Narrative paintings depict 'War' unmanned by 'Love' in the form of a seductive Venus and a semi-nude Mars who has removed his armour; Danae reclining as Jupiter disguised as a shower of golden coins targets her suggestively parted thighs; Paris awarding a golden apple to the most beautiful of the three goddesses twirling in glorious nudity around him.

Artists tended to keep their political opinions to themselves, or at least away from their employers. Goya was circumspect about his horrifying etchings of *The Disasters of War* made between 1810 and 1820. When they were finally published in 1863, long after his death in 1828, they could do no harm to his position as painter of the Spanish great and good. In a similar self-imposed censorship, Joan Miró produced fifty anti-fascist lithographs around 1940, when the Franco government controlled Spain, which he kept quiet about for several years.

When Rubens painted his huge *Peace and War* in 1629–30 to encourage a peace treaty between Spain and England, he was working as the envoy to the Spanish king Philip IV and was ennobled by both countries as a result. The voluptuous nudity of Ceres the goddess of plenty in the centre represents the bounty that results from peace.

Today when artists such as Gilbert & George produce huge works based on their own naked bodies, they also win praise and prizes, but the difference is that they are working for themselves and expressing their own opinions as politicized men in contemporary Britain: 'We always say our art is campaigning art, we are not trying to make a beautiful picture, we are trying to provoke … have ideas, and that's it.'[1] The art that once supported the state now offers a critique.

Gilbert & George's freedom to speak their minds did not come overnight. You could say that although the right to self-expression was won by the mid-20th century, there remained another taboo, that against art with narrative or social content. It was a kind of 20th century parallel for the earlier control of artists held in the past by those who paid the bills. When Gilbert & George started their career at the end of the 1960s, minimal and abstract art were the styles that absorbed the attention of the art world. Art was 'to do with colour, shape, form, weight, and you discussed art in those terms, you never discussed feeling, meanings, sex, race, religion, money, none of those things came into the discussion about art,' recalls George of his time in the mid-1960s at St Martin's School of Art in London. 'So everything had to be on a sheet of paper or it had to be wood or coal or lead, and it had to be true to materials. And the bad things in art then were emotion, colour, sentiment, feeling, sexuality, all these were taboo.'[2]

At art school, says George, 'They taught you to think solely about form. Extraordinary! The entire course was about the work's form, colour, shape, weight. The teachers didn't think about content, meaning didn't come into it: it had to look good, be effective. … I remember this student who'd made this sculpture, a pile of oranges spilling out of a horn. We were discussing his work, and I merely asked, "Are they from Israel or South Africa?" And he immediately flew into a rage, taking it for some cheap political jibe. "But they must be from somewhere," I said.'[3]

These days content is allowed, content that can be extremely shocking when it comes from the handful of artists who cannot resist turning the handle to the door that hides the forbidden and the taboo. Artists deal with this in different ways. The German artist Thomas Ruff, who has based a series of nude images on pornography, coats their crudeness with his own particular style. A decade ago he began digitally modifying thumbnail images of pornography he downloaded from the internet. As a result of the process they become larger but also blurrier, creating a barrier between the shocking subject matter and the viewer, turning it into art, you could say, as well as confusing the conventional belief in photography's power to capture the 'real'. Uninterested in making judgments, Ruff has always claimed that his only concern is with the surface of his photographic images, not their meaning, and in an odd way his use of shocking imagery can be seen as a test of his intention.

Gilbert & George chose a more confrontational path. Once they found their format of huge grids of photographs in the 1970s, they set about breaking all the taboos that interested them. And for a decade, the way they did this was by removing their clothes. The 1990s was the great decade of their nakedness: in 1991 came the *New Democratic Pictures*, in 1994 the *Naked Shit Pictures*, in 1996, the *Fundamental*

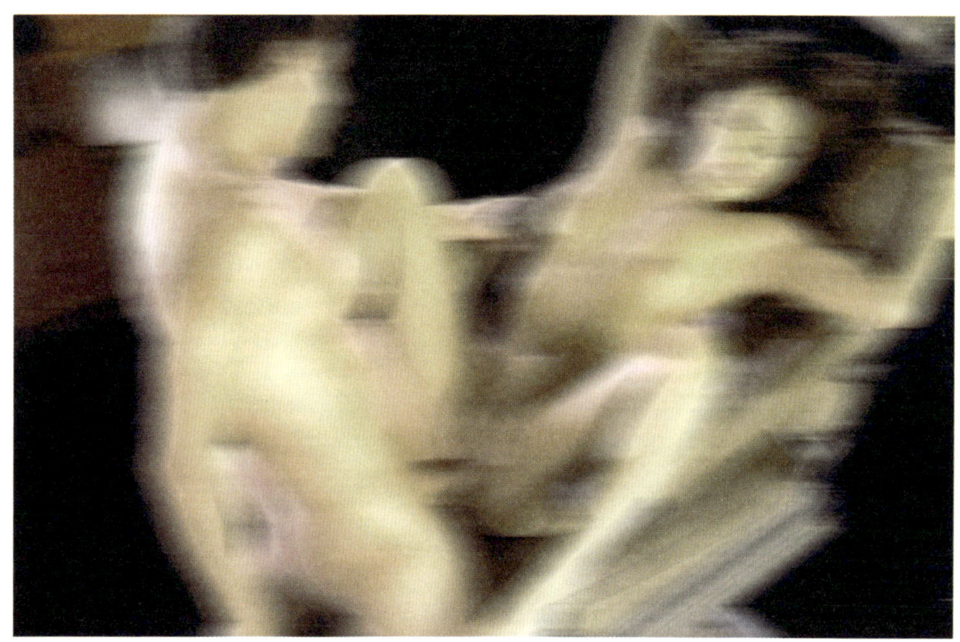

Thomas Ruff, *nude em08*, 2000, C-print. Ruff blurs the shocking reality of the
pornography he downloads from the internet, turning the images into abstracted forms
and colours.

Pictures, in 1997 the *New Testamental Pictures*. Their choices were inspired by their feelings about politics, sex and religion: 'To free ourselves we said we were low-class Tories. That got us free from everybody. But we are the most socialistic, mad subversive artists that exist in the world. I think we are nearer to anarchists than anything else because we are totally self-sufficient.'[4]

Gilbert & George want to reach two completely different kinds of audience, those who think art is not for them, like the neighbourhood boys who appear in their images, as well as those who visit galleries. To do this, they communicate with both their audiences via provocation and confrontation. Their outrageous imagery, inspired by the young men, the sexuality and the graffiti they find around them in the East End street where they have their London home, is conveyed through repetition, overwhelming scale, limited bright colours and shiny surfaces in their art. The result is guaranteed to grab anyone's attention, even someone whose eyes usually glaze over at the sight of art. 'We never liked the idea of the artist using a language which excludes 99% of the world's population, we don't think it's necessary. That it's only white people in London, Paris and New York in certain boroughs who would even understand the work, we think that's so elitist and cruel to the vast general public.'[5]

At the same time, the artistry of Gilbert & George's work appeals to the initiated. The gallery audience sees the same thing but is involved for different reasons. The artists' strategy here, particularly in the naked work of the 1990s, is to deny the educated viewer the comfort of a familiar response. By presenting themselves naked and middle aged, surrounded by young men of assorted ethnic origins and between the wastes and fluids of the body, in giant works resembling altarpieces, they leave the viewers unsure how to respond. While the grid and the kaleidoscopic arrangements of the subject matter aestheticize the work in ways the gallery-goers understand by encouraging an analysis in terms of form and colour, the uncompromising subject matter works against the impulse to aestheticize.

Some of the most shocking imagery is found in their *Naked Shit Pictures*, which are exactly what the title says: a series of huge photographic compilations of excrement and Gilbert & George with no clothes on. But when you look at the works with their smooth surfaces and black divisions, it is stained-glass windows that come to mind, a religious reference that adds an extra element of shock to the already shocking content of nudity, swear words, urine and faeces. It is not a comforting art and it guarantees attention, although they say they are not out to shock: 'Shocking is a media idea, it is not an artist idea. Our pictures are not attacking or confronting, but exploring.'[6]

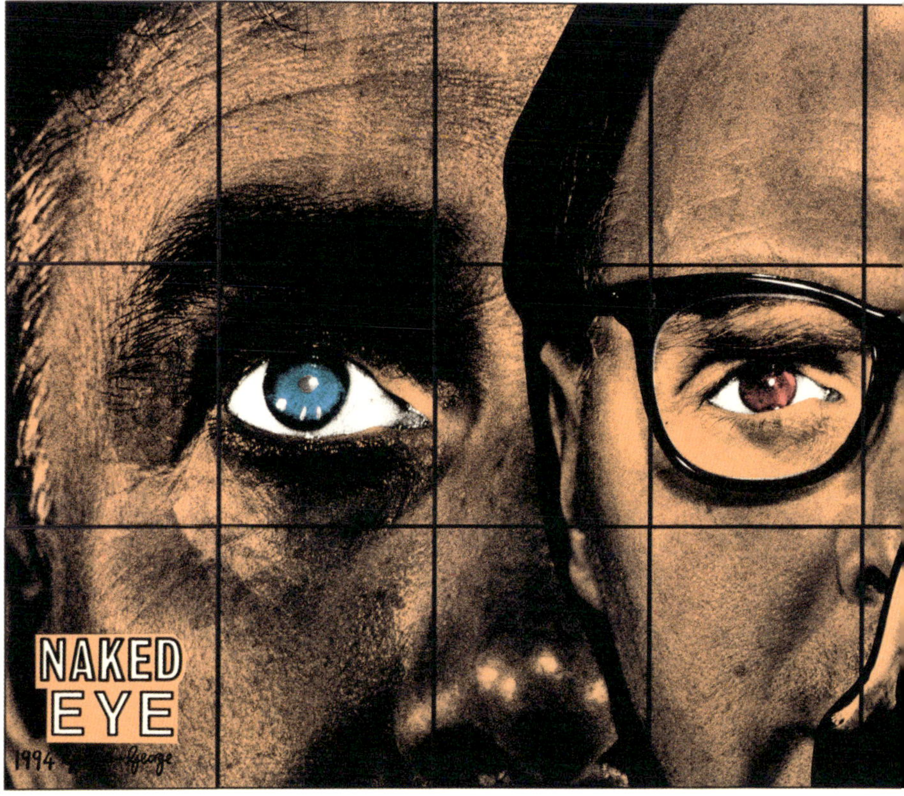

For a couple who have always been willing to be interviewed, Gilbert & George
are remarkably coy about the meaning of their images. *Naked Eye*, 1994, shows
the couple unclothed and with their hands over their eyes, recalling the depiction
of the shamed Adam and Eve as, newly aware of their nakedness, they are expelled
from the Garden of Eden. Typically, they have a double response to this interpretation. 'For us, being naked in front of the public, we are trying to make ourselves
vulnerable in front of the viewer,' says Gilbert. 'So many people said "But isn't it a
reference to Adam and Eve?" and we said, "Surely it's more like Adam and Steve,"'
says George.[7] This jokiness, this refusal to deny or admit or apologize for their
outrageous imagery, is a strategy: they want their art to speak for itself and also
perhaps want the viewer to work at making sense of its shocking imagery.

Though they would not admit to anything so crass as a wish to change society,
the Adam and Steve comment reveals a deep intent to put across their point of

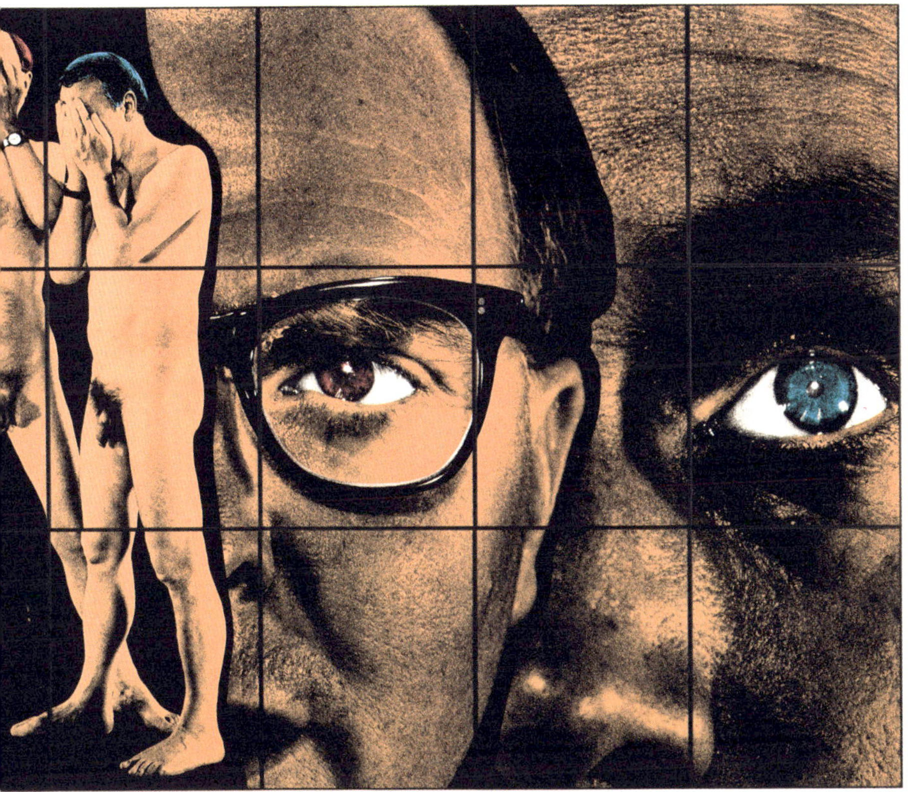

view through art not argument. Gilbert & George claim that they are painting not the present but some future state, picturing things that have not yet come about. They are not mirroring reality so much as imagining what it could be: 'We like to think that we're forming our tomorrows, that we're making pictures that don't exist in reality, that maybe tomorrow will be a little bit more like our pictures than it would otherwise.'[8] It is certainly true that these works, which seemed so shocking in the 1990s, seem much less so today.

Gilbert & George's images are clearly imbued with a point and a passion. This is not always the case with artists who itch to break out of the rooms marked 'Good

Gilbert & George, *Naked Eye*, 1994, mixed media. In huge works that resemble stained-glass windows, Gilbert & George expose their middle-aged naked bodies in order to explore the taboos that interest them. Their pose here suggests and explodes conventional ideas of shame.

'Taste' and 'Acceptability'. A particularly bewildering group of work is *Made in Heaven*, 1989–91, which depicts heterosexual intercourse. In these, the American Jeff Koons, known for remaking popular kitsch items in fine materials, applies this approach to sexually explicit images of himself and his then wife, the Italian porn star and politician Ilona Staller (La Cicciolina), in life-size sculptures, prints and paintings.

Is Koons making fun of our credulity when faced by work by a famous artist? Perhaps he felt it was the best joke ever to put himself, his wife and the studio where she made her pornographic films into images destined for the world's most prestigious galleries. Perhaps he was merely doing what many modern artists have done, taking inspiration from the commonplace stuff of society. One theory relates his work to the way that American artists began to achieve great celebrity in the 1980s. In this view, Koons's art is not so much about absolving the shame of sex as about the avant-garde's courtship of celebrity: 'His bid to achieve a broader audience and a new form of artistic celebrity while maintaining his art world credentials was a far greater gamble than his other forms of self-exposure, and in this he certainly succeeded like no artists ever before.'[9]

Theories aside, what is certain is that despite the explicit poses and genitalia on show, Koons has ensured that gratuitous sexuality is not all these works offer the viewer. By providing the clues necessary for a respectful analysis, Koons makes it possible to approach them with the eye of an art historian: some of the poses in the group, for example, can be compared with those of classical statues, a respectable art-historical exercise, and their glossy, colourful surfaces share an aesthetic with animated films, a hallowed borrowing practice of the Pop artist. We comfortably accept that the manga comics of his native Japan lie behind Takashi Murakami's two sculptures from 1998 in which the sperm from the penis of a cowboy turns into a lasso, and milk from his female counterpart's breasts becomes a skipping rope, so why not accept pornography as the source of Koons's work? To make it even easier for the viewer to rise above the explicit sexuality, he provides, in line with current fashion, a dash of irony by superimposing fairy-tale butterflies over an image of sexual intercourse, *Ilona on Top (Rosa Background)* of 1990, as he turns his head quizzically to meet the viewer's eye.

Sarah Lucas disconcerts her audience by outdoing the stereotypical crudeness of the media presentation of sexuality. She does not so much criticize the breasts and bottoms falling out of flimsy underwear favoured by pop stars and the gracefully named 'glamour models', as offer them back to us stripped of any shreds of glamour they might have. Her art is a kind of visual version of the fairy tale of

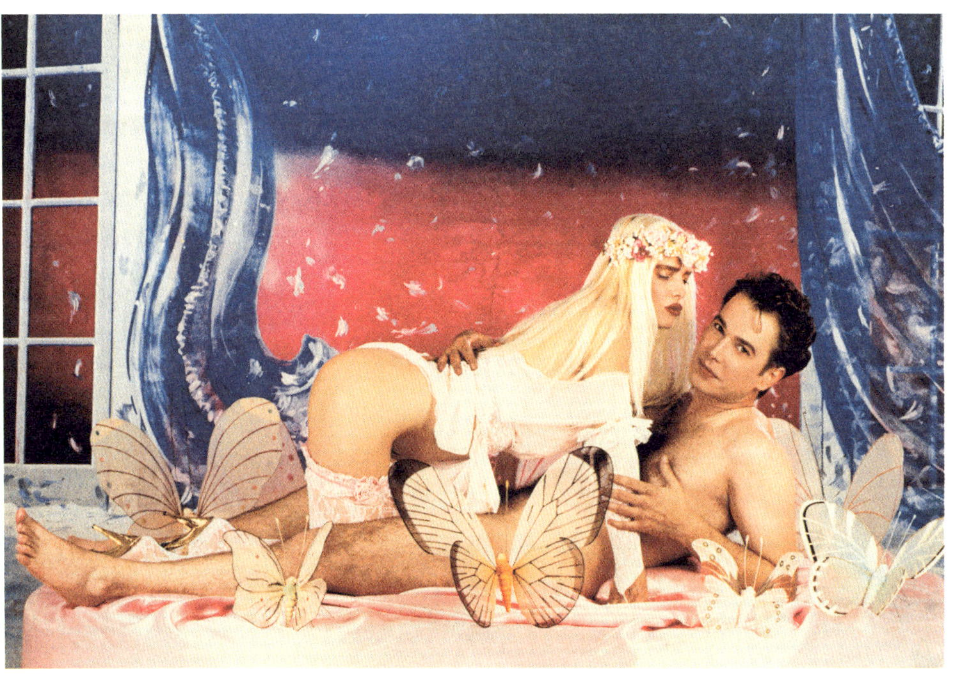

Jeff Koons, *Ilona on Top (Rosa Background)*, 1990, oil inks on canvas. Koons, the master of kitsch items sculpted in materials of the greatest quality, turned his sexual relationship with his wife into a series called *Made in Heaven*, perhaps ironic, definitely beautiful and absolutely the kind of work that previously would have been kept for a private viewing.

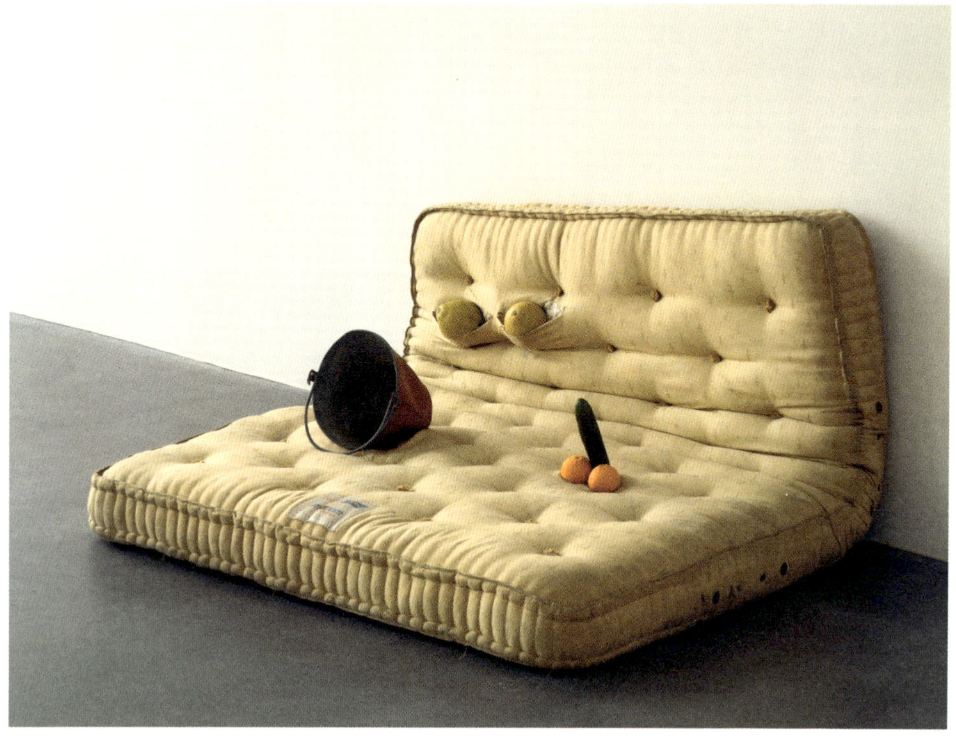

Sarah Lucas, *Au Naturel*, 1994, mattress, melons, oranges, cucumber and bucket. Lucas's work speaks with the crudity of casual conversation, but sits inside the pure white walls of the modern gallery. Her mattress, bucket and fruit that stands in for sexual parts critique contemporary attitudes to sexuality.

the emperor's new clothes. The crudity of conception of the couple on the bed in *Au Naturel*, 1994, the female a bucket to receive the male cucumber and oranges, forces viewers to confront their own attitudes, or those in the pages of the tabloid newspapers. It is a horrible image, but then so are many of the attitudes of our society. Woman as receptacle, sometimes in the form of a lavatory, is a theme Lucas returns to. One of her most disturbing works, *Chicken Knickers*, shows a standing female torso with a chicken placed over her genitals, its cavity gaping towards the viewer. One may wish to dismiss it as disgusting, but how can one in the light of society's ever-coarsening attitudes to sexuality? Compared to Koons, Lucas is a crusader. Her serious critique of the attitudes that most of us dismiss, campaign against or meet with a mix of tolerance and unease is also funny, a disarming approach to making a point.

Ellen Altfest's painting *The Penis*, 2006, illustrates the change from Kenneth Clark's notion of the nude as 'the body re-formed' for art. All of this American artist's work is the result of an intense act of looking, whether at a tangle of tumbleweed or a naked and middle-aged male bottom sat squarely on a paint-spattered stool. Every infinitesimally small hair is delineated rising free of the skin, and every fold and wrinkle is suggestive of weight and mass. Neither medical illustration nor genitals tidied up for art, this is in fact a portrait of a penis. Its owner's fingertips and the fraction of his leg bent back against the stool add humanity and context in a new and contemporary version of the nude.

Jake and Dinos Chapman offend every rule of good taste with their explorations of matters more familiar from horror films than art. Their interest in testing the extremes of what is allowed into art is not limited to sexual matters. Their

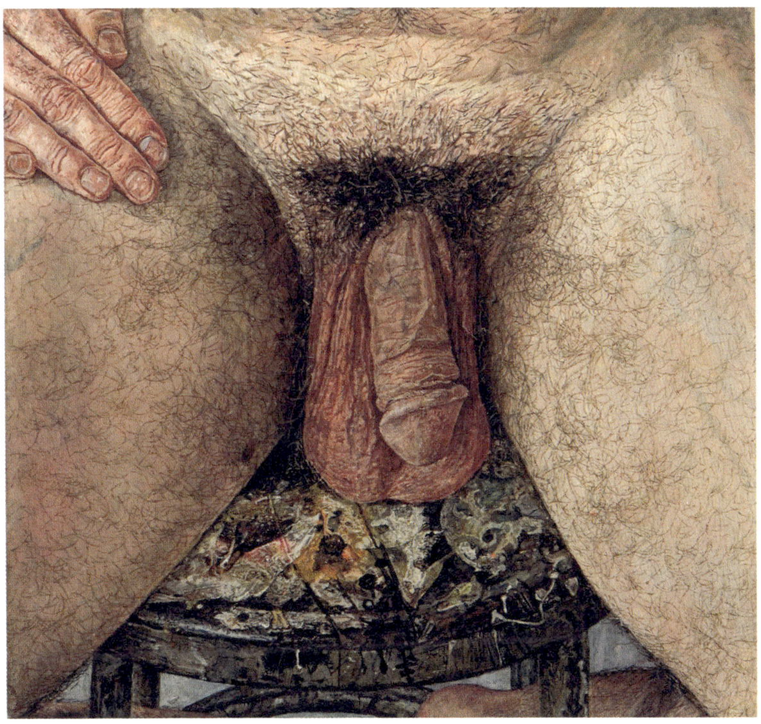

Ellen Altfest, *The Penis*, 2006, oil on canvas. The precise detail of Altfest's work is decades away from the nude as the body generalized, idealized and improved for art. The minute observation of the penis and pubic hair and inclusion of the closely observed fingers and thighs give this work the individualized quality of a portrait.

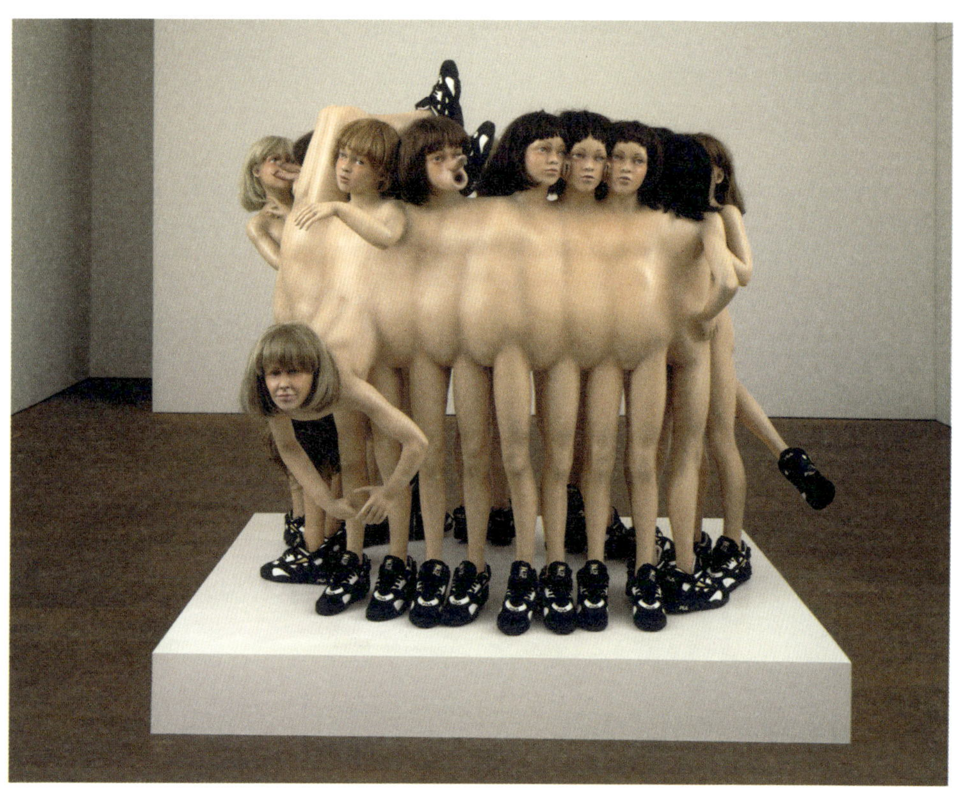

Jake and Dinos Chapman, *Zygotic Acceleration, Biogenetic De-sublimated Libidinal Model (Enlarged x 1000)*, 1995, fibreglass, resin, paint, wigs and trainers. The taboo of linking children and sexuality is explored by Jakes and Dinos Chapman. Their mutant group of disturbingly fused naked children in trainers has male and female genitals in unexpected places.

sculptures include brutally hacked off limbs after Goya's etchings of the *Horrors of War* and miniature concentration camps, which are like perverse adult versions of the model set-ups beloved of children (and their fathers). The difference is that unlike the farmyard or the railway layout, the Chapmans' recreation of unspeakable activities both draws and repels the eye – the equivalent of looking through one's fingers at the cinema.

In 1994 the Chapmans exhibited the first of their sculptures of child mannequins grotesquely adorned with sexual parts. In 1995 came *Zygotic Acceleration, Biogenetic, De-sublimated Libidinal Model (Enlarged x 1000)*, a mutant family of naked children in trainers, victims of genetic engineering, which the brothers describe as a 'post-Freudian pseudo-scientific vision of a self-reproducing cell fizzing with rampant sexual energy'. These pretty naked child mannequins are horribly fused together, each one equipped with genitals in unexpected places and anuses in place of mouths. 'The process was basically this: we went to one shop, bought something, went to another shop, bought something else. Then stuck them together. It's just that the shops happened to be a second-hand mannequin shop and Ann Summers (a sex shop). Those works are a marriage between things that don't physically belong together but, mentally, stem from the same place. The idea of a mannequin is that it shows off clothes to its best ability, therefore it has to be attractive, and therefore sex is involved in some way. So, to have mannequins of little children …'[10] In 2003 came *Death*, a grotesque coupling of two blow-up dolls lying on a blue pool mattress on the gallery floor engaged in sexual intercourse. Apparently made of garishly coloured plastic, the work was actually made of bronze.

Today's artists want to deal with the contemporary tolerance of the sexual and violent in daily life, in cinema, and on TV as well as in the lap-dancing and strip clubs that can be found in even the smallest towns. The expression of personal opinions and the resulting creation of images that can be very hard to look at present problems. They can provoke outrage in the public sphere and for the individual gallery-goer a very private embarrassment.

Public outrage is expressed through shrieks of horror in the media and entails the risk of prosecution. When artists use the nude in these extreme ways, controversy follows. A group of legal demons – 'obscenity', 'pornography', 'outrage to public decency' – prowl the museums and galleries of every country, licking their lips for prey. You could say that risking prosecution is an occupational hazard for artists who 'go to extremes'.

Marlene Dumas is aware of the hazards in her choice of strippers as a subject. 'At the moment my art is situated between the pornographic tendency to reveal everything and the erotic inclination to hide what it's all about,' she said in 2007.[11] 'The aim is to "reveal", not to display. It is the discourse of the lover. I am intimately involved with my subject matter … I am not disengaged from the subject of my gaze.'[12] Her work is very near the edge of acceptability. Admiring painter Alex Katz is reported to have said at her show at New York's Museum of Modern Art in 2008: 'There is a lot of explicit stuff that I wouldn't have the nerve to do.'[13]

Dumas's defence operates on two fronts. She aims to arouse empathy in the viewer for her subjects. And she transmutes her subject matter into art. She makes it clear that far from straightforward realism, with its pretence that there is nothing between the viewer and the subject, she, the artist, is the medium through which the subject matter has passed. However shocking her painting, say, of a stripper revealing the most intimate parts of her anatomy, it is the bruising colour and brilliant manner of the painting that you see first; and it is this artistic skill that makes her a deeply respected contemporary painter.

Like Dumas, most artists manage to outwit the law. Their defence works because the legal definition of pornography is as difficult to pin down as a confidence trickster. Not only does it vary from country to country, but the definition can seem absurdly subjective. In Canada, for example, pornography is defined as the portrayal of acts purely for sexual arousal, while in Britain there is no agreed legal definition at all. Furthermore, terms like obscenity or pornography are not static. What one decade views as obscenity, another may see as art – as the British legal verdict on D.H. Lawrence's *Lady Chatterley's Lover* showed in 1962, when a judge declared it no longer obscene and free to be read by all.

Given the amount of noise works of art arouse in the media, it is surprising how much outspoken art gets past the censors. Even when the police are brought in, the outrage usually evaporates like the cloud that follows an explosion. The difficulty of proving transgression of the law, combined with such mitigating factors as intention, context and increased public tolerance, tends to mean that few of the artists are prosecuted and some probably benefit from the publicity.

Spencer Tunick was arrested several times in the United States early in his career because, he has said, there were no precedents for his kind of work with artistically arranged naked bodies. He convinced the courts with his defence that they represented a way for people to connect with each other's humanity, to warm up anonymous public spaces and to replace the contemporary tendency to see the human body in terms of violence and sex with something more humanitarian. The court decided not only that were no laws being broken, but also that Tunick was protected within his First Amendment rights of freedom of expression. All charges

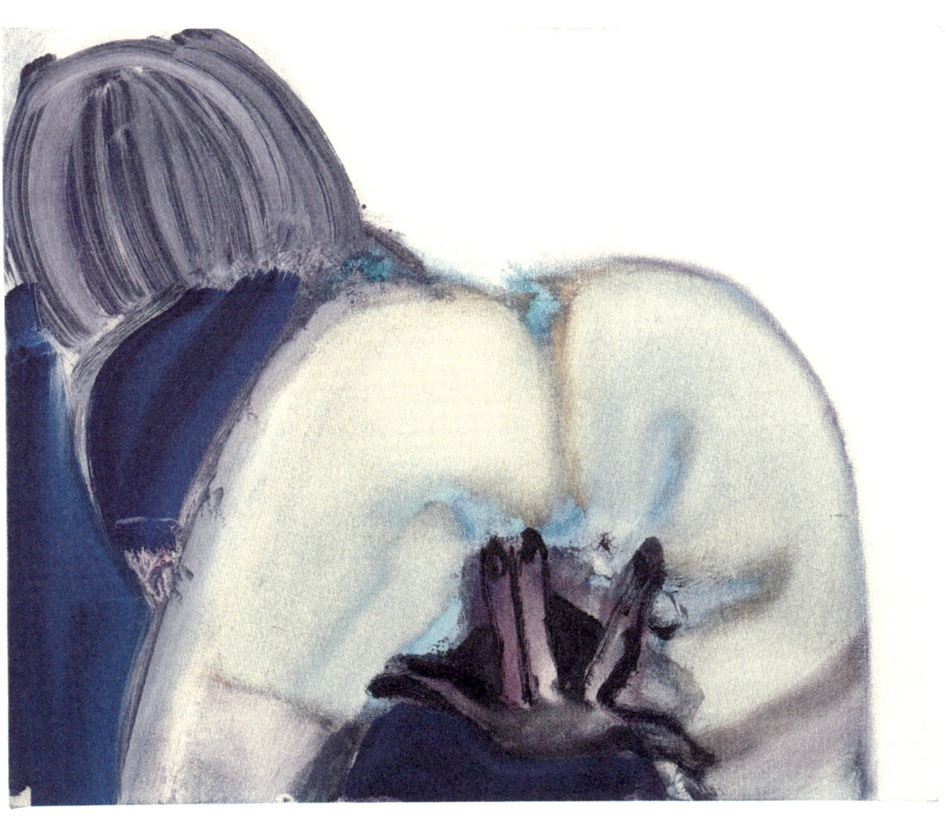

Marlene Dumas, *Fingers*, 1999, oil on canvas. Dumas's subtle colours,
striking composition and style of drawing with her paintbrush transmute
this outspoken image of a stripper into a work of beauty.

were dropped, an outcome more frequent in such cases than one might expect if one were to judge only by the initial shouts of shock reported in the media.

On the whole, nudity comes off lightly. It is religion, the wilder shores of sexuality, violence and children that cause offence today. Robert Mapplethorpe's combination of violence and homosexual sexuality in his images of gay men is a visual step too far for many. Art that does not treat religion with deference can get the exhibiting institutions into trouble. This was the case in 1987 with Andres Serrano's *Piss Christ*, a photograph of a crucifix immersed in the artist's urine; in 1999 with Chris Ofili's *The Holy Virgin Mary* incorporating elephant dung and images of genitals, which outraged New York mayor Rudy Giuliani; and in 2010 when the Smithsonian decided to remove David Wojnarowicz's *A Fire in My Belly* from an exhibition due to a short clip depicting a crucifix covered in ants.

While lawyers try to pin down the ever-shifting definitions of 'indecent', 'pornographic' and 'obscene', there is greater clarity about the unacceptability of displaying images of naked children. For one thing, a legal definition of a child exists and for another children are in the legal care of adults. We expect the adults, which in these cases means the artists, the viewers or the gallery owners, to protect the children who cannot speak for themselves and who, when they reach maturity, might be horrified about the way they had been represented. These days the police appear with increasing frequency when photographs of naked children are exhibited on gallery walls. In Britain, the Protection of Children Act 1978 makes it an offence to possess and display indecent photographs of a child under sixteen. The removal of children's naked photographs from the country's galleries accounts for most of the police action in connection with the exhibition of art in the last ten years.

The 'Pop Life' exhibition held at Tate Modern, London, in 2009 contained some openly sexual and violent works of art, including Jeff Koons's *Ilona's Asshole*, a close-up silkscreen of the subject plus a penis entering a vagina, but it was Richard Prince's reworking of a 1970 *Playboy* photo of a sexualized nude Brooke Shields, made when the actor was ten years old, that drew a visit from the police. Titled *Spiritual America*, and made in 1983, it appeared in the catalogue as an empty gold frame with a grey square in the centre on which were the words: 'This image has been obscured on legal advice.'

Sexual suggestiveness involving children is the one area today where most people's tolerance breaks down and where they willingly support the police in carrying out their duty. How would today's audience react if Mary Cassatt's *Little Girl in a Blue Armchair* painted in 1878 were to appear on the walls of a contemporary portrait exhibition? To our less-than-innocent eyes, the pose of the little girl seems disturbingly sexualized, an aspect that is ignored in the art-historical literature about it.

The artists who 'go to extremes' want to reach us. They want to make us think again by shaking us out of our comfortable attitudes. They understand that in the empty white spaces of a modern gallery, the spectator is a sort of prisoner who has nowhere else to look.

Though the Chapman Brothers refuse to claim any element of morality for their art, they admit to a drive to break through the complacent, closed circle of the gallery and its visitors. They want their art to be uncomfortable but say 'shock is the wrong response to art'. Laughter, they feel, is a better response 'because it breaks through language and morality'.[14] They have a point. All of us have a protective filter of some kind when faced with shocking imagery. It may be horror or it may be worldly-wise dismissal. The Chapmans would rather their references to body-part grafts or childhood sexuality be met with bemused stares and nervous giggles than with cool acceptance, because that would show that awkward questions are forming and seeds of doubt are being planted.

Gilbert & George are another couple who want to make us feel uncomfortable. They exploit our comfort in looking at conventional nudes and our discomfort at looking at men, particularly two men together with ageing bodies like their own. 'We use the male,' Gilbert said in 1987, 'because the image is not so used up. A woman is immediately seen as a sex symbol. We are the first artists to tip the balance.'[15] They went open-eyed into their decision to use their own naked bodies in their work. It was a strategy informed by their knowledge of the role of the nude in past centuries.

In a discussion with the sexologist Shere Hite, they explain how they deny the audience the safety net of conventional artistic nudity: 'If it's something from central Africa or something from Florence from the 15th century, it's much easier then. But if it's living art saying that, that's already something different ... If it's actual and truthful, then it's much more complicated to view it.'[16]

This desire to break through our defences is what poses problems for the spectator. Art like this forces viewers to realize the absence of a code of etiquette for looking at sexually explicit works of art in public in a contemporary art gallery. Ideal nudes destined for public viewing are traditionally 'clothed' in the heroic identities of Mars or Venus, their genitals expunged, their pubic hair at most suggested and their activities above reproach. Occasionally classically endorsed sexual activity may be alluded to, as in the cloud enveloping Io, actually Jupiter in disguise, but so tactfully imagined and intellectually sanctioned by the mythology familiar to

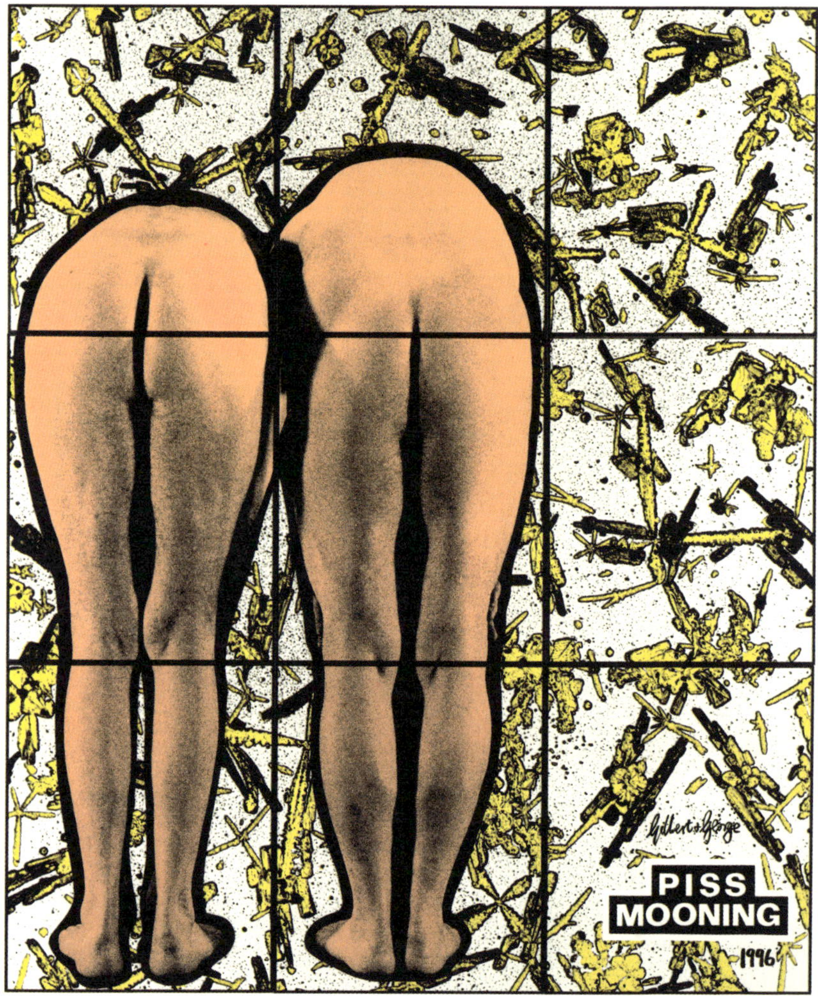

Gilbert & George, *Piss Mooning*, 1996, mixed media. Centuries of veneration of the handsome male nude body in painting and sculpture gives power to *Piss Mooning*, in which Gilbert & George offer their unidealized backsides to viewers against a background of urine magnified through a microscope.

the educationally and artistically initiated that no one need call for the smelling salts. The transformation from sexual misdeeds to elevated art gives Jupiter and Io a respectability that makes them a suitable sight for either sex.

As Gilbert & George discuss their divergence from the classic nudes of the past, their goal becomes clearer: 'People who talk about the nakedness in our pictures could pass without batting an eyelid at a marble naked, a bronze naked, a water-colour naked, but when you see ours it's a totally different experience.'[17] Discussing a critic's response to the *Naked Shit Pictures*:

George: 'It was very interesting that David Sylvester, having seen these pictures, said something which we hadn't realized entirely. He said that all of the modern artists tried to do pictures and only succeeded in doing nudes, which they were very unhappy about, but that we have done naked.

Gilbert: Because the pin-up magazine is not naked, it is a sexual stimulant. It is different.

George: We believe that if you look at pin-up magazines you are looking at those models, you are looking at that material. We believe that people looking at our pictures where we are naked are looking at their own nakedness as well. It's not just us. They realize their own nakedness under their clothes at that moment. In that way the pictures are as much about the viewer as about us really.[18]

Sexually explicit art has always existed, but the cameos, prints and drawings of past centuries that showed the sexual act in all its variety were treated differently from the public nudity which merely flirted with the subject. These sexually explicit works were housed in secret rooms and cabinets, to be brought out for the delectation and entertainment of the owner and his, one imagines mostly male, friends.

This division between the two viewing conventions, one private, the other public, was made very clear at an exhibition called 'Seduced' at London's Barbican Art Gallery in 2007–8, an assembly of objects, prints, film, paintings and draw-ings from antiquity to the present 'concerned with the depictions of the sexual act – whether before, during or after'.[19] Much of the work on display from past centuries was designed to be viewed in private: tiny carvings and cameos intended solely for the sight and handling of the owner and his circle, graphics you had to peer at to see what was going on, folios of explicit Japanese prints of courtesans and their lovers. All were intended to be viewed in places where one's reactions could remain unseen. The modern section of the show was equally explicit with the difference that these works were much bigger and made for public exhibition. Robert Mapplethorpe was there, of course, as was Jeff Koons penetrating Ilona. *Requiem*, a thirty-minute video by k r buxey fixed on the artist's face as someone or something unseen brought her to orgasm.

This public display of sexual subject matter, not just the objects designed for private viewing but some of the modern works as well, brought home to me the problem of embarrassment. I found the whole show a nightmare to go round. I realized within the first minutes that I had no way of behaving in this context. If I sneaked (the only word for my desire to be invisible) into a dark booth to see an excerpt from a film with sexual content, included because it had been made by an artist, I felt, as a woman with behaviour learned in my good-girl youth, like a man in a grubby mackintosh, my only point of reference for looking at such things. If I went up close to inspect a tiny print, which had been put on the wall for just that purpose, I felt embarrassed by displaying my curiosity in public. Faced by Jeff Koons's giant portraits of himself and his wife in poses that would shame a sex manual, I analysed the imagery in art-historical terms while feeling great discomfort. Neither as a woman nor as a museum visitor had I any learned behaviour for looking at work that flouted the conventions of public nudity. Refusal to capitulate to what I understood was only a conventional and learned response made me go round the show, but I felt self-conscious. It made me realize what a triumph was the creation of the fine-art category of the nude. It removed any taint of pornography; it only occasionally, and most tactfully, touched on the erotic; and it presented the viewer with a subject which could be viewed in public without embarrassment.

The new nudity shows how the boundaries between public and private are crumbling inside the galleries of contemporary art. A proportion of today's art is so shocking that it demands all the viewers' strength to hold on to their appreciation of it as art over their unease about its content. It can lead to the absurd situation in which a Mapplethorpe print of a leather-clad man with objects protruding from his most intimate areas is discussed only in terms of its clarity and tonal values. At one level it should be, given Mapplethorpe's fine technique; but such analysis ignores the fact that at another level he was a photographer who chose to deploy his skill on a certain sort of previously private subject matter that he wanted to bring to our attention. In his metaphor in *The Nude*, Clark concludes that art can hold a great deal of the erotic suspended in solution. Can it be that this balance is changing as the nude becomes the naked? Or will art once more rise to the occasion and absorb the contradiction between outrageous content and our clinging feeling that art should exist above the everyday?

Artists who deal with the extreme like to complicate our certainties. They ignore the barriers of good taste and have the courage to tackle all the issues of our day from pornography to gender reassignment. I do not believe they present extreme images because, as the cynics suggest, they want the publicity. They do it because they are not convinced by the comforting stories we all tell ourselves. Their curiosity about humanity in all its naked variety sensitizes viewers to the commonly held attitudes of our time and sometimes suggests alternative ways to think about them.

Mainstream entertainment goes as far as it dares, but even when dealing with bodily functions and malfunctions or the cruder kind of extrovert sexuality, it tends to sensationalize or medicalize. Unlike art, it is not in the business of encouraging doubts and thoughts. Artists who deal with the body bring humanity back to art. It might seem old fashioned to use the word humanity in a science-dominated world, in which the Marxist theory of false consciousness still has a grip and the idea of a thinking 'self' is seen as naive and theorized into oblivion. And yet we do feel and think and see and react on the basis of our bodies and our experience. We may not have control of the world but we live in it, as do the artists in this book, and it is this shared experience that makes their insights so important.

It is often said that art today is opaque and only comprehensible to those who already speak the language. But the artists who take the body as their subject involve us all by offering a way out of contemporary art's tendency to speak only to the converted. It may be bewildering or uncomfortable, but their use of the body offers the viewer a point of contact. By using an imagery with which we can all identify, artists extend the spectator a hand in to the art they have created. By replacing the ideal nude with the naked nude, recycling it for our times, they have brought the heart back to art, the blood into its arteries and ideas back into its brain.

POSTSCRIPT:
TEN YEARS LATER

THE ADJECTIVES USED TO DESCRIBE an exhibition of nudes in 1956, the year Kenneth Clark's *The Nude* was published, and one today, have nothing in common with each other. Ideal, classical, realistic and beautiful have been replaced with surprising, sexual, raw and shocking. The trend from ideal nude, so brilliantly explained by Clark as the body re-formed for art, to the naked nude we see on gallery walls today has grown into a subject, which, sleeves rolled up, is ready to take on the newest issues of our times. In the years since I wrote this book, the naked nude has continued to expand its scope. Queer, trans and non-binary artists have begun to come to the fore, presenting us with images and bodies that defy traditional gender categories, while artists of colour use a range of strategies to disrupt Western-centric histories of art and challenge conventional white appropriations of the black body as hyper-sexualized or exoticized.

The nude was never solely owned by art. It is a contested subject, one that is also claimed by medicine, by sexual studies, by gender studies, by ethnography, by pornography. But for centuries these other meanings were not allowed to set foot in fine art. Through an elaborate set of arguments that demand the credulity of the spectators admiring the emperor's new clothes, the educated art lover was convinced that the ideal nude was elevated above the everyday, a belief that legitimized a woman with no clothes on to be viewed by men, women and children as something pure, artistic, even improving. Somehow the gate-keepers to art – the art schools and national academies, the theoreticians, the galleries and museums – had turned the naked body into something devoid of any reminder of its disturbing animal elements.

I can see as I look back that the ghost of Clark, or at least his formulation of the nude as a construct made for art, as opposed to the naked, which is the basic body – or as I think of it, the body as it looks, wrinkled and mottled, when you get out of a hot bath – has haunted this book. Clark had no idea in 1956 that an unidealized nude resulting from modern ideas and attitudes was prowling hungrily

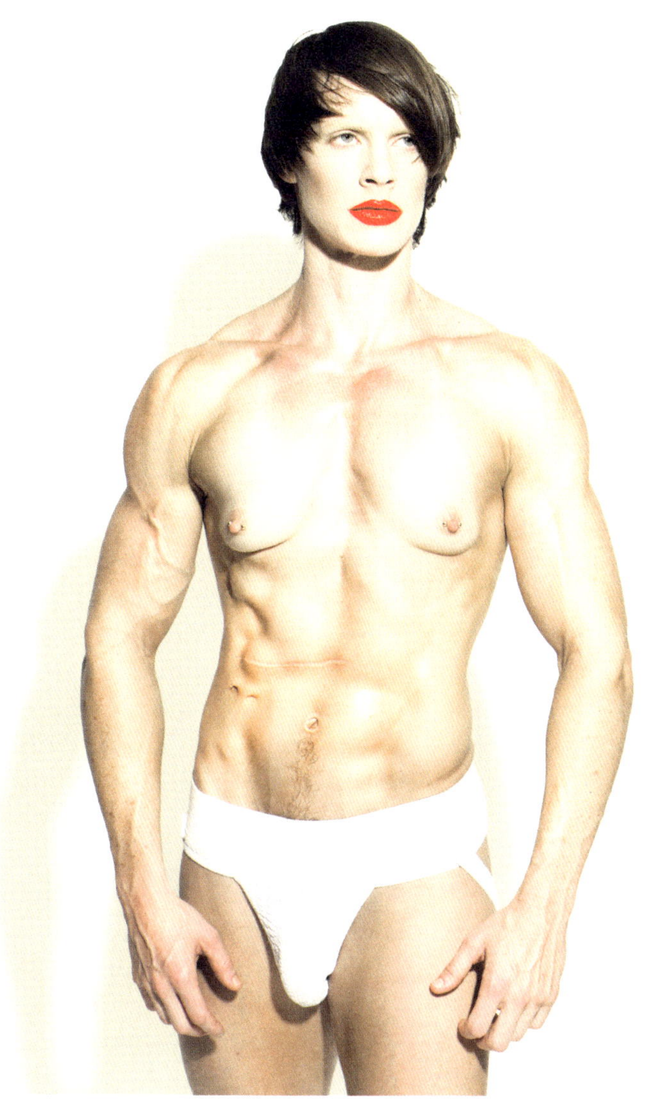

Cassils, *Advertisement: Homage to Benglis*, 2011, archival pigment print.
Cassils and their collaborator, the photographer and make-up artist Robin Black,
distributed this image to gay fashion and art publications, rather than paying for
a slot in *Artforum* as Lynda Benglis did (see page 75).

around his images of perfection. Of course, the entrance of the new naked nudes into our books and galleries has not destroyed the ideal nudes. These still exist, like flower pieces or landscapes, as a category of art history, alongside Clark's way of viewing them.

It is possible now to look at an artwork such as Titian's *Venus of Urbino* or Manet's *Olympia* (page 120), which intentionally rivalled it, and discuss the subject intellectually and aesthetically – at a step removed from the work's erotic overtones. When these two paintings were brought together for the first time in Florence, I stood behind a glamorous Italian family who were carefully going through the time-honoured process of compare and contrast familiar to all students of art history. We looked at the little dog in the Titian, an image of fidelity, and at the cat, an image of lasciviousness, in the Manet. We compared the skill with which the respective bed sheets were painted – white fabric being a challenge for any artist – and we noted that Titian's nude reclined whereas Manet's sat alert and upright on her couch.

It is difficult to imagine the same conversation being had regarding Marlene Dumas's *Fingers* (page 191). Like Manet and Titian, Dumas painted women who remove their clothes for a living, but whereas theirs fit into an art-historical category of the reclining nude, Dumas represents her nude, based on a pornographic image, in a manner not fit for the art of previous centuries. It is easy to forget, however, that Manet's *Olympia* was just as shocking in its time. The viewers it scandalized knew it was a real woman, the model Victorine Meurent, who looked brazenly out at us 'dressed' in nothing but jewelry and tiny heel-less slippers as she awaits the client who is preceded by the bouquet.

Although Manet's *Olympia* is daring in its depiction of a courtesan, a century and a half have added a tasteful gloss to the image, and rubbed off the raw edges of realism that so shocked contemporary viewers. Despite Manet's modernity, to our eyes 150 years later, it remains closer to the reclining nude of centuries-old tradition than to the outspokenness of today's images. It is Manet's relationship to this tradition – for he was, after all, consciously updating the earlier work – that qualifies it for its place in the line of ideal nudes and turns the story behind it into 'history' not scandal.

Another feature of this tradition – the history of the nude as described by Clark – is that it represents a more-or-less linear progression from ancient Greek sculpture, through the Renaissance, to the works of the great, European, modernists. In 2021 the British-Nigerian artist Yinka Shonibare staged a black takeover of one of the great male nude sculptures of Western culture, Donatello's bronze

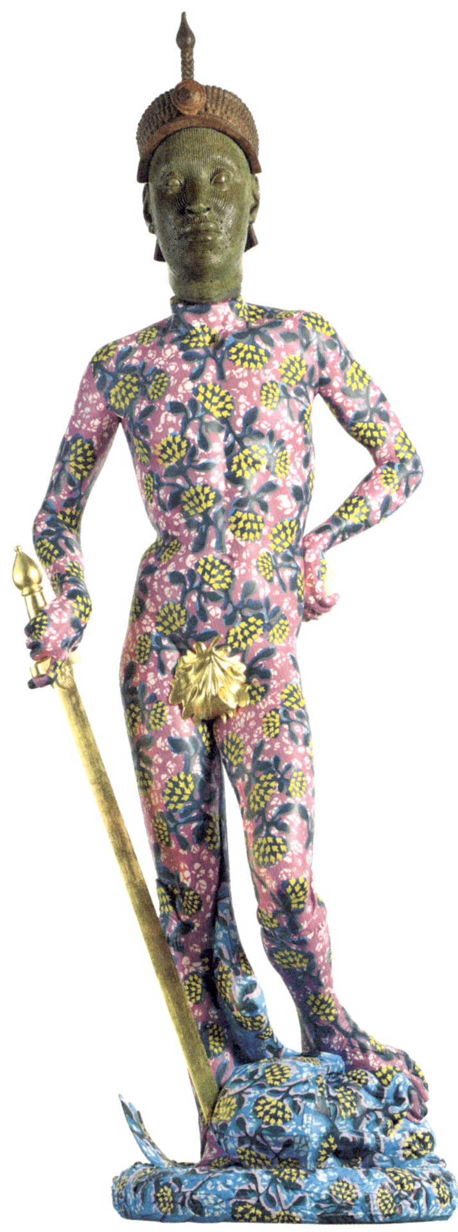

Yinka Shonibare, *Unintended Sculpture*, fibreglass sculpture, 2021. The Ife Head Shonibare
chose to sit atop his replica of David is currently held by the British Museum. The discovery of heads
such as this by the German archaeologist Leo Frobenius shook Eurocentric ideas about Western
supremacy in art, causing Frobenius to claim that he had in fact discovered evidence of ancient
Greek migrants in Africa – distributed as evidence of Plato's Atlantis by news outlets in 1911.

David, made in late 1440s Florence to stand in the Medici Palace courtyard. In *Unintended Sculpture*, Shonibare recreated Donatello's masterpiece and covered it with a swirling multi-coloured *batik* pattern. Then he replaced its rather effeminate head with an imposing replica of one of the Heads of Ife, Yoruba sculptures made around the same time as Donatello was creating *David*. The result presents the viewer with a thought-provoking consideration of a great artistic African culture through a bold reinvention of a Western artistic icon: one culture inhabits another.

In the decade since the publication of this book queer politics, and transgender politics in particular, have entered the mainstream. The depictions of trans people by Jenny Saville and Marc Quinn – shocking to many in the 1990s and early 2000s – have lost much of their edge, as trans people have begun to occupy a hyper-visible role in the media. The categories of male and female have been joined by a variety of other genders, some of which have begun to be legally recognized across the world, while some artists and activists aim to abolish the very notion of gender. The vocabulary that has developed to describe this ever-evolving landscape, from now well-established terms such as 'cis' and 'trans' to the increasingly widely used singular pronoun 'they', has made an undeniable impact on modern life and societal expectations around gender.

These linguistic developments, driven by years of trans activism and accompanied by fierce debates on trans issues, have been mirrored by a shift in the visual languages that artists use, inevitably posing a challenge to traditional depictions of the nude. In 1999, interested in what she called the state of in-betweenness, Jenny Saville painted *Matrix* (page 110), a portrait of Del LaGrace Volcano. Fifteen years later, in *INTER*me*, Volcano investigated the way photographs of intersex bodies taken by sexologists such as Magnus Hirschfeld functioned to regulate gender. Rather than medicalizing the non-conventional body, Volcano's work aims to challenge traditional categories of sex and gender through the medium of self-portraiture.

This desire to use art to celebrate the body while simultaneously challenging the preconceptions of the viewer is common to many transgender and non-binary artists. In 2011, with a nod to Eleanor Antin's *Carving: A Traditional Sculpture* of 1972 (page 79), the multi-disciplinary artist Cassils produced a six-month durational performance series entitled *Cuts: A Traditional Sculpture*. Cassils is a transgender artist for whom performance is a form of social sculpture, and in *Cuts* they showed their mastery of bodybuilding and nutrition to gain 23 pounds (10.5 kg) of muscle over 23 weeks; a powerful inversion of Antin's commentary on femininity and weight loss. In *Advertisement: Homage to Benglis*, Cassils used their physique, honed during *Cuts*, as a substitute for the double-ended phallus in Lynda Benglis's *Artforum* advertisement (page 75). Just as Manet referred his new type of modern nude back to Titian, one of the greatest painters of female nudes in history, it is fascinating to see these trans and non-binary artists linking their subject matter to their art-historical and feminist predecessors.

It is of particular importance to this book that the body plays so central a part in the work of these artists. When so many are interested in changing the way their bodies are perceived and interpreted, it is hardly surprising that so many choose to use their own bodies to make their points in a kind of extended self-portraiture. In 2015 Juliana Huxtable depicted herself naked in *Untitled in the Rage (Niburu Cataclysm)*; an image that at first seems pure pin-up, albeit a pin-up designed through an afrofuturist lens. Huxtable's purpose was to celebrate her body – the body of a black, intersex, trans woman – while at the same time forcing viewers to examine their attitudes towards gender, blackness and overtly queer sexuality.

The photographer Zanele Muholi, who has risen to global prominence over the last decade with their stunning portraits of queer people in South Africa, sces themself as a visual activist rather than an artist. Although homosexuality is not outlawed – South Africa is the only African country to have legalized same-sex marriage – lesbians, particularly black lesbians, are targeted there for 'corrective rape', a phrase that glosses over the often murderous intent of its practitioners. It was Muholi's agenda in a series of photographs made for a magazine focused on LGBTI issues to counter the view of lesbians as deviant by presenting them in images of beauty and dignity. *Caitlin and I*, 2009, is an extraordinary image of racial harmony and gender difference, beautifully lit and totally original, by a photographer whose intimate relationships with those they depict has sensitized them to the situations of those the state ignores or bullies. The couple face the camera as a unit, meeting the gaze of the viewer with a calm confidence. With echoes of Mapplethorpe's provocative and formally beautiful images of gay men, Muholi offers an image that does not only dazzle aesthetically, but also radiates trust and acceptance of difference as they and Caitlin literally lay their bodies on the line.

Meanwhile, the traditional ideal nude shows it still has blood in its veins. A decade ago, I referred to its new and perhaps final home in photography, but now it is clear that it has found an even newer one in social media. The nude selfie, taken above all by women with a smartphone in the privacy of their bedrooms,

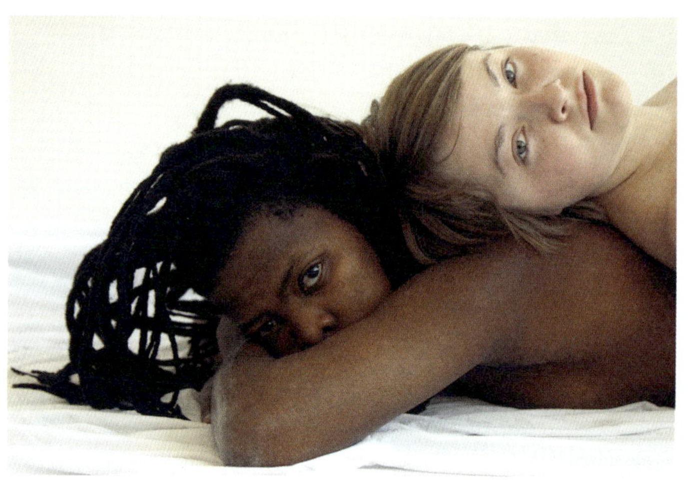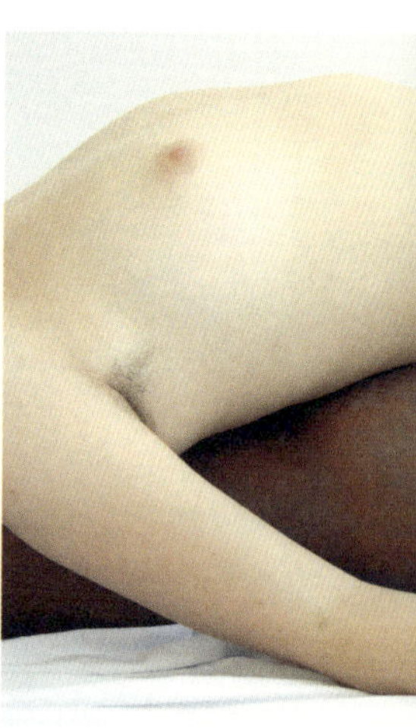

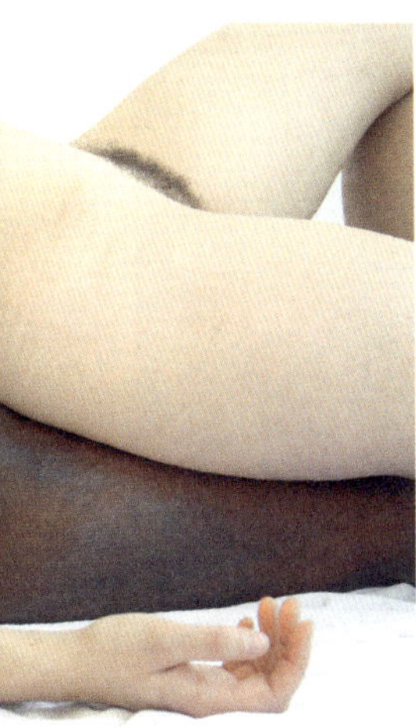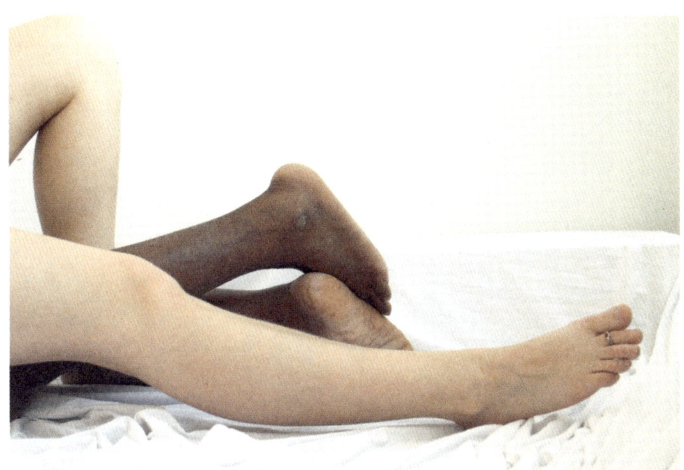

Zanele Muholi, *Caitlin and I*, 2009, C-print. As with the work of Cassils, Muholi's intimate portraits of queer South Africans were printed in a magazine focused on LGBTI issues. Their aim is to displace the negative stigma around queer identity, rewriting 'a black queer and trans visual history of South Africa for the world to know of our resistance and existence'.[1]

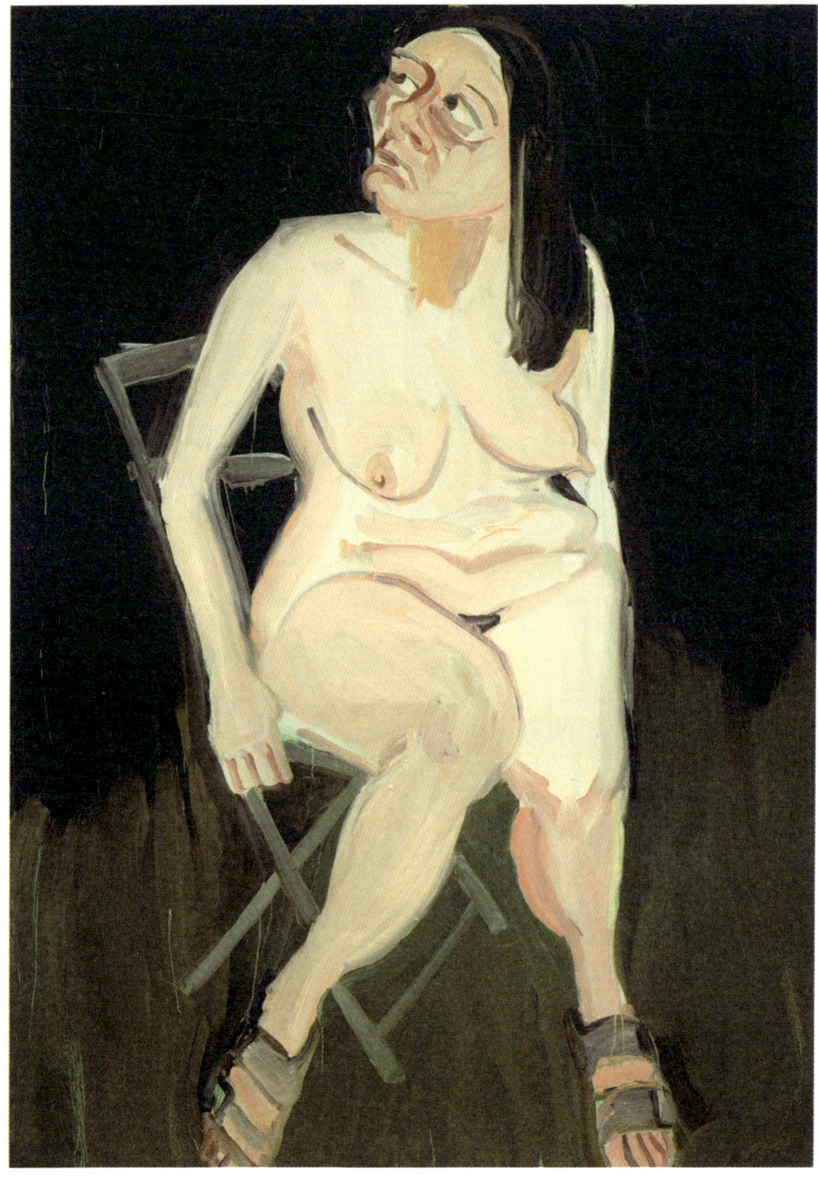

Chantal Joffe, *Self-Portrait in the Garden at Night*, 2016, oil on board. Joffe presents the opposite of a selfie in this unfiltered mid-life image of herself, looking off into the distance.

has generated much excited chatter in the art world – is the selfie the art form of our times? – as well as serious concern over the fact that it is often teens who are taking the photographs.

Looked at from the perspective of this book, you could argue that the nude selfie represents the democratization of the ideal nude, above all in its self-conscious glamorization. The words the critic John Berger wrote in 1972 about women in *Ways of Seeing* have taken on a whole new relevance: 'Whilst she is walking across a room or whilst she is weeping at the death of her father, she can scarcely avoid envisaging herself walking or weeping. … Her own sense of being in herself is supplanted by a sense of being appreciated as herself by another. … The surveyor of woman in herself is male: the surveyed female. Thus she turns herself into an object – and most particularly an object of vision: a sight.'[2] He was talking about the ideal nude in art, but his words apply to the takers of today's nude selfies. They present themselves with all the artifice and skills that a trained artist brings to the traditional nude, managing the lighting and finding the artful pose that hides the defects and exaggerates the good points. They are 'dressed' for nudity, as the ideal nude has always been, with perfect breasts, well-chosen jewelry, judicious depilation and a graceful pose. And it is there, on social media, that we leave her, the descendent of all those glorious nudes who decorate the walls of the world's greatest galleries.

Meanwhile contemporary artists get on with the job of reinterpreting the nude, raising issues, picturing the taboo, and facing us with the raw honesty of their work, as Chantal Joffe does in her semi-naked self-portraits of her middle-aged body. Dedicated to telling the truth of what she sees and feels, the bold brush strokes and lack of glamour of Joffe's self-presentations bear no relationship either to Kenneth Clark's ideal nude of the past or to the sucked-in stomachs and blow-dried hair of today's selfies. Today there is still no comfortable way to view the new naked nude, particularly as artists continue to produce new variations on the theme. It is as if we spectators are at the frontier of something new with no agreed way of dealing with it. Now that the veil of agreed and accepted poses has been removed, visitors to art galleries have no protection against what they may find shocking or unacceptable. Perhaps time will do its job, as it has with the Manet, and neutralize the shock. But maybe it won't, since today's artists seem so set on making a break with the past as a strategy to open our eyes to difficult issues.

NOTES

Introduction
THE RECYCLED NUDE
1   Kenneth Clark, *The Nude: A Study in Ideal Form*, London, 1956, p. 1.
2   Ibid.

Chapter 1
THE NUDE: ITS LIFE, DEATH AND RESURRECTION
1   Clark, p. 357.
2   Frances Borzello, *The Artist's Model*, London, 1982; new ed. 2010, p. 123.
3   Clark, p. 6.
4   Ibid.
5   It began to change after that, with – as just one example – the founding of the New York Academy of Art in 1982 to provide instruction in the lost art of rigorous figure drawing. Thanks to Dr Gregory Gilbert, Knox College, Galesburg, Illinois, for contributing this.
6   In conversation with the author, 2010.
7   Carl Goldstein, *Teaching Art: Academies and Schools from Vasari to Albers*, Cambridge, 1996, p. 280.
8   Howard Singerman, *Art Subjects: Making Artists in the American University*, Berkeley and Los Angeles, 1999, p. 127.
9   Ministry of Education, Examination in Art, Form 707 F. E. (1951).
10   First Report of the National Advisory Council on Art Education, known as the Coldstream Report, after its chairman, Sir William Coldstream. In case there was anyone who had not got the message, the Second Report of the National Council for Diplomas in Art Design, 1970, stated: 'The Council wishes to emphasize that it has never assumed a rigid or doctrinaire attitude as regards course development. On the contrary it would expect to find all course programmes flexible and capable of progressive modification within whatever terms of reference are established from time to time.'
11   In conversation with the author.
12   Hester R. Westley, 'Tradition and Transition: St Martin's Sculpture Department 1960–1979', PhD thesis, University of London (Courtauld Institute of Art), 2007, 2 vols, vol. 1, p. 68.

Chapter 2
BODY ART: THE JOURNEY INTO NAKEDNESS
1   Theodore Tucker (pseud. Allan Kaprow), 'Allan Kaprow's "Apple Shrine"', in *Village Voice*, 12 January 1961, p. 7.
2   Allan Kaprow, 'The Legacy of Jackson Pollock', in *ARTnews* 57:6 (1958); repr. in Kaprow, *Essays on the Blurring of Life and Art*, Berkeley and London, 1993.
3   Ira Licht, *Bodyworks*, exh. cat. Museum of Contemporary Art, Chicago, 1975.
4   *Marina Abramović: The Artist is Present*, exh. cat. Museum of Modern Art, New York, 2010, p. 17.
5   Stuart Jeffries, 'Orlan's Art of Sex and Surgery', Guardian.co.uk, 1 July 2009.
6   John Berger, *Ways of Seeing*, London, 1972, p. 47.
7   Laura Mulvey, 'Visual Pleasure and Narrative Cinema', in *Screen* (Autumn 1975), pp. 6–18.

Chapter 3
THE CHANGING ROOM: FEMALE PERSPECTIVES
1   Berger, pp. 63–4.
2   Linda Nochlin, 'Why Have There Been No Great Women Artists?', in *ARTnews* (1971), pp. 22–39, 67–71.
3   Nancy Spero, 'Woman as Protagonist'; repr. in K. Stiles and P. Selz, eds, *Theories and Documents of Contemporary Art*, Berkeley, 1996, p. 246.
4   *Hannah Wilke: A Retrospective*, exh. cat. University of Missouri Press, Columbia, 1989.
5   Sarah Kent, 'The Erotic Male Nude', in Sarah Kent and Jacqueline Morreau, eds, *Women's Images of Men*, London, 1985, pp. 75–104.
6   Mark C. Taylor, Amanda Sharp and Matthew Higgs,

PressPLAY: Contemporary Artists in Conversation, London, 2005, p. 521.

7   Ibid., p. 522.
8   Andrew Pulver, 'Elinor Carucci's Best Shot', in *The Guardian*, 21 January 2010, G2, p. 23.
9   Anthony Vidler, et al., *Antony Gormley: Blind Light*, exh. cat. Hayward Gallery, London, 2007, p. 42.
10 'Gormley and Gombrich in Conversation', *Prospect* (August/September 1996), p. 59; repr. in *PressPLAY: Contemporary Artists in Conversation*, pp. 229–42.

Chapter 4
FORGIVE ME, I'M A PAINTER

1   Mildred Glimcher, ed., *Willem de Kooning – Jean Dubuffet: The Women*, exh. cat. Pace Gallery, New York, 1990, p. 8.
2   *ARTnews* 61:4 (Summer 1962), p. 39, quoted in Jerome Viola, *The Painting and Teaching of Philip Pearlstein*, New York, 1982, p. 24.
3   Robert Storr, *Philip Pearlstein Since 1983*, New York, 2002, p. 29.
4   Patricia Sheridan, *Pittsburgh Post-Gazette*, 18 June 2007.
5   William Feaver, *Lucian Freud*, exh. cat. Tate Britain, London, 2002, p. 41.
6   Ibid., p. 45.
7   Ibid., p. 41.
8   Martin Gayford, *Man with a Blue Scarf: On Sitting for a Portrait by Lucian Freud*, London, 2010, p. 208. Refers to Lucian Freud's article 'Some Thoughts on Painting', in *Encounter* 3:1 (July 1954), p. 23.
9   Gayford, p. 72.
10 Slim Stealingworth (pseud. Tom Wesselmann), *Tom Wesselmann*, New York, 1980, p. 15.
11 Ibid., p. 23.
12 Arthur C. Danto, Robert Enright and Steve Martin, *Eric Fischl 1970–2007*, New York, 2008, p. 40.
13 Dominic van den Boogerd, et al., *Marlene Dumas*, London, 1999, p. 8.
14 Ibid., p. 21.
15 Lisa Gabrielle Mark, ed., *Marlene Dumas: Measuring Your Own Grave*, exh. cat. D. A. P./Museum of Contemporary Art, Los Angeles, 2008, p. 211.
16 Mark Vallen, 'Eric Fischl and the "Death of Painting"', 20 April 2006, Mark Vallen's Art for a Change blog, http://art-for-a-change.com/blog/2006/4.
17 Simon Schama, et al., *Jenny Saville*, New York, 2005, p. 128.
18 Suzie Mackenzie, 'Under the Skin', in *The Guardian*, 22 October 2005, Weekend, p. 38.
19 In conversation with the author.
20 Schama, p. 126.
21 Mackenzie, 'Under the Skin'.
22 *Jenny Saville*, exh. cat. Museo d'Arte Contemporanea, Rome, 2005, p. 93.
23 Zefrey Throwell, interview with Cecily Brown, Frank Prattle Show, 8 January 2009.
24 Gaby Wood, 'Cecily Brown: I Like the Cheap and Nasty', in *Observer*, 12 June 2005.
25 Dore Ashton, et al., *Cecily Brown*, New York, 2008, p. 26.
26 www.interviewmagazine.com/art/john-currin.
27 *John Currin*, exh. cat. Museum of Contemporary Art, Chicago, 2003, p. 83.

Chapter 5
THE NAKED PORTRAIT

1   Elisabeth Vigée-Le Brun, *The Memoirs of Elisabeth Vigée-Le Brun*, London, 1989, p. 28.
2   John Hayes, ed., *Thomas Gainsborough*, exh. cat. Tate, London, 1980, p. 108.
3   Vigée-Le Brun, pp. 354–5.
4   Clark, pp. 300–334
5   Feaver, p. 44.
6   Berger, p. 64.
7   Patricia Hills, *Alice Neel*, New York, 1993, p. 49.
8   Phoebe Hoban, 'Portraits: Alice Neel's Legacy of Realism', in *The New York Times*, 22 April 2010.
9   Danto, Enright and Martin, p. 116.
10 Ibid., p. 30.
11 Hoban, 'Portraits: Alice Neel's Legacy of Realism', *New York Times*.
12 Robin Knight, 'Portrait of Perfection', in *BP Magazine*, 3, 2006, p. 34.

Chapter 6
AFTER RODIN, IS THERE ANYTHING LEFT TO SAY?

1 Joachim Pissarro, *Marc Quinn: Allanah, Buck, Catman, Chelsea, Michael, Pamela and Thomas*, exh. cat. White Cube, London, 2010, p. 102.
2 'Gormley and Gombrich in Conversation', *Prospect*, 1996; reprinted in *PressPLAY: Contemporary Artists in Conversation*, London, 2005, pp. 229–42.
3 Ibid., p. 59.
4 Ibid., p. 57.
5 Vidler, et al., *Antony Gormley: Blind Light*, pp. 43, 44.
6 Antony Gormley, 'The Iron Men', *Guardian*, 7 August 2010, Review, p. 14.
7 Phil Daoust, 'The Many Faces and Bodies of Antony Gormley', *Guardian*, 23 June 2010, G2, p. 2.
8 Gerald Matt, *Interviews Volume 2*, Kunsthall, Vienna, Cologne, 2008, p. 287.
9 Ibid., p. 288.
10 Ibid., p. 285.
11 Ibid.
12 Jeffrey Deitch, 'Performance that Makes Itself', in *Vanessa Beecroft Performances 1993–2003*, exh. cat. Castello di Rivoli Museo d'Arte Contemporanea, Turin, 2004.
13 Hans Ulrich Obrist et al., eds, *Louise Bourgeois: Destruction of the Father/ Reconstruction of the Father, Writings and Interviews 1923–1997*, London and Cambridge, Massachusetts, 1998, p. 101; reprinted in U. Kittelmann, et al., eds, *Hans Bellmer/ Louise Bourgeois*, exh. cat. Nationalgalerie, Staatliche Museen zu Berlin, 2010, p. 89.
14 Kathryn Rattee, et al., eds, *Rebecca Warren*, exh. cat. Serpentine Gallery, London, 2009, pp. 62–3.
15 'Summer Kisses Winter Tears – Sarah Lucas', interview with Kiriaki-Domenika Chandra and Eleni Malami, *Ozon Magazine*, ozonweb.com/en/art/7274.

Chapter 7
GOING TO EXTREMES

1 John Tusa, interview with Gilbert & George, www.bbc.co.uk/ programmes/poonc2dn.
2 Ibid.
3 François Jonquet, *Gilbert & George: Intimate Conversations with François Jonquet*, London, 2004, p. 58.
4 Hans Ulrich Obrist, ed., *The Words of Gilbert & George*, London, 1997, p. 277.
5 Tusa, interview with Gilbert & George
6 Jan Debbaut, et al., *Gilbert & George*, exh. cat. Tate Modern, London, 2007, p. 11.
7 Obrist, ed., pp. 290–1.
8 Tusa, interview with Gilbert & George.
9 Scott Rothkopf, 'Made in Heaven: Jeff Koons and the Invention of the Art Star', in Jack Bankowsky, Alison Gingoras and Catherine Wood, eds, *Pop Life: Art in a Material World*, exh. cat. Tate Modern, London, 2009, p. 44.
10 David Barrett and Lucy Head, eds, *Jake & Dinos Chapman*, London, 2007, p. 3.
11 *Marlene Dumas: Intimate Relations*, exh. cat. Iziko South African National Gallery, Capetown, 2007–8, p. 42.
12 Mark, ed., p. 211.
13 Goldstein, Andrew, 'Marlene Dumas Retrospective Stays Just This Side of Pornography', Vulture, 2008
14 Barrett and Head, eds, p. 6.
15 Obrist, ed., p. 167.
16 Ibid., p. 285.
17 Ibid., p. 273.
18 Ibid., pp. 249–50.
19 Marina Wallace, Martin Kemp and Joanne Bernstein, *Seduced: Art and Sex from Antiquity to Now*, exh. cat. Barbican Art Gallery, London, 2007, p. 11.

Postscript
TEN YEARS LATER

1 www.yanceyrichardson.com/artists/zanele-muholi.
2 Berger, pp. 46–7.

SELECTED BIBLIOGRAPHY

Adler, Kathleen and Marcia Pointon, eds, *The Body Imaged: The Human Form and Visual Culture since the Renaissance*, Cambridge, 1993

Ashton, Dore, et al., *Cecily Brown*, New York, 2008

Barcan, Ruth, *Nudity: A Cultural Anatomy*, Oxford, 2004

Berger, John, *Ways of Seeing*, London, 1972

Bernadac, Marie-Laure and Jonas Storsve, eds, *Louise Bourgeois*, exh. cat. Centre Pompidou, Paris; Tate Modern, London, 2007

Black Male: Representations of Masculinity in Contemporary American Art, Whitney Museum of American Art, New York, 1994

Black Womanhood: Images, Icons and Ideologies of the African Body, Hood Museum of Art, New Hampshire, 2008

Body, exh. cat. Art Gallery of New South Wales, Sydney, 1997

Body: New Art from the UK, exh. cat Vancouver Art Gallery, 2005

Broude, Norma and Mary D. Garrard, eds, *The Power of Feminist Art*, New York, 1994

Clark, Kenneth, *The Nude: A Study in Ideal Form*, London, 1956

Cooper, Emmanuel, *Fully Exposed: The Male Nude in Photography*, London, 1989; 2nd ed. 1995

——, *The Sexual Perspective: Homosexuality and Art in the Last 100 Years in the West*, London, 2nd ed., 1994

Danto, Arthur C., et al., *Eric Fischl 1970–2007*, New York, 2008

Debbaut, Jan, et al., *Gilbert & George*, exh. cat. Tate Modern, London, 2007

Duncan, Carol, *The Aesthetics of Power: Essays in the Critical History of Art*, Cambridge, 1993

Esanu, Octavian, ed., *Art, Awakening and Modernity in the Middle East: The Arab Nude*, New York and London, 2018

Feaver, William, *Lucian Freud*, exh. cat. Tate Britain, London, 2002

Gayford, Martin, *Man with a Blue Scarf: On Sitting for a Portrait by Lucian Freud*, London, 2010

Geiss, Suzanne and Marzia Branca, eds, *Vanessa Beecroft Performances 1993–2003*, exh. cat. Castello di Rivoli Museo d'Arte Contemporanea, Turin, 2004

Gilbert & George, and Rudi Fuchs, *Gilbert & George: The Complete Pictures, 1971–2005*, 2 vols, London, 2007

Goldstein, Carl, *Teaching Art: Academies and Schools from Vasari to Albers*, Cambridge, 1996

Hammer, Martin, *The Naked Portrait, 1900–2007*, exh. cat. Scottish National Portrait Gallery, Edinburgh, 2007

Hannah Wilke: A Retrospective, exh. cat. University of Missouri Press, Columbia, 1989

Herzog, Hans-Michael, et al., eds, *The Body – Le Corps: Contemporary Canadian Art*, Zurich, 1994

Hills, Patricia, *Alice Neel*, New York, 1993

Hudson, Anna, et al., *Woman as Goddess: Liberated Nudes by Robert Markle and Joyce Wieland*, exh. cat. Art Gallery of Ontario, Toronto, 2003

John Currin, exh. cat. Museum of Contemporary Art, Chicago, 2003

Kent, Sarah and Jacqueline Morreau, eds, *Women's Images of Men*, London, 1985

Kiss My Genders, exh. cat. Hayward Gallery, London, 2019

Lewinski, Jorge, *The Naked and the Nude: A History of the Nude in Photographs 1839 to the Present*, London, 1987

Licht, Ira, *Bodyworks*, exh. cat. Museum of Contemporary Art, Chicago, 1975

Lloyd, Fran, ed., *Consuming Bodies: Sex and Contemporary Japanese Art*, London, 2007

McCarthy, David, *The Nude in American Painting, 1950–1980*, Cambridge, 1998

McDonald, Helen, *Erotic Ambiguities: The Female Nude in Art*, London, 2001

Macdonald, Stuart, *The History and Philosophy of Art Education*, London, 1970

Mahon, Alyce, *Eroticism and Art*, Oxford, 2005

Martineau, Paul, *The Nude in Photography*, J. Paul Getty Museum, Los Angeles, 2014

Marina Abramović: The Artist Is Present, exh. cat. Museum of Modern Art, New York, 2010

Mark, Lisa Gabrielle, ed., *Marlene Dumas: Measuring Your Own Grave*, exh. cat. D. A. P./Museum of Contemporary Art, Los Angeles, 2008

Mark, Lisa Gabrielle and

Cornelia Butler, eds., *Wack! Art and the Feminist Revolution*, exh. cat. Museum of Contemporary Art, Los Angeles, Cambridge, Massachusetts, 2007

Miglietti, Francesca Alfano, *Extreme Bodies: The Use and Abuse of the Body in Art*, Milan and London, 2003

Naked Since 1950, exh. cat. L & M Arts, New York, 2001

Natter, Tobias and Elizabeth Leopold, eds., *Nude Men: From 1800 to the Present Day*, Leopold Museum, Vienna, 2012

Nead, Lynda, *The Female Nude: Art, Obscenity and Sexuality*, London, 1992

Nelson, Charmaine, *Representing the Black Female Subject in Western Art*, New York, 2010

Neri, Louise, *Go Figure*, exh. cat. Gagosian Gallery, New York, 2009

Obrist, Hans Ulrich, et al., eds, *Louise Bourgeois: Destruction of the Father/Reconstruction of the Father, Writings and Interviews 1923–1997*, London and Cambridge, Massachusetts, 1998

O'Reilly, Sally, *The Body in Contemporary Art*, London, 2009

Pevsner, Nikolaus, *Academies of Art Past and Present*, London, 1940

Philbrick, Harry, et al., *The Nude in Contemporary Art*, exh. cat. Aldrich Museum of Contemporary Art, Ridgefield, Connecticut, 1999

Pissarro, Joachim, *Marc Quinn: Allanah, Buck, Catman, Chelsea, Michael, Pamela and Thomas*, exh. cat. White Cube, London, 2010

Pitts, Victoria, *In the Flesh: The Cultural Politics of Body Modification*, Basingstoke, 2003

Rattee, Kathryn, et al., eds, *Rebecca Warren*, exh. cat. Serpentine Gallery, London, 2009

Rifkin, Benjamin, et al., *Human Anatomy: Depicting the Body from the Renaissance to Today*, London, 2006

Ruff, Thomas, with an excerpt from a Michel Houellebecq novel, *Thomas Ruff Nudes*, Munich, 2003

Salaman, Naomi, ed., *What She Wants: Women Artists Look at Men*, London, 1994

Saunders, Gill, *The Nude: A New Perspective*, London, 1989

Scala, Mark W., ed., *Paint Made Flesh*, exh. cat. First Center for the Visual Arts, Nashville, 2009

Schama, Simon, et al., *Jenny Saville*, New York, 2005

Singerman, Howard, *Art Subjects: Making Artists in the American University*, Berkeley and Los Angeles, 1999

Solomon-Godeau, Abigail, *Male Trouble: A Crisis in Representation*, London, 1997

Spivey, Nigel, *Understanding Greek Sculpture: Ancient Meanings, Modern Readings*, London, 1996

Stealingworth, Slim (pseud. Tom Wesselmann), *Tom Wesselmann*, New York, 1980

Storr, Robert, *Philip Pearlstein Since 1983*, New York, 2002

Townsend, Chris, *Vile Bodies: Photography and the Crisis of Looking*, Munich, New York and London, 1998

Van den Boogerd, Dominic, et al., *Marlene Dumas*, London, 1999

Vergine, Lea, ed., *Body Art and Performance: The Body as Language*, Milan, 2000

Vidler, Anthony, et al., *Antony Gormley: Blind Light*, exh. cat. Hayward Gallery, London, 2007

Viola, Jerome, *The Painting and Teaching of Philip Pearlstein*, New York, 1982

Walters, Margaret, *The Nude Male: A New Perspective*, New York and London, 1978

Wallace, Marina, et al, *Seduced: Art and Sex from Antiquity to Now*, exh. cat. Barbican Art Gallery, London, 2007

Warhol, Andy and Simon Goldhill, *Andy Warhol: Eros and Mortality: The Late Male Nudes*, exh. cat. Anthony D'Offay/Cheim & Read, London and New York, 2005

Warr, Tracey, ed., *The Artist's Body*, London, 2000

Weiermair, Peter, ed., *Ideal and Reality: The Image of the Body in 20th-Century Art from Bonnard to Warhol*, exh. cat. Salzburg Museum of Modern and Contemporary Art, Zurich, 1998

——, ed., *The Nude: Ideal and Reality from the Invention of Photography to Today*, exh. cat. Galleria d'Arte Moderna, Bologna, 2004

Worton, Michael and Judith Still, *Typical Men: Recent Photography of the Male Body by Men*, exh. cat. Djanogly Art Gallery, Nottingham, 2001

LIST OF ILLUSTRATIONS

Measurements are given in centimetres, followed by inches, height before width before depth. Page numbers reflect the page on which the illustration appears.

Page 2. Jemima Stehli, *Strip No. 7*, 1999. Chromogenic photograph mounted on aluminium, 43.8 × 26.7 cm (17¼ × 10½ in.). Courtesy of Jemima Stehli

Page 6. Lucian Freud, *David and Eli*, 2003–4. Oil on canvas, 162.5 × 174 cm (64 × 68½ in.). Lucian Freud Archive: photography by John Riddy

Page 8. Jenny Saville, *Plan*, 1993. Oil on canvas, 274.3 × 213.4 cm (108 × 84 in.). © 2011 Jenny Saville. Courtesy Gagosian Gallery

Page 9. Philip Pearlstein, *Female Nude on a Platform Rocker*, 1977–8. Oil on canvas, 243.84 × 183.5 cm (96 × 72¼ in.). Brooklyn Museum, New York, J.B. Woodward Fund. Courtesy artist and Betty Conningham Gallery

Page 11. Marc Quinn, *Alison Lapper Pregnant*, 2005. Marble, 355 × 180.5 × 260 cm (139¾ × 7⅝ × 102⅜ in.). Photo Marc Quinn Studio, courtesy White Cube

Page 14. *Apollo Belvedere*, plaster cast of a Roman marble copy, *c.* 130–140 AD, after the bronze original attributed to Leochares. Statue without the 1532/33 additions of Montorsoli. 225 × 113 × 82 cm (76⅝ × 42½ × 32¼ in.). Vatican Museums. Photo akg-images

Pages 16–17. Giorgione, *Sleeping Venus*, *c.* 1508–10. Oil on canvas, 108.5 × 175 cm (42¾ × 68⅞ in.). Gemaldegalerie, Dresden. Photo akg-images/Erich Lessing

Page 18. Théodore Géricault, *Nude Study of a Man*, 1816. Oil on canvas, 79 × 62 cm (31⅛ × 24⅜ in.). Musée du Louvre, Paris

Page 26 top. Gustave Courbet, *The Studio of the Painter* (detail), 1855. Oil on canvas, 598 × 361 cm (235¾ × 132⅛ in.). Musée du Louvre, Paris. Photo akg-images/ Erich Lessing

Page 26 bottom. Julien Vallou de Villeneuve, *Nude Study*, 1854. Print on salted paper from a paper negative, 16.5 × 12.3 cm (6½ × 4¾ in.). Bibliothèque Nationale de France, Paris

Page 28. Edgar Hilaire Degas, *The Tub*, 1886. Pastel on paper, 69.8 × 69.8 cm (27½ × 27½ in.). Alfred Atmore Pope Collection, Hill-Stead Museum, Farmington, CT

Page 29. Pablo Picasso, *Les Demoiselles d'Avignon*, 1907. Oil on canvas, 243.9 × 233.7 cm (96 × 64 in.). MoMA, New York, acquired through the Lillie P. Bliss Bequest. © Succession Picasso/DACS, London 2011

Page 30. René Magritte, *La Magie noire*, 1945. Oil on canvas, 80 × 60 cm (31½ × 23⅝ in.). Musées Royaux des Beaux Arts, Brussels. Photo Scala.

© ADAGP, Paris and DACS, London 2011

Page 31. Paul Delvaux, *Les Mains*, 1941. Oil on canvas, 110 × 130 cm (43¼ × 51¼ in.). Delvaux Museum. © DACS 2011

Page 32. Francis Picabia, *Femmes au bull-dog*, 1941–2. Oil on board, 106 × 76 cm (41¾ × 29⅞ in.). Collection Centre Pompidou, Paris. Photo RMN/Jean-Claude Planchet. © ADAGP, Paris and DACS, London 2011

Page 33. Constantin Brancusi, *Torso of a Young Man II*, 1923. Walnut, 42.7 × 28.4 × 14.6 cm (16¾ × 11⅛ × 5¾ in.); limestone base, 13.4 × 22.5 × 18.4 cm (5⅜ × 8⅞ × 7¼ in.). Collection Centre Pompidou, Paris, Brancusi Bequest, 1957. © ADAGP, Paris and DACS, London 2011

Page 35 top. Aristide Maillol, *La Méditerranée*, 1902–5. Bronze, 113 × 110 × 77.5 cm (44½ × 43¼ × 30½ in.). Museum Boijmans van Beuningen. © ADAGP, Paris and DACS, London 2011

Page 35 bottom. Henry Moore, *Recumbent Figure*, 1938. Green Hornton stone, 88.9 × 132.7 × 73.7 cm (35 × 52¼ × 29 in.). Tate, London. Reproduced by permission of The Henry Moore Foundation

Page 39. Valie Export, *Action Pants: Genital Panic*,

1968. Screenprint on paper, 65.8 × 45.9 cm (25⅞ × 18⅛ in.). © DACS 2011

Page 41. Carolee Schneemann, *Meat Joy*, 1964. Performance: raw fish, chickens, sausages, wet paint, plastic, rope, paper scrap. Photo Al Giese. © Carolee Schneemann

Page 42. Yves Klein, *Untitled Anthropometry*, 1960. Pure pigment and synthetic resin on paper mounted on canvas, 37.1 × 129.2 cm (14⅝ × 50⅞ in.). Private collection. © ADAGP, Paris and DACS, London 2011

Page 43. Yves Klein, *Anthropometries of the Blue Period*, 9 March 1960. Performance at the Galerie Internationale d'Art Contemporain, Paris. © ADAGP, Paris and DACS, London 2011

Page 44. Rebecca Horn, *Arm Extensions*, 1968. Fabric, wood and metal, 60 × 123 × 51 cm (23⅝ × 48⅜ × 20⅛ in.). Tate, London. © DACS 2011

Page 45. Carolee Schneemann, *Interior Scroll*, 1975. Photo collage with text: beet juice, urine and coffee photographic print, 121.9 × 182.8 cm (48 × 72 in.). Photo Anthony McCall. © Carolee Schneemann

Page 46. Marina Abramović, *Imponderabilia*, performance, Galleria Communale d'Arte Bologna, 1977. Photo Giovanna dal Magro. © Marina Abramović. Courtesy of Marina Abramović and Sean Kelly Gallery, New York. DACS 2011

Page 48. Marina Abramović, *Rhythm O*, performance Studio Morra Naples, 1974. Photo Donatelli Sbarra. © Marina Abramović. Courtesy of Marina Abramović and Sean Kelly Gallery, New York. DACS 2011

Page 49. Orlan, *The Kiss of the Artist (Le Baiser de l'artiste): Automatic dispenser, well, almost!*, 1977. Black-and-white photograph, 165 × 110 cm (65 × 43⅜ in.). Collection Maison Européenne de la Photographie, Paris, France. Courtesy of the artist

Page 50. Stelarc, *Sitting/Swaying: Event for Rock Suspension*, Tamura Gallery, Tokyo, 1980. Photographer – Keisuke Oki/ Stelarc

Pages 52–3. Jemima Stehli, *Strip*, 1999. Set of ten chromogenic photographs mounted on aluminium, each 43.8 × 26.7 cm (17¼ × 10½ in.). Courtesy of Jemima Stehli

Page 54. Anna Bilińska-Bohdanowiczowa, *Male Semi-Nude*, 1885. Oil and gouache on canvas, 95 × 67 cm (37⅜ × 26⅜ in.). Photo Żółtowska-Huszcza Teresa/ Muzeum Narodowe w Warszawie

Page 57. Dame Laura Knight, *Ella Louise Naper (née Champion)*, 1913. Oil on canvas, 152.4 × 127.6 cm (60 × 50¼ in.). National Portrait Gallery, London. © Reproduced with permission of The Estate of Dame Laura Knight DBE RA 2011

Pages 60–1. Paula Modersohn-Becker, *Mother and Child*, 1906. Oil on canvas, 82.5 × 124.7 cm (32½ × 49⅛ in.). Paula Modersohn-Becker Museum, Bremen

Page 62. Gwen John, *Nude Girl*, 1909–10. Oil on canvas, 44.5 × 27.9 cm (17½ × 11 in.). Tate, London

Page 63. Elena Luksch-Makowsky, *Adolescentia*, 1903. Oil on canvas, 171 × 78 cm (67¼ × 30¾ in.). Oesterreichische Galerie im Belvedere, Vienna. Photo akg-images/Erich Lessing

Page 64. Edvard Munch, *Puberty*, 1894–5. Oil on canvas, 151.5 × 110 cm (57⅝ × 43⅜ in.). © Munch Museum/Munch – Ellingsen Group, BONO, Oslo/DACS, London 2011

Page 65. Gwen John, *Self-Portrait Sitting Naked on Her Bed*, c. 1908–9. Gouache and pencil on paper, 25 × 16 cm (9¾ × 6¼ in.). Private Collection

Page 66. Paula Modersohn-Becker, *Self-Portrait*, 1906. Oil on card, 101.8 × 70.2 cm (40⅛ × 27⅝ in.). Paula Modersohn-Becker Museum, Bremen

Page 68. Lotte Laserstein, *Morning Toilette*, 1930.

Oil on panel, 99.7 × 65 cm (39¼ × 25⅝ in.). National Museum of Women in the Arts, Washington DC, Gift of the Board of Directors

Page 69. Alice Neel, *Rhoda Myers with Blue Hat*, 1930. Oil on canvas, 69.2 × 59 cm (27¼ × 23¼ in.). Private Collection. © Estate of Alice Neel

Page 70. Alice Neel, *Isabetta*, 1934–5. Oil on canvas, 109.2 × 66 cm (43 × 26 in.). © Estate of Alice Neel

Page 71. Frida Kahlo, *Henry Ford Hospital*, 1932. Oil on metal, 30.5 × 38 cm (12 × 15 in.). Museo Dolores Olmedo Patino, Mexico City. © 2011 Banco de México Diego Rivera Frida Kahlo Museums Trust, Mexico, D.F./DACS

Page 74. Sandy Orgel, *Linen Closet* from *Womanhouse*, 1971. Mixed media. Photo courtesy Through the Flower Archives

Page 75. Lynda Benglis, *Artforum* advertisement, November 1974. Courtesy the artist and Cheim & Reid. © Lynda Benglis. DACS, London/VAGA, New York 2011

Pages 76–7. Joan Semmel, *Intimacy-Autonomy*, 1974. Oil on canvas, 127 × 248.9 cm (50 × 98 in.). Brooklyn Museum, anonymous gift, 2004.117. © Joan Semmel

Page 79 top. Hannah Wilke, *S.O.S. Starification Object Series*, 1974–82.

10 black-and-white gelatin silver prints with 15 chewing gum sculptures mounted on board, 104.1 × 147.3 cm (41 × 58 in.), framed. Collection of The Museum of Modern Art, New York. Image Courtesy Alison Jacques Gallery, London. © Marsie, Emanuelle, Damon and Andrew Scharlatt/DACS, London/VAGA, New York 2011

Page 79 bottom. Eleanor Antin, *Carving: A Traditional Sculpture* (detail), 1972. 144 black-and-white photographs and text panel, 17.8 × 12.7 cm (7 × 5 in.) each. Collection of The Art Institute of Chicago. Courtesy Ronald Feldman Fine Arts, New York/www.feldmangallery.com

Pages 82–3. Sylvia Sleigh, *Philip Golub Reclining*, 1971. Oil on canvas, 106.7 × 152.4 cm (42 × 60 in.). Courtesy of the Estate of Sylvia Sleigh

Page 84. Ana Mendieta, *Imagen de Yagul*, 1973. Lifetime colour photograph, 48.3 × 31.8 cm (19 × 12½ in.). © The Estate of Ana Mendieta Collection Courtesy Galerie Lelong, New York. Collection Glenstone

Page 85. Rineke Dijkstra, *Tecla, Amsterdam, Netherlands, May 16 1994*, 1994. Photograph on paper, 117.5 × 94.5 cm (46¼ × 37¼ in.). Tate, London. © Rineke Dijkstra

Page 86. Sam Taylor-Wood, *Brontosaurus*, 1995. Video projection and sound, duration: 10 minutes. Courtesy White Cube

Page 87. Cindy Sherman, *Untitled*, 1992. Courtesy the artist and Metro Pictures

Page 88 top. Kiki Smith, *Train*, 1993. Wax and glass beads, 134.6 × 426.7 × 139.6 cm (4 ft 5 in. × 14 ft × 4 ft 7 in.). Photography courtesy The Pace Gallery. © Kiki Smith, courtesy The Pace Gallery

Page 88 bottom. Pipilotti Rist, *Blutclip* (Blood Clip), 1993. Video by Pipilotti Rist (video still). Courtesy the artist and Hauser & Wirth

Page 90. Elinor Carucci, *My Mother and I*, 2002. Chromogenic print, 76.2 × 101.6 cm (30 × 40 in.). Courtesy Fifty One Fine Art Photography, Antwerp, Belgium. © Elinor Carucci

Page 91. Melanie Manchot, *Liminal Portraits 1999–2000: With Mountains I*. C-print. Courtesy Melanie Manchot

Page 92. Kiki Smith, *Tied to Her Nature*, 2002. Bronze, 31.8 × 15.2 × 48.3 cm (12½ × 6 × 19 in.). Edition of 6. Photography by Ellen Page Wilson, courtesy The Pace Gallery. © Kiki Smith, courtesy The Pace Gallery

Page 95. John Coplans, *Self-Portrait (Torso, Front)*, 1984. Photograph on paper, 115.6 × 81.7 cm (45½ × 30¼ in.). Tate, London. © John Coplans Trust

Page 96. Willem de Kooning, *Woman I*, 1950–2. Oil on

canvas, 192.7 × 147.3 cm (6 ft 3⅞ in. × 4 ft 10 in.). MoMA, New York. © The Willem de Kooning Foundation, New York/ARS, NY and DACS, London 2011

Page 99. Philip Pearlstein, *Male and Female Nudes with Luna Park Lion and Bamboo Chair*, 1991. Oil on canvas, 152.4 × 152.4 cm (60 × 60 in.). Courtesy artist and Betty Conningham Gallery

Page 101. Lucian Freud, *Benefits Supervisor Resting*, 1994. Oil on canvas, 160 × 150 cm (63 × 59⅛ in.). Lucian Freud Archive: photography by John Riddy

Page 102. Tom Wesselmann, *Great American Nude No. 48*, 1963. Oil and collage on canvas, acrylic and collage on board, enamelled radiator and assemblage, 213.3 × 271.1 × 102.8 cm (84 × 106¾ × 40½ in.). © Estate of Tom Wesselmann/DACS, London/VAGA, New York, 2011

Page 106. Eric Fischl, *Krefeld Project: Bathroom Scene 2*, 2003. Oil on linen, 182.8 × 274.3 cm (72 × 108 in.). Courtesy Eric Fischl

Page 108. Gustave Courbet, *The Origin of the World*, 1866. Oil on canvas, 46 × 55 cm (18⅛ × 21⅞ in.). Musée d'Orsay, Paris. Photo White Images/Scala, Florence

Page 109. Jenny Saville, *Reflective Flesh*, 2002–3. Oil on canvas, 305.1 × 244 cm (120⅛ × 96⅛ in.). © 2011 Jenny Saville. Courtesy Gagosian Gallery

Page 110. Jenny Saville, *Matrix*, 1999. Oil on canvas, 213.4 × 304.8 cm (84 × 120 in.). © 2011 Jenny Saville. Courtesy Gagosian Gallery

Page 111. Cecily Brown, *The Skin Game*, 1999. Monoprint with gouache on paper, 76.8 × 106.7 cm (30⅛ × 42 in.). © Cecily Brown. Courtesy Gagosian Gallery. Photography by Robert McKeever

Page 113. John Currin, *Fishermen*, 2002. Oil on canvas, 127 × 104.1 cm (50 × 41 in.). © John Currin. Courtesy Gagosian Gallery. Photography by Robert McKeever

Page 114. John Currin, *Honeymoon Nude*, 1998. Oil on canvas, 116.8 × 91.4 × 3.3 cm (46 × 36 × 1¼ in.). © John Currin. Courtesy Gagosian Gallery. Photo Tate

Page 116. Agnolo Bronzino, *Andrea Doria as Neptune*, c. 1530. Oil on canvas, 115 × 52 cm (45¼ × 20½ in.). Pinacoteca de Brera, Milan

Page 119 top. Diego Velázquez, *The Toilet of Venus* (Rokeby Venus), 1647–51. Oil on canvas, 122.5 × 177 cm (48¼ × 69¾ in.). National Gallery, London

Page 119 bottom. Francisco de Goya y Lucientes, *Naked Maja* (*Maja Desnuda*), c. 1797. Oil on canvas, 98 × 191 cm (38⅝ × 63⅛ in.). Museo del Prado, Madrid

Page 120. Édouard Manet, *Olympia*, 1863. Oil on canvas, 130.5 × 190 cm (51⅜ × 62¾ in.). Musée d'Orsay, Paris. Photo White Images/Scala, Florence

Page 121. François Clouet, *A Lady in Her Bath*, c. 1571. Oil on oak, 92.3 × 81.2 cm (36¼ × 311¼ in). Samuel H. Kress Collection, National Gallery of Art, Washington DC

Page 123. Albrecht Dürer, *Old Woman with a Bag of Money*, 1507. Oil on panel, 35 × 29 cm (13¾ × 11⅜ in.). Kunsthistorisches Museum, Vienna. Photo akg-images/Erich Lessing

Page 124. Richard Gerstl, *Semi-Nude Self-Portrait*, 1904–5. Oil on canvas, 159 × 109 cm (6⅝ × 42⅞ in.). Leopold Museum, Vienna

Page 125. Richard Gerstl, *Nude Self-Portrait with Palette*, 1908. Oil on canvas, 139.3 × 100 cm (52¾ × 39⅜ in.). Leopold Museum, Vienna

Page 126. Edvard Munch, *Self-Portrait in Hell*, 1903. Oil on canvas, 82 × 66 cm (30⅛ × 26 in.). Photo Scala, Florence. © Munch Museum/ Munch – Ellingsen Group, BONO, Oslo/DACS, London 2011

Page 127. Georg Baselitz, *Fingerpainting – Nude (Fingermalerei – Akt)*, 1972. Oil on canvas, 200 × 162 cm (78¾ × 63¾ in.). Photo: Friedrich Rosenstiel, Cologne. © Georg Baselitz

Page 129. Lucian Freud, *Painter Working: Reflection*, 1993.

Oil on canvas, 101.6 × 81.7 cm (40 × 32¼ in.). Lucian Freud Archive: photography by John Riddy

Pages 132–3. Sylvia Sleigh, *The Turkish Bath*, 1973. Oil on canvas, 193 × 254 cm (76 × 100 in.). The David and Alfred Smart Museum of Art, University of Chicago. Courtesy of the Estate of Sylvia Sleigh

Page 134. Alice Neel, *Self-Portrait*, 1980. Oil on canvas, 137.1 × 101.6 cm (54 × 40 in.). National Portrait Gallery, Smithsonian Institution, Washington DC. © Estate of Alice Neel

Page 136. Alice Neel, *Andy Warhol*, 1970. Oil on canvas, 152.4 × 101.6 cm (60 × 40 in.). Whitney Museum of American Art, New York. © Estate of Alice Neel

Page 137. Elizabeth Peyton, *Alice Neel in 1931*, 2007–8. Oil on linen over board, 34.3 × 25.4 cm (13½ × 10 in.). Courtesy of the artist and Gavin Brown's enterprise. © The artist

Page 138. Eric Fischl, *Simon and Anh*, 2003. Oil on linen, 182.8 × 266.7 cm (72 × 105 in.). Courtesy Eric Fischl

Page 139. Marlene Dumas, *The Painter*, 1994. Oil on canvas, 200 × 100 cm (78⅝ × 39⅜ in.). Courtesy the artist and Frith Street Gallery, London

Page 140. Lucian Freud, *Naked Portrait 2002* (Kate Moss).

Oil on canvas, 152.7 × 122.2 cm (60⅛ × 48⅛ in.). Lucian Freud Archive: photography by John Riddy

Page 142. Victoria Kate Russell, *Fiona Mary Shaw*, 2002. Oil on canvas, 182.8 × 122 cm (72 × 48 in.). Commissioned as part of the First Prize, BP Portrait Award, 2000, 2002. National Portrait Gallery, London

Page 143. Ishbel Myerscough, *Two Girls*, 1991. Oil on canvas. 58.4 × 99.0 cm (23 × 39 in.). National Portrait Gallery, London

Page 145. Robert Mapplethorpe, *Lisa Lyon*, 1982. Gelatin silver print, 50.8 × 40.6 cm (20 × 16 in.). © Copyright The Robert Mapplethorpe Foundation. Courtesy Art + Commerce

Page 146. Ryan McGinley, *Tree No. 3*, 2005. C-print, 183 × 122 cm (72 × 48 in.). Courtesy of the artist and Team Gallery, NY

Page 147. Wolfgang Tillmans, *Lutz and Alex Sitting in the Trees*, 1992. Inkjet print, 195 × 135 cm (76¾ × 53⅛ in.). © Wolfgang Tillmans, courtesy Maureen Paley, London

Page 148. Panayiotis Lamprou, *Portrait of My British Wife*, 2010. Digital chromogenic Fujicolor Chrystal Archive print, 85 × 85 cm (33½ × 33½ in.). Courtesy of the artist

Page 150. Spencer Tunick, *Nevada*, 1977. Gelatin silver print, 152.4 × 121.9 cm (60 × 48 in.). Edition of 6. Courtesy of the artist

Page 152 left. *Venus of Willendorf, c.* 20,000 BC. Sandstone with red chalk decoration, 10.5 cm (4⅛ in.) high. Naturhistorisches Museum, Vienna

Page 152 right. Auguste Rodin, *The Walking Man, c.* 1890–5. Bronze, 85.7 × 55.9 × 28 cm (33¾ × 22 × 11 in.). Digital image, The Museum of Modern Art, New York/Scala, Florence

Page 154 left. Joana Vasconcelos, *Juliet*, 2010. Concrete statue, acrylic paint, handmade cotton crochet, plastic globe, light bulb, electric system, 260 × 50 × 50 cm (102⅜ × 19¾ × 19¾ in.). Private collection, Seoul. Photo Peter Mallet, courtesy Haunch of Venison, London/Atelier Joana Vasconcelos

Page 154 right. Joana Vasconcelos, *Guinevere*, 2010. Concrete statue, acrylic paint, handmade cotton crochet, plastic globe, light bulb, electric system, 276 × 40 × 40 cm (108¾ × 15¾ × 15¾ in.). Photow Peter Mallet, courtesy Haunch of Venison, London/Atelier Joana Vasconcelos

Page 157. Marc Quinn, *Peter Hull, Selma Mustajbasic, Jamie Gillespie, Alexia Westmoquette, Tom Yendell, Catherine Long, Stuart Penn, Helen Smith*, 1999–2000.

ACKNOWLEDGMENTS

Page 191. Marlene Dumas, *Fingers*, 1999. Oil on canvas, 40 × 50 cm (15¾ × 19¾ in.). Courtesy the artist and Frith Street Gallery, London

Page 194. Gilbert & George, *Piss Mooning*, 1996. Mixed media, 226 × 190 cm (89 × 74¾ in.). © the artist, courtesy White Cube

Page 199. *Cassils, Advertisment: Homage to Benglis*, 2011. Archival pigment print, 101.6 × 76.2 cm (40 × 30 in.).Photo Cassils with Robin Black. Courtesy of the artist

Page 201. Yinka Shonibare CBE, *Unintended Sculpture (Donatello's David and Ife Head)*, 2021. Fibreglass sculpture, hand-painted with Dutch wax pattern, patinated bronze, gold leaf, 154.5 × 57 × 58 cm (60¾ × 22½ × 22⅞ in.). Image courtesy the artist. Photographer: Stephen White & Co. © Yinka Shonibare CBE. All rights reserved, DACS 2022

Pages 204–5. Zanele Muholi, *Caitlin and I*, 2009. C-print, 43.2 × 59.7 cm (17 × 23½ in.) each. © Zanele Muholi. Courtesy of Stevenson, Amsterdam/Cape Town/ Johannesburg and Yancey Richardson, New York

Page 206. Chantal Joffe, *Self-Portrait in the Garden at Night*, 2016. Oil on board, 214 × 152.5 × 6 cm (84¼ × 60⅛ × 2⅜ in.). © Chantal Joffe. Courtesy the artist and Victoria Miro

I wrote this book by looking at art and arguing with myself and the words of other authors. Though the internet helpfully tipped information into my lap at home, I am grateful to informed librarians for their courtesy and knowledge. In particular, thank you staff at the London Library and the Hyman Kreitman Reading Rooms at the Tate Gallery Library and Research Centre. The team at Thames & Hudson smoothed my path, and their suggestions and questions made this a better book. And thank you family and friends, especially Ann Cook, for so patiently enduring the anxieties that resulted from producing this work.

INDEX